**EZWebGuides is about saving you time -
300 years of it, give or take a few.**

There are more than 10 million websites on the internet which have reference to golf. It would take someone more than 300 years at 8 hours a day to look at them all ...

We review the best ones and in doing so save your time...

www.**ezwebguides.com**

Publisher
EZ Webguides.com Ltd

Author
EZ Webguides.com Ltd

Editors
Chris Alexandre
Rich Alexandre
Kathryn Heathcote

Design, Artwork
Robyn Frew

Printed by
Lemon Press

ISBN
1-904085-00-8

Contents

EZ Webguides - Introduction

about EZ Webguides

EZWebGuides is a series of Webguides on very specific subjects with the aim of saving you time when you want to find good quality and RELEVANT information on the Internet.

Search Engines and Web directories propose to do this but often fall short when dealing with the large numbers of websites on the Internet. Whether they return 1,000 or 10,000,000 results in a search, there's no doubt that having to sift through all the irrelevant content to find the information that you really want is very time consuming.

Our team of content collectors and reviewers spend many hours searching for the best, most relevant sites on the subject, and then review them in detail, with helpful ratings to make your search quick and easy.

EZWebGuides Golf is the first in the series with plenty more to come.

The EZWebGuides.com website will keep you up to date on the immediate releases, and there's plenty of other information that you'll find useful. Sign up to receive first hand news on releases up to two months in advance so you can be sure to book your copy. The website also allows you to download FREE mini versions of all EZWebGuides as a sampler to the full versions.

EZWebGuides are always available in electronic format from the website.

Every EZWebGuide will be updated on a regular basis to keep the content fresh and current.

We hope you enjoy the guide.

The EZWebGuides team.
www.ezwebguides.com

EZ Webguides - Introduction

description of ratings

Overall Rating:

Covers the general experience of using the site and its overall feel.

Ease of Use:

Covers ease of navigation, sensible ordering of information and clarity of layout.

Content:

Covers the relevance, quality and quantity of the information on the site with regards to the subject.

Look & Feel:

Covers the aesthetical aspects of the site and whether the images, layout and design are pleasing to view.

Customer Service:

Covers the length of time taken for the site to respond to queries we sent them using the contact options on the site

5 = less than 12 hrs
4 = 12-18hrs
3 = 18-24hrs
2 = 24-36hrs
1 = 36-48hrs
0 = more than 48hrs
NA = no apparent contact information

Site Speed:

Covers the site's speed of loading and reaction times to clickable links. (Note: These tests based on a 56K modem Internet connection)

Technical:

Covers more technical issues of the site, such as broken links, errors while browsing etc.

RATING

Overall Rating	✪✪✪
Ease of Use	✪✪
Content	✪✪
Look & Feel	✪✪✪
Customer Service	✪✪✪
Site Speed	✪✪
Technical	✪✪✪

Key:

✪✪✪✪✪ Excellent
✪ Poor

EZ Webguides

why register?

REGISTER YOUR PURCHASE WITH US ON THE EZWebGuides website.

Why Register?

When you register the purchase of your ezwebguide online at www.ezwebguides.com we'll send you the next electronic update of that guide on the day it's released, absolutely FREE.

You'll also benefit from:

>> Massive discounts on all other EZWebGuides.

>> Advance notification on updates for your guide, new guides released, discounts and special offers only for registered users.

>> Draws, prizes and gifts from one of the sites we have reviewed or other sponsors on the subject.

>> Online access to all the content on the subject from any web browser, anywhere in the world.

>> Useful utilities to add the links to your bookmarks or favourites.

>> Free Software Downloads.

>> Product and Event offers (eg. tickets to the US Masters or Ryder Cup).

REGISTRATION IS FREE!
Go to **www.ezwebguides.com** and **register today.**

EZ Webguides
1st hole - art & collectibles

Reviews

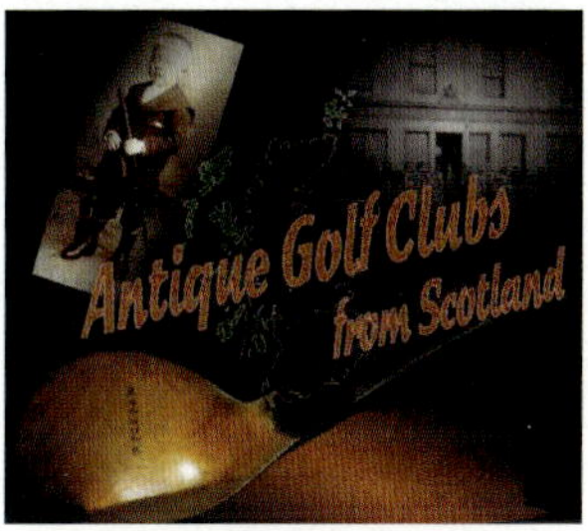

Anitque Golf Clubs from Scotland

http://www.antiquegolfscotland.com

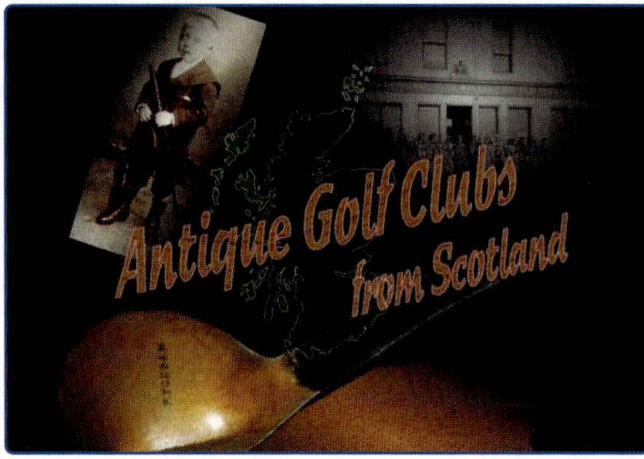

Antique Golf Clubs from Scotland: chances are the name alone tells you all you need to know before deciding whether or not you're going to visit this site. Mind you, that would make this a rather short review, so with that in mind, lets look a little deeper, shall we?

Well, this is a truly impressive site, which begins with an intriguing and fast loading montage style image that successfully manages to draw you in. Once you're in the site itself, you'll find they offer a truly unique service, concentrating on some truly rare examples of Scottish golfing memorabilia. The range of clubs and other golf related antiquities is awesome, while the site itself is slick and professional.

A F.A.Q. section gives invaluable information about the old clubs, including advice on how to ascertain if your own are valuable or not. There is also an auction component to the site, as well as the ubiquitous shopping cart.

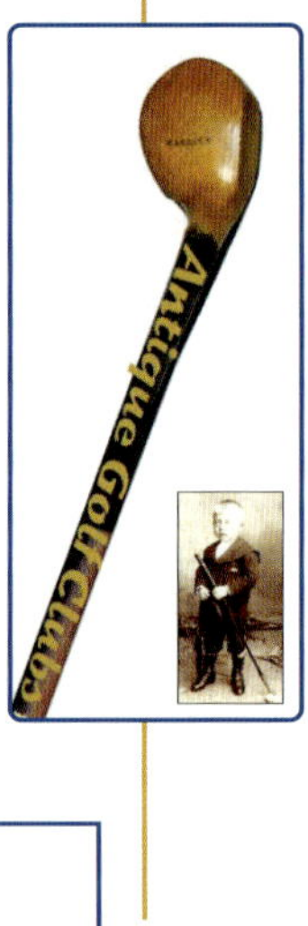

If you're looking to sell, rather than buy, you can do that here too. The content goes even further than this though, and also presents interesting information on Scottish club makers themselves.

They get top marks for maintaining the site: when we visited, the last update was only two days previously. This is what we like to see. Ultimately, this is a site that is worth visiting.

RATING Refer to pg8 for rating explanations.

Overall Rating	✪✪✪✪
Ease of Use	✪✪✪✪
Content	✪✪✪✪✪
Look & Feel	✪✪✪✪✪
Customer Service	✪✪✪
Site Speed	✪✪✪✪
Technical	✪✪✪✪

MAIN POINTS:
>> Good, unique content, with slick presentation.

Antique Golf

http://www.antiquegolf.com

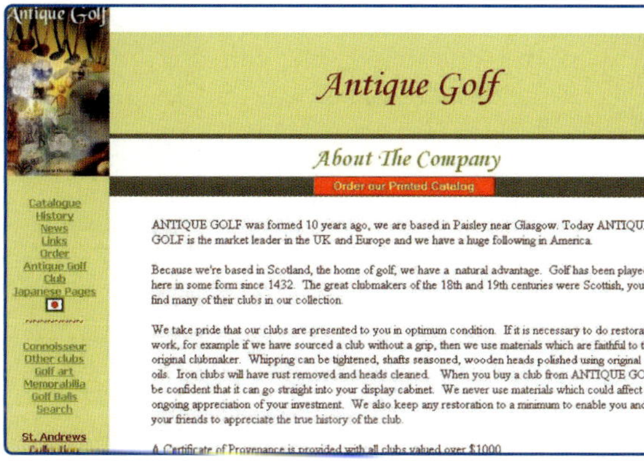

Almost every golfer has heard it said that Scotland is the place from where the great game originates. And if you believe that, then you'll believe Scotland-based company Antique Golf since, as they put it "we have a natural advantage. Golf has been played here in some form since 1432." And indeed, Antique Golf does have a lot of old items, which should catch any collectors eye, including collectible clubs that date back to the early 1900's. They offer a decent level of information on each product, with a fairly well written summary of your potential purchase.

Unfortunately, as far as we can gather, there are no pictures of any of the clubs. Instead, if you email them, they will send you a picture of the item you're interested in. This seems unnecessary at best and will definitely not be a very viable option for those who like to browse. It's too cumbersome and demanding for the average casual Internet shopper. Ordering is done via a secure server, but product numbers must be jotted down as you browse as the site lacks a shopping cart facility. Despite this, the site is definitely worth a look, as they have some items that would be very hard to find elsewhere.

RATING Refer to pg8 for rating explanations.

Overall Rating	✪ ✪
Ease of Use	✪
Content	✪ ✪ ✪
Look & Feel	✪ ✪
Customer Service	✪
Site Speed	✪ ✪ ✪
Technical	✪ ✪

MAIN POINTS:

>> Home to several very rare golfing antiques.

>> Lack of pictures and Shopping Cart.

Golf Art

http://www.golf-art.com

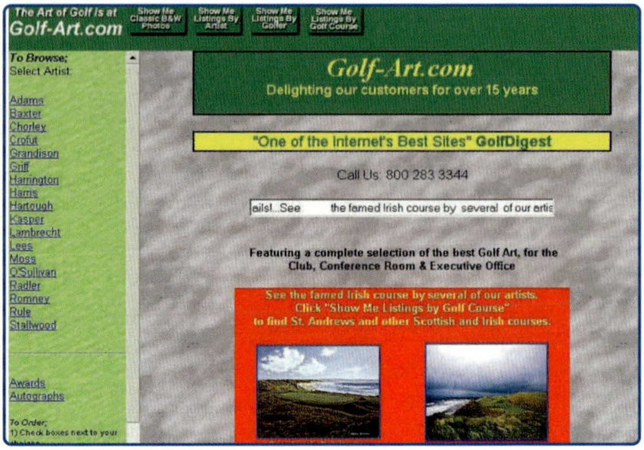

On the one hand, we can almost understand why a website such as Golf Art might opt for having a less than impressive looking site. After all, when the main focus of your business is the art you sell, then you're going to want it to look as good as it possibly can. This site is not particularly well designed and the images are not attractively presented.

Still, it's much more likely that the low quality design wasn't intentional, but more by accident, for everything else on the site is done well. The various prints, photographs and art images, are of golfers, courses etc and date from the 1940's to the present day. They are all good quality images viewable at reasonable sizes. Should you be interested in purchasing one of these works, then you'll have no problem finding out exactly what you'll be getting. If you're looking for one particular photographer, artist or subject, then you'll find it reasonably easy to locate, as the site has divided up its gallery of work in a intuitive and easy to follow way. This is fortunate, as with so many different pieces on display, it could be a little daunting trying to find exactly the right one to adorn your living room wall.

RATING Refer to pg8 for rating explanations.

Overall Rating	✪ ✪ ✪
Ease of Use	✪ ✪ ✪ ✪
Content	✪ ✪ ✪
Look & Feel	✪
Customer Service	✪ ✪
Site Speed	✪ ✪ ✪ ✪
Technical	✪ ✪

MAIN POINTS:
>> User friendly and well stocked.

Golf Collectibles

http://www.golfcollectible.com

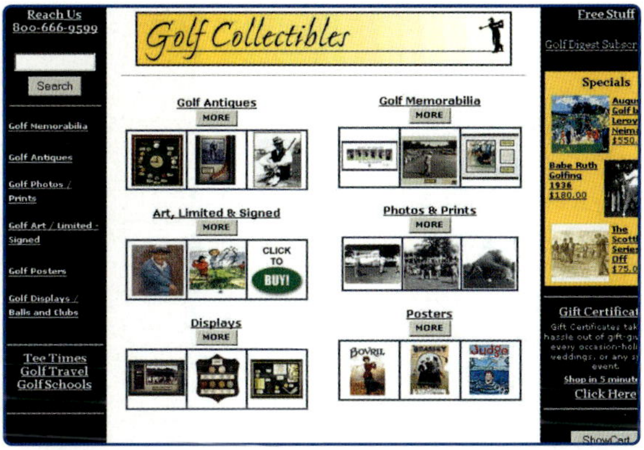

One of the great appealing elements of a game of golf isn't simply the enjoyment of competing, or the challenge of bettering your own performance, but rather the stunning surroundings in which the game is played. Although the game has often been unfairly dubbed a "good walk, spoiled" there's no denying the often magnificent settings in which golfers can find themselves.

It's with this in mind that we turn to Golf Collectibles, a site that realises such a visual sport deserves to be captured for all time through sculpture, paintings or photographs. Yet you'll find much more than art here. There's also an impressive range of golf related antiques, memorabilia and displays (ideal if you've always wanted to frame that magic ball that gave you a hole in one). The only criticism we have is that there was no discernable means of communication other than via a telephone number. Considering that anyone who has visited their site must be able to access the Internet, it seems odd that there's no email link included here.

Overall, this site is still worthy of your time.

RATING Refer to pg8 for rating explanations.

Overall Rating	✪✪✪
Ease of Use	✪✪✪✪
Content	✪✪✪
Look & Feel	✪✪✪
Customer Service	N/A
Site Speed	✪✪✪
Technical	✪✪✪

MAIN POINTS:
>> Excellent range of golfing antiques.

Golf Photos

http://www.golfphotos.com

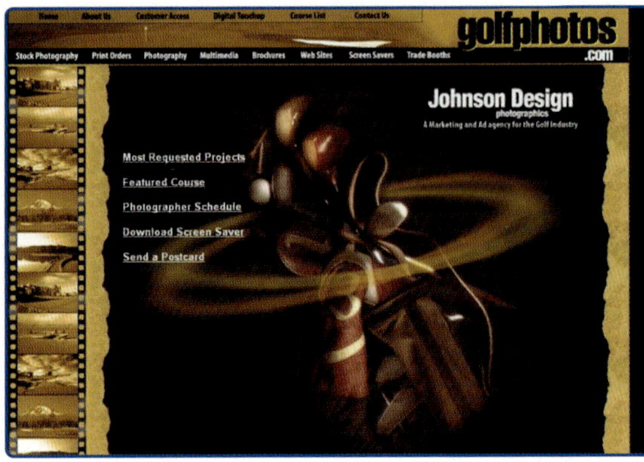

The first thing that you notice about this site is that it looks absolutely fantastic.

The Flash intro alone is worth a look, as a crosshair moves around the screen, stopping every few seconds to "take a picture". It's really quite well done.

The rest of the site maintains this high standard. The backgrounds feature very high quality graphics while the site in general has a number of good, clear photos on a golfing theme. Really, the fact that the site looks so good is pretty much the only reason that most of us will visit it. It is mainly geared towards business people that are looking for certain images for brochures, advertising projects, magazines and the like.

All sample images are stamped with the golfphotos.com logo and are small – until you purchase them, that is - so don't think you can just go in and steal one or two pictures for your desktop wallpaper.

If you are in a golf-related business though, you should definitely check this site out. With a wide range of pictures under topics such as fairways, bunkers and water, this site might have exactly the shot you're looking for.

RATING Refer to pg8 for rating explanations.

Overall Rating	★★★
Ease of Use	★★★★
Content	★★
Look & Feel	★★★★★
Customer Service	★★★
Site Speed	★★★
Technical	★★★★

MAIN POINTS:

>> Great golfing images.

>> Aimed at business user.

Silver Stone Publishing

http://www.silverstoneart.com

Siver Stone Publishing covers a variety of sports including fishing, skiing and of course golf. The section for each sport is rather limited, as is often the case when a publisher covers a range of subjects.

Those interested in multiple sports and fine art prints however, will definitely find this site worth taking a look at. Based on the sample pictures that they show on the site (all of which can be enlarged) the pieces all appear to be of high quality and would look good in most offices or homes.

The site itself is simple, but that only seems to enhance the appeal of the prints themselves.

Since they don't have a secure server, credit card ordering must be done over the phone while money orders or cheques can be sent via mail.

There is not a huge selection of golf prints, but what there is is of high quality.

Overall, if you're looking for some high quality art, then give this site a look.

RATING Refer to pg8 for rating explanations.

Overall Rating	✪✪
Ease of Use	✪✪✪
Content	✪✪
Look & Feel	✪✪
Customer Service	✪✪✪✪
Site Speed	✪✪✪
Technical	✪✪

MAIN POINTS:

>> Some fine, high quality sports themed prints.

SMA Golf Art

http://www.smagolfart.com

If you're in the market to purchase gold oriented art items, then you should definitely give SMA Golf Art a look. With a wide variety of items ranging from lithographs to original pieces and sculptures to clocks, there's a very good chance that SMA will have the golf art item you're looking for.

The site specialises in high value, good quality pieces and the large pictures of each item help give you an idea of exactly what you are purchasing. Also, although this may only apply to a select few, members of the PGA of America will be given a special rate. Membership, as they say, has its privileges. The site itself is very plain and not golf themed at all with the exception of the tees that are used in the place of bullets on the bottom of the page. Luckily, should something capture your fancy, all ordering is done via a secure server so you can feel pretty safe in using your credit card to order anything. Overall, if you're a golfer who's looking for some nice pieces to fill an empty office, game room or other such space, then give SMA Golf Art a try.

RATING Refer to pg8 for rating explanations.

Overall Rating	✪✪✪
Ease of Use	✪✪✪
Content	✪✪✪
Look & Feel	✪✪
Customer Service	✪✪✪✪
Site Speed	✪✪
Technical	✪✪✪

MAIN POINTS:

>> Impressive range of hard to find golfing antiques.

Other Art & Collectibles Link Listings

Other Art & Collectibles related sites reviewed		Page
GolfAndTravel.com	http://www.golfandtravel.com	215
ParGolf.com	http://www.pargolf.com	196
United States Golf Association	http://www.usga.org	136

Other Art & Collectibles related sites

http://graphicgolf.com
http://interoz.com/gallery/milo1.htm
http://users.erols.com/golferjim
http://werple.net.au/pmann
http://www.aei.ca/chase
http://www.angelfire.com/ny/flagstik
http://www.antique-golf.com
http://www.golf-antiques.com
http://www.appletreegolfinc.com
http://www.artistsgolf.com
http://www.blimpguy.com
http://www.cardmall.com
http://www.cartoonwebsite.com
http://www.coplu.com
http://www.crocker.com/golf
http://www.cu-online.com/klharney
http://www.discoverydirect.com
http://www.dmcsoft.com/antiquegolf
http://www.fortherecord.org
http://www.golfiana.com
http://www.golfartcollections.com
http://www.golfinggallery.com
http://www.golfoto.com
http://www.golfpix.net
http://www.golfsculptures.com
http://www.greenviewgolf.com
http://www.greynet.net/classic
http://www.hickorystx.com
http://www.homesandgolf.com
http://www.looksee.com/barry
http://www.malibuplace.com
http://www.mastersofgolf.com
http://www.mtechpub.com/golf
http://www.northwestgifts.com
http://www.oldcourse.com
http://www.pgaprotour.com
http://www.rsc.co.uk/ddd/golf.html
http://www.rwga.com/g2.htm
http://www.rwga.com/humor1.htm
http://www.sandhillartstudio.com
http://www.scottishgolfgifts.com
http://www.scottish-valley.co.uk
http://www.vintagegolfhouse.com
http://www.webeesports.com
http://www.yagigolf.com

EZ Webguides

2nd hole - books & videos

Reviews

Amazon.com

http://www.amazon.com

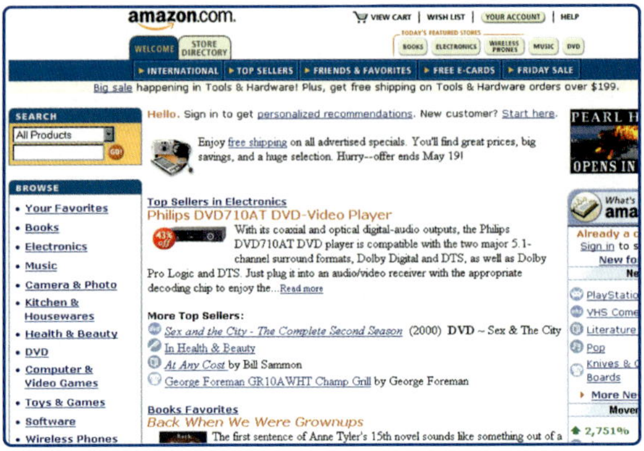

Chances are that if you've got Internet access and have been surfing the web for a while, or even if you've picked up a newspaper or turned on the TV news, you'll probably have heard of Amazon.com. And, as one of the biggest all-purpose shopping sites on the net, buying from Amazon has become something of a rite of passage for net users so there's no reason why online golfers shouldn't do so too.

Selling golf related computer and video games, instructional videos and literally thousands of books on golf, they truly offer an unparalleled array of products.

The site is plain looking yet well structured so that you can find any product, as long as they have it, within minutes if not seconds. Their search engine is one of the most user friendly you'll find, enabling you to do a store-wide search, or narrow your focus down to certain departments including books, DVDs, videos, games, music and so on. Orders are placed on a secure server, and for those of us who prefer not to use credit cards, Amazon also offers the option of placing your order then sending in a cheque or money order to pay. You can happily shop with confidence, as Amazon is the undisputed leader in online shopping.

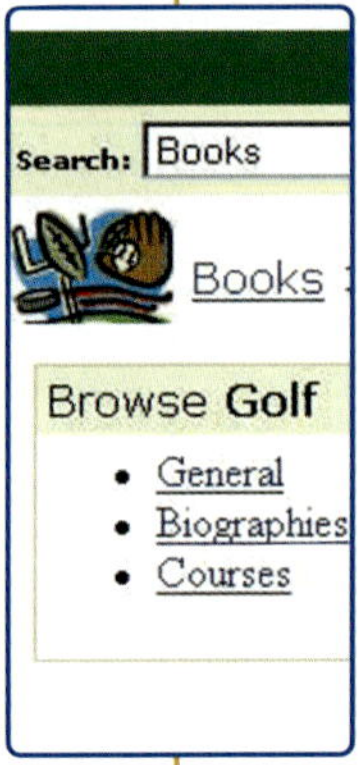

Overall, this is a great site with hundreds of items that will appeal to the golf lover.

RATING Refer to pg8 for rating explanations.

Overall Rating	✪✪✪✪✪
Ease of Use	✪✪✪✪
Content	✪✪✪✪
Look & Feel	✪✪✪✪
Customer Service	✪✪✪✪✪
Site Speed	✪✪✪✪
Technical	✪✪✪✪✪

MAIN POINTS:

>> The leading name in online shopping. Reliable, fast and secure with a huge range of products.

Barnes & Noble

http://www.bn.com

Even if you're not looking for golfing books, you should definitely give Barnes & Noble's online store a visit because, quite simply, they have available for order almost every book currently in publication - and even a few that aren't.

Just a simple search using "golf" as our keyword brought up nearly three thousand results. It'll take even the most hardened golf fan a while to get through all those choices.

The site also offers significant discounts on most books, allowing you to offset shipping costs if you live outside the US.

The site itself is very professionally laid out and is the next best thing to being in a store, flipping through books yourself. It offers a description of each title, photos of most books covers and reader reviews, although some of them look less than 100% objective. As would be expected from a site of this calibre, Barnes & Noble collects all information on a secure server.

The site also sells items such as videos, DVDs and computer games, but without doubt the main reason for checking the site out is the books.

So, even if you're not looking for something new to read, give the site a look. With so much content, you're bound to find something that catches your eye.

RATING Refer to pg8 for rating explanations.

Overall Rating	✪✪✪✪
Ease of Use	✪✪✪✪
Content	✪✪✪✪✪
Look & Feel	✪✪✪
Customer Service	✪✪✪✪
Site Speed	✪✪✪
Technical	✪✪✪

MAIN POINTS:

>> Impressive array of golf related books, videos and games.

Books On Golf

http://www.booksongolf.com

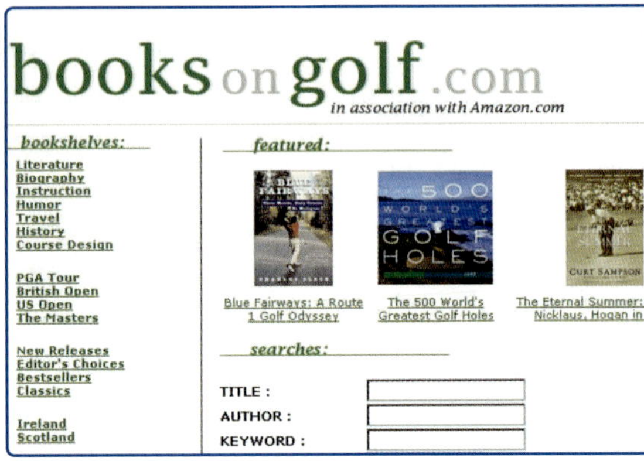

Don't be fooled by Books On Golf.com! Although it looks like an online bookstore in its own right, in reality it's just a shell which helps you find books on golf through Amazon.com. Every "buy the book" type link merely opens a new window which takes you to that exact book on the Amazon website.

However, the reason for including this site in the guide is that this site makes finding golf-related books on the Amazon website a whole lot easier than looking for them on the Amazon site itself.

The side navigation panel divides everything into separate categories such as biographies, travel and, of course, a section devoted to Tiger Woods.

The real star of this site however, is the extremely comprehensive search engine which allows you to narrow down your search to specific years, regions and other sub-divisions.

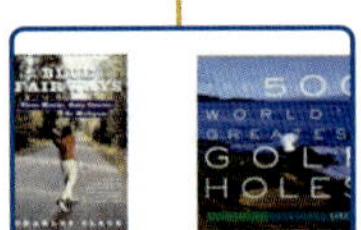

The look and feel of the site is nothing special and very nearly approaches boring with a lot of plain text on white backgrounds. However it serves its purpose well and its exclusive coverage of golf ensures you only search through relevant material.

RATING Refer to pg8 for rating explanations.

Overall Rating	✪✪✪
Ease of Use	✪✪✪✪
Content	✪✪
Look & Feel	✪✪
Customer Service	✪✪✪
Site Speed	✪✪
Technical	✪✪✪

MAIN POINTS:

>> Great search facility that should make shopping at Amazon for golf books much easier.

Other Books & Video Link Listings

Other Books & Videos related sites

http://golfbook.freeyellow.com
http://home.clara.net/bobsteiner
http://maxwellsbookmark.com
http://members.home.net/botheball
http://showcase.netins.net
http://www.accessthezone.com
http://www.advancedgolf.itgo.com
http://www.cloverleafgolf.com
http://www.coyotegolf.com
http://www.dalink.com/golf/ed.html
http://www.depernodevelopment.com/mindgolf.html
http://www.ecsports.net
http://www.free-golf.com
http://www.gate.net/raymillr/golf/golfhome.htm
http://www.golfbtb.com
http://www.golfcpons.com
http://www.golfingbooks.com
http://www.golfingkey.com
http://www.golflearning.com
http://www.golfpassbook.com
http://www.golfpoet.com
http://www.harpercollins.com/baggervance
http://www.hawaii-discounts.com
http://www.holebyhole.com
http://www.lakesidepress.com/golf/contents.htm
http://www.mavenvideo.com
http://www.mbagolf.com
http://www.mentalkeys.com
http://www.new1.com/jkohl/toons/luckypants.htm
http://www.pepegolf.com
http://www.playgolfnow.com
http://www.powersgolf.com
http://www.puttingmagic.com
http://www.ricd2.com/forenomore
http://www.sleepingbearpress.com
http://www.whygolf.net

EZ Webguides

3rd hole - clothing

Reviews

Footjoy

http://www.footjoy.com

Footjoy's site has plenty of information and pictures about their clothing and footwear.

The site opens with a flash intro which is quite large in size and so can take some time to load on a 56K modem. There's an option to skip the intro and once inside, there's plenty of high quality images, information and a strong customer service area that answers most of the questions you might have about their products pre and post purchase.

Finding products is easy with the way they are laid out, and the high quality images give you a very good idea of the product.

The customer service section offers you a worldwide office locator which is easy to use, as well as information on product warranty registration (you can do it online) as well as a section on "shoe care" and a live help system during US business hours with the option to send an email out of hours.

A really nice idea, and a good way to get people to visit them regularly is their auction section. Not like other auctions, this one has only one product in it replaced each week. A footjoy product autographed by a Pro and you can bid on it to add it to your collection. an excellent "interactive" feature.

RATING Refer to pg8 for rating explanations.

Overall Rating	✪✪✪✪
Ease of Use	✪✪✪
Content	✪✪✪✪
Look & Feel	✪✪✪✪
Customer Service	✪✪✪
Site Speed	✪
Technical	✪✪✪✪✪

MAIN POINTS:

>> Genuinely international. Impressive, media intensive design.

Golfshoes Plus

http://www.golfshoesplus.com

Can half a million visitors be wrong? We certainly hope not, because that's how many people have paid a visit to Golfshoes Plus since its launch. Quite an impressive figure, which implies they must be doing something right. Investigate further and you'll find that they're doing just that.

Essentially, whatever brand name of golfing shoe that you care to mention you're sure to find it here. Whether it's Dunlop, Nike, Reebok, Footjoy or Bite, you'll find exactly the shoe you're after somewhere amongst their extensive range.

The online ordering system is not quite up to scratch since you're required to remember the details of what you want, and fill them in on their secure order form...maybe time for a site of this supposed popularity to invest in a shopping basket?

They claim to have had some fraud problems with international customers, and so if you're not in the US, they ask you to first fill out a pre-order form and fax it to them along with copies of your Passport, Drivers License and the Credit Card you propose to use. Seems a little excessive and I'm sure that they would go a long way in investing in a shopping basket that hooks into one of the credit card clearing houses with fraud protection. If you're up to it, the prices look good, and it would be worth a visit.

RATING Refer to pg8 for rating explanations.

Overall Rating	✪ ✪ ✪
Ease of Use	✪ ✪ ✪
Content	✪ ✪ ✪
Look & Feel	✪ ✪ ✪
Customer Service	N/A
Site Speed	✪ ✪ ✪
Technical	✪ ✪ ✪

MAIN POINTS:

>> Appears highly popular, large range semi-online store.

St Andrews Golf

http://www.stagolf.co.uk

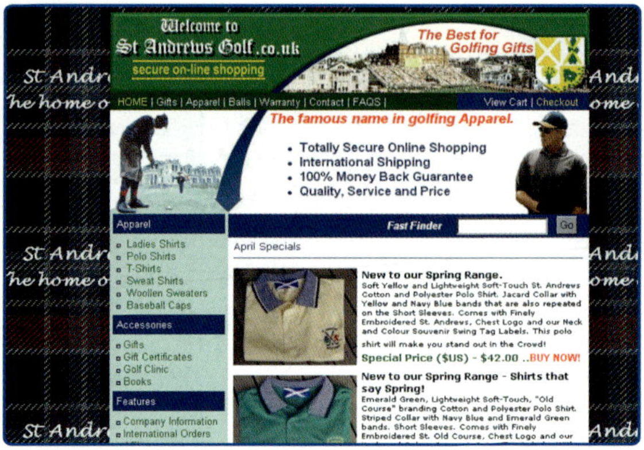

St Andrews Golf makes it's offering clear right on their front page. "Everyone wants a piece of St Andrews - Get yours Now" is the greeting they offer, closely followed by "Totally secure online shopping. International shipping. 100% money back guarantee. Quality, service and price" - the kinds of things that we are starting to expect from our online retailers.

The site offers a wide range of branded St Andrews clothing and gifts. Many golfers are passionate about the "home of golf" and anyone in any country is proud to wear the name St Andrews.

There's a handy gift search which will allow you to search for gifts of certain prices, which means you don't have to sift through everything, but get a list of the gifts that will suit your budget.

The site is of UK origin and displays it's prices in $ - not the usual way it's done, but is accompanied by an ever present link to a currency converter which allows you to quickly check the price in your local currency.

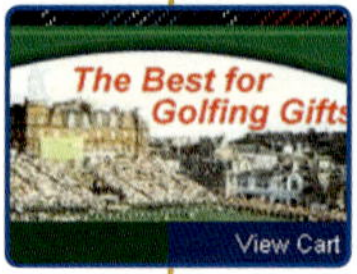

The site offers you the chance to join their monthly newsletter which provides interesting reading, and a refreshing feature of this, was that they offer you the chance to read, print or pass-on their back issues. This way you get to see what you could expect to receive from them on a monthly basis.

A few of the links we tried weren't working, but all in all, well worth a visit and a place where you're sure to get "...a piece of St Andrews..."

RATING Refer to pg8 for rating explanations.

Overall Rating	✪✪✪✪
Ease of Use	✪✪✪✪
Content	✪✪✪✪
Look & Feel	✪✪✪
Customer Service	✪✪✪✪
Site Speed	✪✪✪✪
Technical	✪✪

MAIN POINTS:

>> A good range of clothing and gifts for men and women golfers with international appeal.

Wee Generation

http://www.weegeneration.com

As the name suggests, Wee Generation.com is devoted to the more junior golfer who is often overlooked at some of the more adult oriented shopping sites. After all, if you're going to take the kids around the green with you and introduce them to the game then they deserve to look the part!

In addition to the traditional golfing apparel that you'll find on this site (shirts, polo necks, sweaters, caps, shorts and shoes) you'll also be able to pick up golfing gloves, kid sized golfbags and carts, and even a set of junior clubs - perfect if your kids are eager to learn but have difficulty swinging a club that is twice their size. Prices are reasonable, although we're not looking at bargain basement ranges, so expect to pay out a fair amount of money if you're planning on fitting out the next Tiger Woods in head-to-toe Wee Generation clothing.

Clothing sizes are all given in the USA measurement system with no conversion information for shoppers from other countries. Still, a great site to kit out your junior golfer.

RATING Refer to pg8 for rating explanations.

Overall Rating	✪✪✪
Ease of Use	✪✪✪✪
Content	✪✪✪
Look & Feel	✪✪✪
Customer Service	✪✪
Site Speed	✪✪✪
Technical	✪✪✪

MAIN POINTS:

>> Well designed site, packed with well designed clothes.

Other Clothing Link Listings

Other Clothing related sites reviewed		Page
BestValueGolf.com	http://www.bestvaluegolf.com	184
Bird Of Prey	http://www.birdofprey.com	185
Blue Chip Socks	http://www.bluechipsocks.com	186
Global Golf	http://www.globalgolf.com	86
Lady Classic	http://www.ladyclassic.com	228
Liquid Golf	http://www.liquidgolf.com	56
Nike Golf	http://www.nikegolf.com	195
She Golfs	http://www.shegolfs.com	230
The Golf Warehouse	http://www.tgw.com	198

Other Clothing related sites

http://www.allamericanspecialty.com

http://www.bette-court.com

http://www.blacksheepusa.com

http://www.golfstore.com/apparel.htm

http://www.golfwholesale.com/golf_wsle.htm

http://www.gtigolf.com/apparel.html

http://www.jps.net/pazzo

http://www.off2golf.com/womensgifts.html

http://www.pureadrenalin.com/golf.html

http://www.puremagazine.com

EZ Webguides

4th hole - directories & discussion

Reviews

Golf Farm

http://www.golffarm.com

If you've lost as many golf balls in your time as we have, then we're going to break this to you gently: Golf Farm isn't a place where they've finally made golfballs grow on trees. Unfortunately.

Instead, what you'll find here is a links site, which essentially acts as a portal to different golfing areas on the Internet. At first glance, the range of links seems to be fairly comprehensive, covering everything from golf associations to shopping online. There is a classified ads section which sounded promising, but on browsing was revealed to be virtually empty, with some categories only having one entry.

The site is redeemed however, by a fairly comprehensive tips and instructions section, which includes pages devoted to women golfers too. It also offers a subscription newsletter, which simply links you through to other sites.

In conclusion, Golf Farm, although not as comprehensive as one would like, still serves as an easy and useful portal – possibly more suited to beginners than experienced Internet users - and has some reasonable information and links.

RATING Refer to pg8 for rating explanations.

Overall Rating	✪✪✪
Ease of Use	✪✪
Content	✪✪
Look & Feel	✪✪
Customer Service	✪✪✪✪✪
Site Speed	✪✪✪✪
Technical	✪✪✪

MAIN POINTS:
>> Some decent links and information.

Golf Help

http://www.golfhelp.com

It's pretty difficult when you first set out to design a search engine. There's a real need to show that you have plenty of links, and that your visitors are going to be able to find anything they're looking for, and that everything is organised in an easy to understand fashion. While doing that, you have to juggle, keeping everything clean, clear and easy to use. It's a tough balancing act, but Golf Help manages to do it very well.

This is a really good dedicated golf search engine, with links to almost everything that you might need to know. The site is well designed and even with the mass of material does not feel cluttered. The search engine appeared to be very effective: a search on Scotland for example, brought up 236 useful links. The various categories are also well placed and thought out, while the instructional category provided a wealth of links and information.

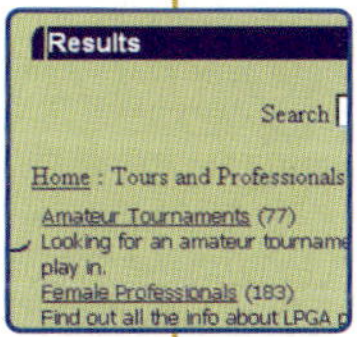

Of special mention is the multimedia section, with over 40 links to instructional and other video sites. There is a very useful directory link to news and statistics, that provides some very insightful bits of info.

Overall, this is one of the best places to go if you are searching for any aspect of golf on the Internet and can't fnd it after using our guide.

RATING Refer to pg8 for rating explanations.

Overall Rating	✪✪✪✪
Ease of Use	✪✪✪✪
Content	✪✪✪
Look & Feel	✪✪✪✪
Customer Service	✪
Site Speed	✪✪✪✪
Technical	✪✪✪✪

MAIN POINTS:

>> Excellent search and directory facilities.

Golf Review

http://www.golfreview.com

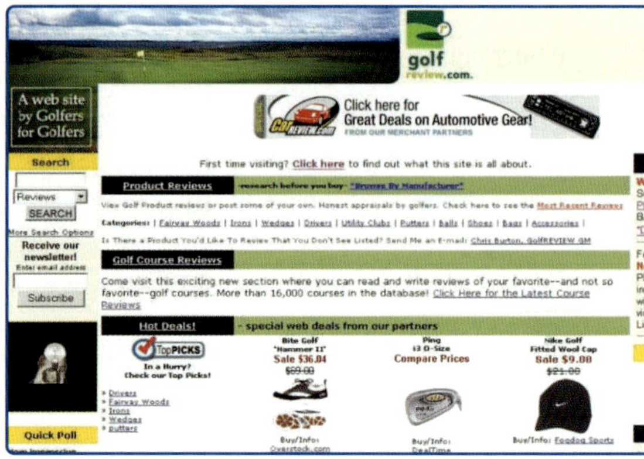

Pop along to this site and you'll find a "website by golfers, for golfers". So says Golf Review.com. Indeed, this is a place where golfers from all over the world have a chance to voice their opinions interactively.

The discussion groups are divided up into different sections, and it's pleasing to see that this is not just another place where visitors alone keep the forums alive. Those running the site also provide regular input, as well as offering some valuable information. This helps to build a sense of community needed for any online discussion forum.

They have sections where consumers can offer product reviews and course reviews, while at the 19th Hole you'll find even more subjects under discussion.

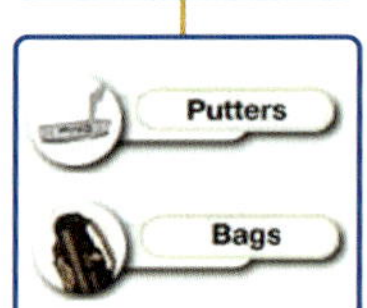

One nice touch is the marketplace, that allows you to view or sell second hand equipment. If you feel the need, you can even send in your own golfing pictures to share with the world.

Finally, there's a helpful section called Golf101 which offers information on Terms, Etiquette, Rules, Governing Bodies, Handicap Help, Games to Play, Equipment Selection Advice and tips on improving your game. Useful stuff, for even the most experienced of golfers.

RATING Refer to pg8 for rating explanations.

Overall Rating	✪✪✪✪
Ease of Use	✪✪✪✪
Content	✪✪✪
Look & Feel	✪✪✪✪
Customer Service	✪✪✪✪✪
Site Speed	✪✪✪✪
Technical	✪✪✪✪

MAIN POINTS:

>> Highly interactive and lively discussion site.

Golf.co.uk

http://www.golf.co.uk

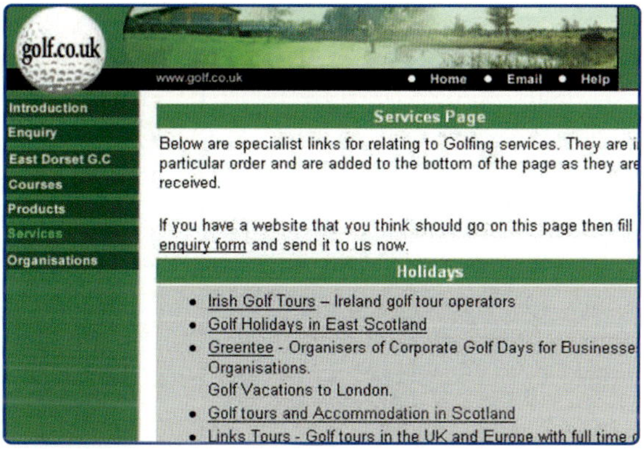

Elsewhere in this guide you'll find a review of Golf.com, where we talk about how it's one of the simplest golf sites to find on the Internet, and many users may stumble across it by accident. Well, the same rules essentially apply to Golf.co.uk. Before we went there, we expected more of the same, only with a slightly more British perspective. Did we get what we expected?

Well, yes and no. Surprisingly, Golf.co.uk wasn't snapped up by the same people who now own and run Golf.com.

Instead, what we have here is essentially a series of links, collected on one site, targeted firmly at a British audience. You'll find this site will direct you to courses in England, Ireland, Scotland and Wales along with links to shopping sites, manufacturers, wholesalers and more. This site has little original content but has some useful links for golfers wishing to play in the UK.

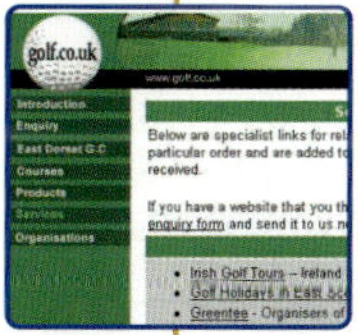

RATING Refer to pg8 for rating explanations.

Overall Rating	✪✪
Ease of Use	✪✪✪
Content	✪
Look & Feel	✪✪
Customer Service	✪✪✪
Site Speed	✪✪✪
Technical	✪✪

MAIN POINTS:

>> Clear design.

GolfBytes

http://www.golfbytes.com

The age-old adage that looks can be deceiving certainly applies to Golf Bytes.

Go to the site and you'll be presented with nothing more than a very plain front page. Aside from a few ads, there's nothing more than a subscription service, a small Link of the Week banner and an icon that will lead you to the main links page.

The subscription service is useful if you're not someone who's inclined to visit a site regularly checking for updates, while the Link of the Week is pretty self explanatory: the webmasters select a site that deserves the spotlight.

But the true value of Golf Bytes can be found by heading into the links section. Here you will find dozens of links to golf related pages arranged in an easy to find manner.

From Betting Services to Golf Schools, Fantasy Golf to Travel Agents, almost any topic you care to mention will have a link on this site. The simple look of Golf Bytes also means that it loads very quickly indeed, which is always a pleasure when searching.

A great place to start exploring the constantly changing world of golf on the web.

RATING Refer to pg8 for rating explanations.

Overall Rating	✪✪✪✪
Ease of Use	✪✪✪
Content	✪✪✪
Look & Feel	✪
Customer Service	✪✪✪✪
Site Speed	✪✪✪✪
Technical	✪✪

MAIN POINTS:

>> Impressive collection of links and easy to use golf search engine.

Golf Link

http://www.golflink.com

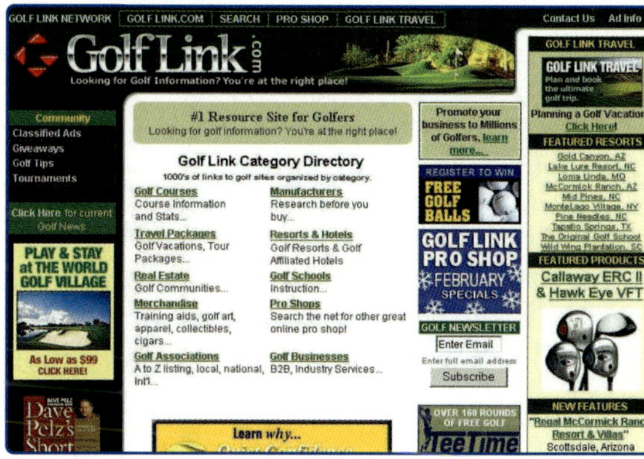

Never has the old saying "if it ain't broke, don't fix it"seemed more appropriate than at Golf Link. You see, you won't find original content. You won't find Golf link sponsored competitions. You won't even find roving reporters bringing you the latest news. Yet this isn't a criticism of the site. Far from it, the reason you won't find any of those things on Golf Link is because it doesn't need them. What it does do, however, it does so well that it more than justifies a visit.

On the Golf Link pages you'll find a large amount of links to golfing sites, making this an excellent portal for searching for almost anything related to golf on the web. If there's a golfing subject that isn't represented here, we can't find it. From links to associations, to golf schools, advertising, womens and junior golf or the latest equipment and reviews, you'll find them here.

The interface is attractive and the mass of material clearly laid out. At no point will you feel adrift in a sea of information.

It is a pity though that, at the time of this review, the search facility was still under construction as this would be a crucial part of a site of this size and nature. Still, we're sure that once it's completed it will follow the trend set by the rest of the site, and excel at its task.

RATING Refer to pg8 for rating explanations.

Overall Rating	✪✪✪✪
Ease of Use	✪✪✪✪
Content	✪✪✪✪
Look & Feel	✪✪✪✪
Customer Service	✪✪✪
Site Speed	✪✪✪✪
Technical	✪✪✪✪

MAIN POINTS:

>> Excellent selection of links.

GolfSearch.com

http://www.golfsearch.com

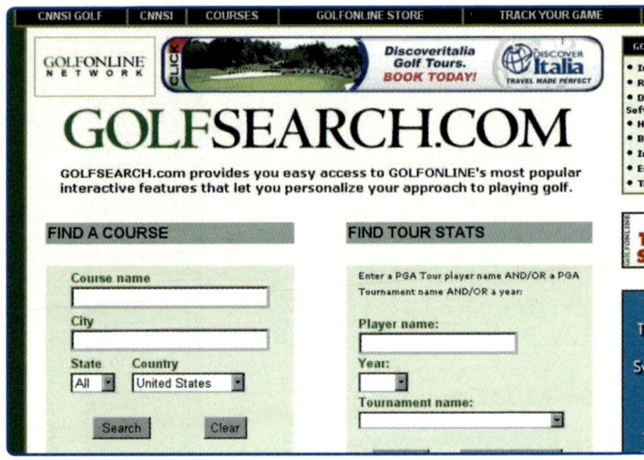

It's difficult when reviewing what is essentially a dedicated search engine for all things golf related to try and do the site justice. More often than not, there's little original content of its own to talk about, so websites like Golfsearch.com live or die on how well their search engine works. Luckily, this one works well – very well.

The home page is divided up into sections, to help you find exactly what you're looking for, with a diverse range of choices. From main headings like Junior Golf, Women's Golf, Rules, Fun & Humour and so on, you'll find subheadings that allow you to refine your search even more. Under Women's Golf, for example, you'll find categories devoted to instruction, organisations, LPGA

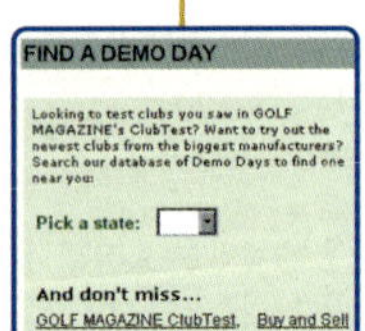

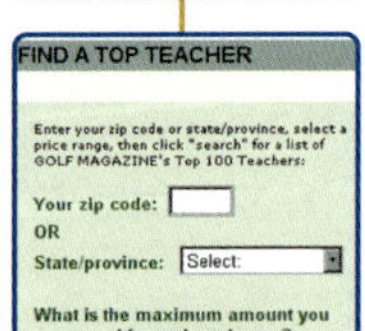

Tournaments and much more.

Chances are if you can't find what you're looking for after using our guide, and a site like this, then it's not out there to be found.

All of the links seem to be constantly updated, checked, and any dead links removed reasonably quickly. When we tested out the site, every single link that was suggested by Golfsearch worked perfectly. When it comes to search engines, you can't ask for much more than that.

RATING Refer to pg8 for rating explanations.

Overall Rating	✪✪✪✪
Ease of Use	✪✪✪✪
Content	✪✪✪✪
Look & Feel	✪✪✪✪
Customer Service	✪
Site Speed	✪✪✪
Technical	✪✪✪

MAIN POINTS:

>> Impressive statistics searcher.

>> Site kept up to date.

My Golf Zone

http://www.mygolfzone.com

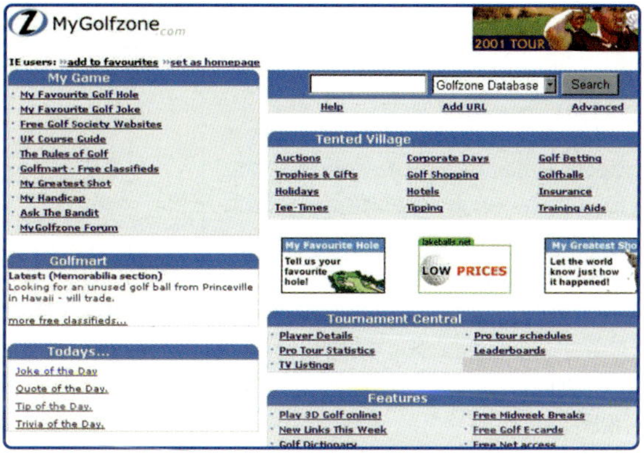

Pay a visit to this golf portal site and the first thing that will hit you is the massive amount of content you'll find on the home page. Tucked away under dozens of clear and logical subheadings, you'll find everything from information about the latest big name golf tournament to golfing jokes to keep your friends laughing at the 19th hole. If you're more of an armchair golf fan, you can play a round or two from the comfort of your home with the great 3D golf game, or alternatively you can subscribe to a host of free online newsletters guaranteed to keep you up to date with all that's happening in the golfing world. The choice can be a little overwhelming.

Indeed, you'll find links to around 30,000 golf related sites on the Internet here, so its unlikely you'll ever truly get to experience everything that MyGolfZone has to offer. With so many links to such a massive number of pages, the relevance of some is inevitably going to be higher than others (will many golfers really want to check their horoscope to see how it will effect their performance?) However if you're serious about your game and want some help in finding your way through all of those golfing sites, then you could do much worse than starting your journey here.

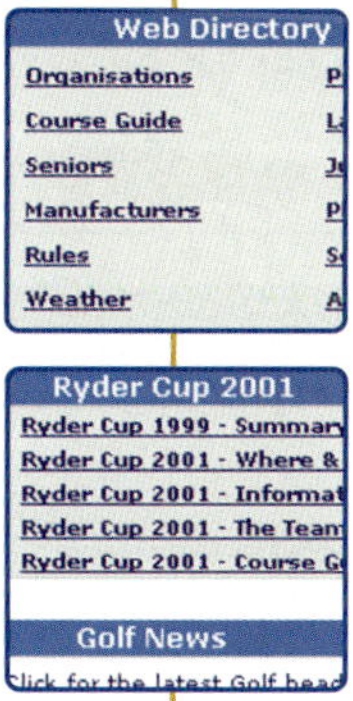

RATING Refer to pg8 for rating explanations.

Overall Rating	✪✪✪✪
Ease of Use	✪✪✪
Content	✪✪✪✪✪
Look & Feel	✪✪✪
Customer Service	✪✪✪✪
Site Speed	✪✪✪✪
Technical	✪✪✪✪

MAIN POINTS:

>> Good set of links to golf sites.

>> Lots of additional features.

Nothing but Golf

http://www.nothingbutgolf.com

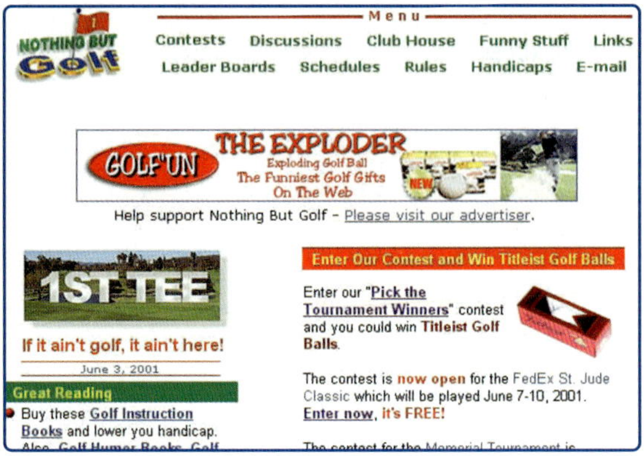

This US based site takes the form of an online golfing magazine, and as such boasts a good selection of jokes, the inevitable embarrassing golfing stories and some truly mind boggling golfing trivia.

One nice touch, the Hole In One boasting-bulletin-board, is clearly there to massage the egos of golfers who may (or may not) have hit that all important shot. Although mostly from the US, there were Hole In One stories from the four corners of the globe, so if nothing else this indicates that the site is visited by an international audience. Indeed, it's such visitors who you'll find in the discussion groups.

Also scattered around the site are reviews of golfing computer games and a "trading place" where equipment can be exchanged or sold. Seemingly, this is only occurring between visitors who live in the USA, but all it takes is enough enthusiastic non-US residents to start the ball rolling, and before you know it there'll be more bartering and haggling going on than there was back in medieval England.

RATING Refer to pg8 for rating explanations.

Overall Rating	✪✪✪
Ease of Use	✪✪✪✪
Content	✪✪✪
Look & Feel	✪✪✪
Customer Service	✪✪
Site Speed	✪✪✪
Technical	✪✪✪

MAIN POINTS:
>> Fun, lively magazine style approach.

Other Directories & Discussion Link Listings

Other Directories & Discussion related sites reviewed		Page
Bad Golf Monthly	http://www.badgolfmonthly.com	147
BunkerShot.com	http://www.bunkershot.com	149
Free Golf Info.	http://www.freegolfinfo.com	71
Golf Europe	http://www.golfeurope.com	88
Golf Magic	http://www.golfmagic.com	152
Golf Monitor	http://www.golfmonitor.com	153
GolfServ	http://www.golfserv.com	128
Golf Journeys in Ireland	http://www.irishgolf.com	90
Little Aussie Golfer	http://www.lag.com.au	74
PGA Net	http://www.pganet.net	94
PGA Professional	http://www.pgaprofessional.com	134
PGA Tour	http://www.pgatour.com	158
The Golf Channel	http://www.thegolfchannel.com	159
Titliest Golf	http://www.titleist.com	63
The Open Championship	http://www.opengolf.com	97
US Senior Open	http://www.ussenioropen.com	160

Other Directories & Discussion related sites

http://golf.start4all.com

http://golfwebcenter.fol.nl

http://members.tripod.co.uk/emr_uk

http://www.bestcoursestoplay.com

http://www.golfalot.com

http://www.golfcourseequipment.com

http://www.golffacilities.com

http://www.golfpublic.com

http://www.golf-select.co.uk

http://www.infohub.com/travel/adventure/recreation/golf.html

http://www.interlog.com/jskrypek/golf.html

http://www.jimzunogolf.com

http://www.linksforall.com

http://www.myrtlebeachsearch.com

http://www.oilcontrol.it/dg/dgindexe.shtml

http://www.onlinegolfclinic.com

http://www.sit.wisc.edu/acjeong/golf

http://www.spaceports.com/keygolf

Reviews

American Golf Auction

http://www.americangolfauction.com

Auctions are funny things. You could put the most worthless piece of golfing memorabilia up for grabs, and its value can be driven through the roof if the right personalities clash over it. It's this drive (no pun intended) to out-do the other bidder that makes them such fascinating things to watch.

This site allows you to buy or sell new and used equipment. To have any access to these facilities, you have to be a registered member, which you can do by filling in a form on the site. You need only register once. Get that out of the way and you're free to buy and sell as you see fit.

When you register, a handicap is calculated for you from the information you've provided. By no means essential to the bidding experience, but still a nice additional touch.

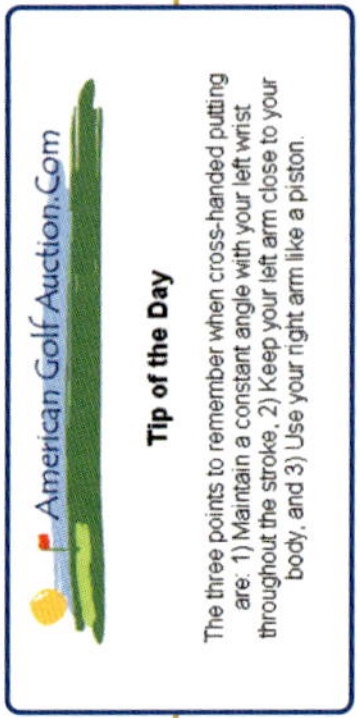

If you have any worries about buying and selling online, they have a frequently asked questions page that will more often than not have the answers you're looking for.

As usual with online auctions, all payments are held until the goods are delivered, which is reassuring to both the buyers and sellers.

RATING Refer to pg8 for rating explanations.

Overall Rating	✪✪✪✪
Ease of Use	✪✪✪
Content	✪✪✪
Look & Feel	✪✪✪
Customer Service	✪✪✪✪✪
Site Speed	✪✪✪✪
Technical	✪✪✪✪

MAIN POINTS:

>> Great way to experience online auctions.

Callaway Golf

http://www.callawaygolf.com

Official home to the major golf equipment brand, we found that visiting Callaway Golf.com was a great experience. From the neat little animation promoting their new range of balls ("more spin, more range, more fun" they promise...), this well designed, professional and easy to navigate site could teach lesser golfing pages a lesson or two about how to make your mark on the Net.

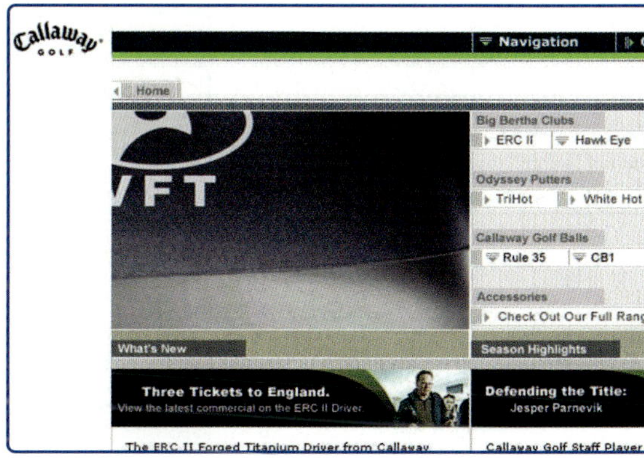

As one would expect, you can find out all the information you could possibly need to know (and quite a bit of interesting trivia) about the current Callaway clubs, putters, balls and accessories. It's all here.

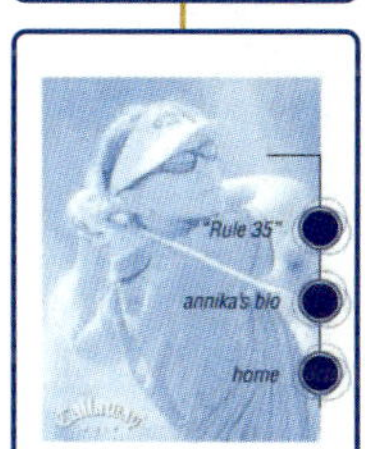

There's a retailer locator, which only covers the USA, but if you live anywhere else in the world, you can use their wholesaler locator, (tucked away in the news section of all places), to find your nearest supplier. Just pick a country from the drop down menu provided and you will have the contact details you need in no time.

It's comforting that the people behind this site, are very accommodating. Their responses to our email enquiries were quick, courteous and concise, so you can be sure that if all else fails, you'll always be able to talk to someone.

RATING Refer to pg8 for rating explanations.

Overall Rating	✪✪✪✪
Ease of Use	✪✪✪
Content	✪✪✪✪
Look & Feel	✪✪✪
Customer Service	✪✪✪✪✪
Site Speed	✪✪✪
Technical	✪✪✪✪

MAIN POINTS:

>> Comprehensive information on products and where to get them. Good response to contact.

Clubfinders Golf

http://www.clubfindersgolf.com

If you're looking to sell off your old golf equipment or fill in a few missing pieces in your set, then Clubfinders Golf claims to be the site for you.

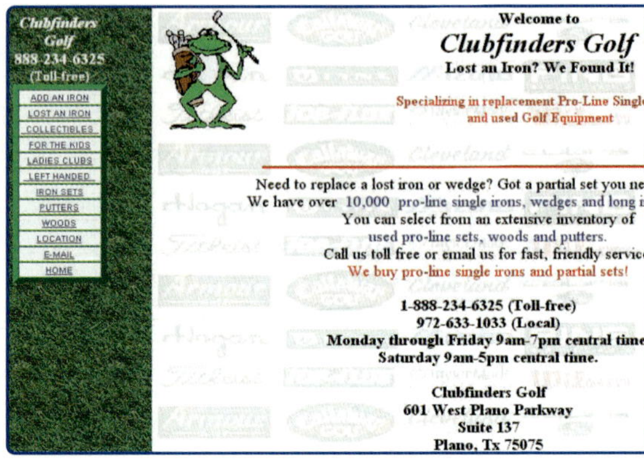

The site offers a large selection of mostly used products, clubs, irons and putters.

All of the information is given on large plain pages, which group each club in stock under their respective manufacturers groupings. The listings themselves offer very little specific information about each club however. All you are presented with is the manufacturer of the club, the name, whether it's new or used and the price that they charge.

The site offers very little information on how much they will pay you for used items, so you'll have to contact them for further information if you're interested in selling.

The product pages are very plain, simply a black and red chart on a white background. Unfortunately the site does not offer online shopping, so should you wish to order something you will have to email or call them.

RATING Refer to pg8 for rating explanations.

Overall Rating	✪✪
Ease of Use	✪✪
Content	✪✪
Look & Feel	✪✪
Customer Service	✪✪✪
Site Speed	✪✪✪
Technical	✪✪

MAIN POINTS:

>> One of the few e-commerce golf sites that buys, as well as sells clubs.

Dandy Golf

http://www.dandygolf.com

The Dandy is a high spec golf putter that this golf website claims will make great improvements to your game.

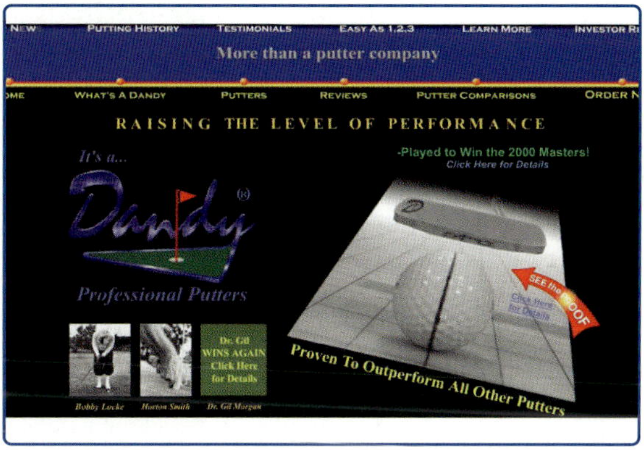

According to the site, the Dandy has a special forward pressing shaft, which is designed so that your hands are positioned in front of the putter's face, which then gives you better control over your putts.

The comparison pictures also show a much-improved view of the ball, which aids you in properly aligning your shots. Such advances don't come without a high price though. Even the cheapest model will cost you close to two hundred US dollars with shipping and handling. Still, the site does a very good job of explaining and demonstrating the Dandy, so you may wish to spend some time checking it out before making any hasty decisions.

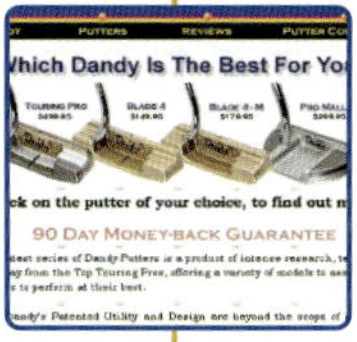

If you do decide to order one, you'll find all orders are taken on a secure server and international shipping is available.

Overall, this is a very well done, professional and informative site. Well worth a look.

RATING Refer to pg8 for rating explanations.

Overall Rating	✪✪✪✪
Ease of Use	✪✪✪
Content	✪✪✪✪
Look & Feel	✪✪✪✪
Customer Service	✪✪✪
Site Speed	✪✪✪
Technical	✪✪✪

MAIN POINTS:

>> Clearly demonstrates the technicalities of the Dandy putter.

Drop Putters

http://www.drop-putters.com

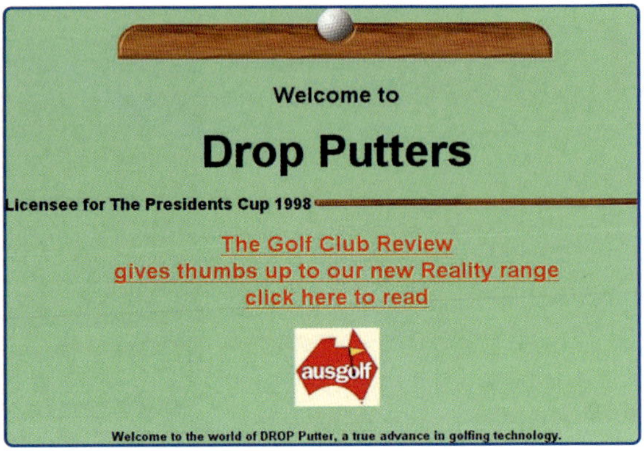

Drop Putters claims to be "better than the almost infinite variety of other putters available today." A bold statement.

This site is simply designed and easy to use with a plain green background and golf ball link buttons. According to the website, their forged blade putters help give you a better feel for your club than with other putters due to the softer metals that are used in the construction of the putters.

The site does a good job of filling you in on almost every conceivable bit of information you could want to know about the Drop Putter.

There's no traditional basket system on the site, so you'll need to remember what you want and select it in on their order form. We strongly suggest that you use their alternate payment methods rather than giving credit card details on their order form which at the time of our visit was NOT SECURE.

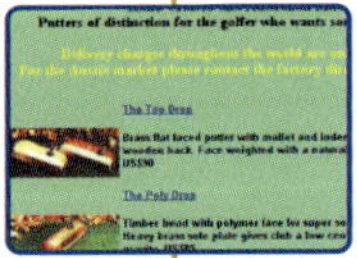

Their prices however, may make it worth looking into, as their specially designed putters come with prices that are largely in line with the upper level mass putters in the market.

An Australian site with prices in US dollars and they will ship worldwide.

RATING Refer to pg8 for rating explanations.

Overall Rating	✪✪✪
Ease of Use	✪✪✪
Content	✪✪
Look & Feel	✪✪✪
Customer Service	✪
Site Speed	✪✪✪
Technical	✪✪✪

MAIN POINTS:

>> Hand made putters at mass market prices.

Golf Judge

http://www.golfjudge.com

Judge, jury and executioner? Well, we're not sure about the last two, but Golf Judge certainly aims to be the standard in golf equipment testing and reviewing.

This is a comprehensive and well-organized site. The aspect of the site that gives Golf Judge its name is a clever button that allows you view the various ratings for each club. These include distance, accuracy and so on, as well as comments from golfing pros.

Probably the most impressive feature of the site is the training pages, which are enhanced by a learning section with video inserts. The video clips are available at different viewer speeds (28k, 56k ISDN and so on) so you'll be sure of playing the clip that is tailored for your connection. You can also choose to play the clips through either Windows Media Player or Real Player. Choices like these are not just cosmetic, and are becoming more important in the streaming media age, so it's nice to see Golf Judge has realised this early on, emphasizing the professional feel of the site.

The site's golf shop is an affiliate site from vstore.com, widely used by many websites and carries a good stock of products, but unfortunately only ships to US destinations.

RATING Refer to pg8 for rating explanations.

Overall Rating	✪✪✪✪
Ease of Use	✪✪✪
Content	✪✪✪✪
Look & Feel	✪✪✪✪
Customer Service	✪✪✪
Site Speed	✪✪✪✪
Technical	✪✪✪

MAIN POINTS:

>> We judged this to be a great site.

GolfMonster.com

http://www.golfmonster.com

"GolfMonster.com brings together a team of dedicated people who love golf and believe it is their job to help you enjoy this great game even more!" proclaims the home page of the site.

"Every employee shares the same commitment to excellence. A commitment that will assure that each and every customer has a rewarding and enjoyable secure online shopping experience." Sounds good so far, doesn't it? "Our goal is to maintain the largest In-Stock inventory of any on-line golf store," they go on to announce.

The most surprising thing, apart from the fact that they've resisted the temptation to go completely over the top and come up with some club carrying creature as their mascot, is that after all the exclamation marks and exuberance, they may just pull it off. The stock listing certainly is large, from Callaway, Taylor Made and Titleist to Nike, Adams and Orlimar, you'll find them all at this online store. Indeed, the question you'll be asking yourself isn't "I wonder if they have my favourite club?" but more likely to be "Which one of these shall I look at first?" because the options available to you from the home page onwards are truly overwhelming. There's some excellent discounts too, making the shop a tempting prospect for golfers from outside the US.

RATING Refer to pg8 for rating explanations.

Overall Rating	✪✪✪✪
Ease of Use	✪✪✪
Content	✪✪✪✪
Look & Feel	✪✪✪✪
Customer Service	✪✪
Site Speed	✪✪✪✪
Technical	✪✪✪✪

MAIN POINTS:

>> Very wide range of latest golf products. User friendly.

Golfonline

http://www.golfonline.com

This site features in a number of categories in our guide bacause it offers plenty of content.

Up to date information on all the latest golf news, all the major tour statistics (which are updated weekly) as well as details on a wide range of courses throughout the world. The details of the courses include a brief description and history of each course, fees, reservation details, handicap requirements, as well as dress code, where applicable.

If you feel the need to hone your game, you'll be able to find out more about golfing instruction here too. There is a facility to search for golf schools by area in the US. Video clips from Golf Magazine TV offer a refreshing distraction, offering classic tips by top teachers, while professional teachers will answer any questions via email. The fundamental rules of the game are discussed, and a useful link is provided to a site that covers all of the official guidelines to the sport. Advice on health and fitness relating to golf is also included.

There are dedicated sections for Women's Golf, Junior Golf and Senior Golf, all featuring articles, tips, schools and leagues.

In addition, an excellent online store is available, which utilises a great search facility that allows you to search by either manufacturer, product, or key word . The equipment buying guide is also very useful, offering monthly reports on the latest golfing gear.

RATING Refer to pg8 for rating explanations.

Overall Rating	★★★★
Ease of Use	★★★★
Content	★★★★
Look & Feel	★★★★
Customer Service	★★★
Site Speed	★★★★
Technical	★★★★★

MAIN POINTS:

>> Packed with good, relevant content

>> Excellent international shop in partnership with golfsmith.com.

Golfspan Pro Shop

http://www.customgolf.com

CustomGolf.com poses as the largest source for custom built "trend design" golf clubs on the Internet They carry most pro-line brands and accessories, but specialize in custom fitting equipment to meet each individual golfer's physical and playing characteristics.

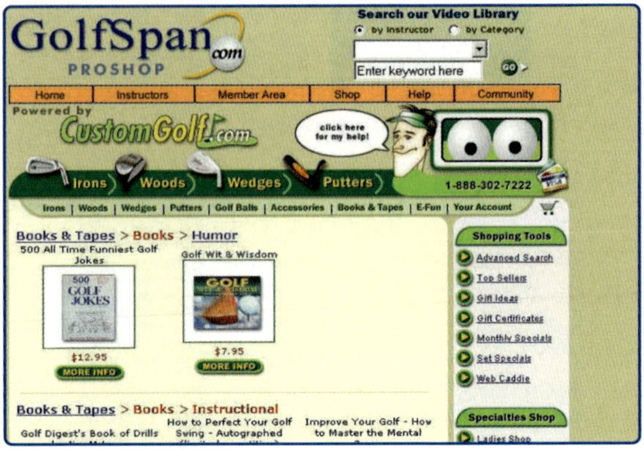

They boast over 3000 products, and provide a comprehensive selection of woods, irons, wedges, putters, golf balls, bags, shoes, and much more. To help you find the equipment that fits your own game, they have a fantastic feature called the Web Caddie. You'll grow to love this virtual chap. He's an online fitting expert, that guides you through each step by asking questions about your physical and playing characteristics. Once Web Caddie learns enough about you and your game, he provides recommendations on various components to be considered in building your equipment. CustomGolf.com was recognized by ZDNet's Top 10 Best Examples of E-Commerce as a result of the Web Caddie feature, so the little fella is clearly something special.

For the advanced golfer, CustomGolf.com provides the option for you to choose from dozens of shaft and grip selections to ensure your clubs are tailored just how you like them. Once you decide which shafts and grips you like, your selections are retained by the site, and automatically become available to you throughout the rest of the pages.

The site stands behind its product too, offering a 30 day unconditional money back guarantee on all custom built equipment.

RATING Refer to pg8 for rating explanations.

Overall Rating	✪✪✪✪✪
Ease of Use	✪✪✪✪✪
Content	✪✪✪✪✪
Look & Feel	✪✪✪✪✪
Customer Service	✪✪✪✪✪
Site Speed	✪✪✪✪
Technical	✪✪✪✪✪

MAIN POINTS:

>> Great Caddie feature.

>> Flawless customer service.

Hole In One Inc

http://www.holeinoneinc.com

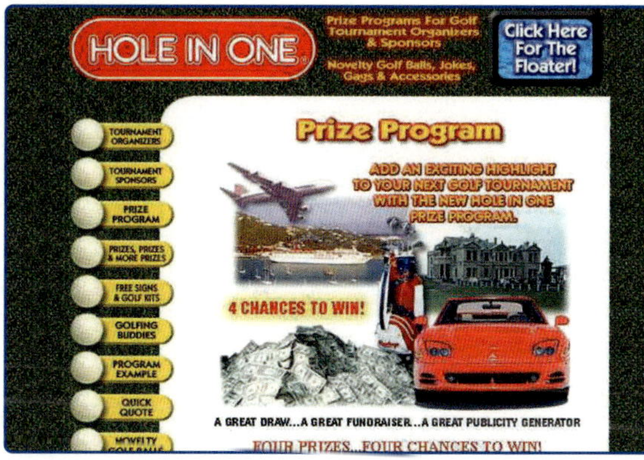

It was difficult to know just where to put this site in the guide, and so we settled for equipment based on the novelty and accessories section they have. These aren't the main focus of the site, but what they do focus on we wanted to show you, but didn't have another section for.

Holeinoneinc.com have a great idea that'll appeal to your competitive side. They market a "hole in one" prize program where, if a club pays a registration fee and signs up to the scheme, they will cover the cost of some great prizes for any hole in one obtained in one of their competitions. Sort of an insurance idea. Worth a look if you think your club would be interested.

The novelty section includes a selection of golf balls that will no doubt be ideal for playing tricks on your golfing buddies the next time you're all on the course. With names such as floater, exploder, wobbler and upputtaball they are sure to provide hours of entertainment.

The small selection of golfing accessories makes up the rest of their e-commerce section.

Orders must be placed by phone, and are more directed to retailers rather than consumers.

RATING Refer to pg8 for rating explanations.

Overall Rating	✪✪✪
Ease of Use	✪✪✪
Content	✪✪
Look & Feel	✪✪
Customer Service	✪✪✪
Site Speed	✪✪✪
Technical	✪✪

MAIN POINTS:

>> Run a special hole in one prize scheme.

>> Great novelty products.

Liquid Golf

http://www.liquidgolf.com

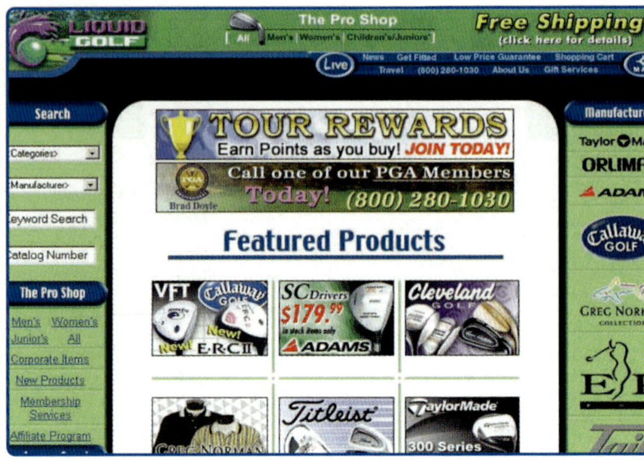

Sometimes you'll find sites that are filled with original content, and want nothing more from you than your time on their site. Others try and stay content heavy, but throw in a shopping section to make a little extra money from their site. At the extreme end of the spectrum, you'll find sites that are purely and simply online stores: no news, no reviews, no features, just products. LiquidGolf is one of those stores.

What it sets out to do it manages to do well. You'll find the latest technologies, new products, accessories, books, videos, magazines and more here, along with links for male and female golfers.

Special mention should be made of the low price guarantee, which reads: "Our low price guarantee is simple: if you find a lower price on new name-brand equipment at a competing web site or proof of a retail ad prior to purchase, LiquidGolf.com will beat the price!" Nice offer, which if honoured, will automatically make this website cheaper than the cheapest e-commerce site on the Net. For this reason alone, LiquidGolf is certainly worthy of a visit.

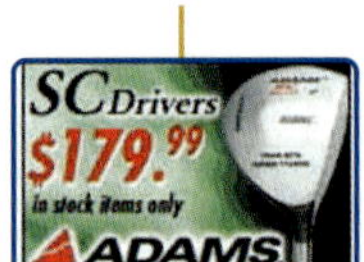

RATING Refer to pg8 for rating explanations.

Overall Rating	✪✪✪✪
Ease of Use	✪✪✪✪
Content	✪✪✪
Look & Feel	✪✪✪✪
Customer Service	✪✪✪
Site Speed	✪✪
Technical	✪✪✪

MAIN POINTS:

>> Excellent low price guarantee.

LouisvilleGolf.com

http://www.louisvillegolf.com

In an age of mass produced, made to identical specification clubs, which admittedly is an inevitable side effect of the incredible popularity of golf, it's nice to find that some corners of the world manage to hold onto a little piece of history. Look hard enough, and you'll still find golf clubs that are crafted by hand, by people who have spent years learning the art of making the perfect club. Specifically, look here.

Because at Louisville Golf, you'll find exactly that: a company that has been producing golf clubs using traditional methods for over 27 years. The site serves to expound the value of the "the world's leading maker of Persimmon golf clubs," and goes into great depth to explore this subject.

A great quiz adds to the enjoyment of a visit and it's added areas of interest like this that pushes the site above the usual limits of promotional pages on the Internet.

Check out the range of hints and "truths" about golf equipment for some real eye opening facts. There is also a corporate logo engraving service here, that seems very reasonably priced indeed.

The site design is impressive, with good graphics and easy navigation.

We had problems reaching the company via email.

RATING Refer to pg8 for rating explanations.

Overall Rating	✪✪✪
Ease of Use	✪✪✪
Content	✪✪✪
Look & Feel	✪✪✪✪
Customer Service	✪
Site Speed	✪✪✪
Technical	✪✪✪

MAIN POINTS:

>> Makers of traditional golf clubs.

>> More than just online shopping.

Ping Golf

http://www.pinggolf.com

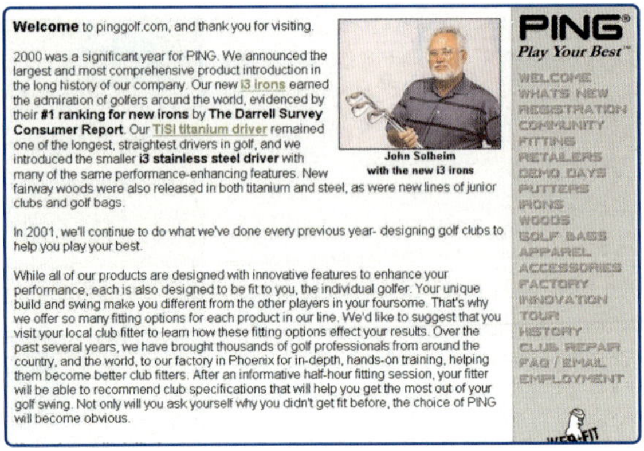
Welcome to pinggolf.com, and thank you for visiting.

2000 was a significant year for PING. We announced the largest and most comprehensive product introduction in the long history of our company. Our new i3 irons earned the admiration of golfers around the world, evidenced by their **#1 ranking for new irons** by **The Darrell Survey Consumer Report**. Our TiSI titanium driver remained one of the longest, straightest drivers in golf, and we introduced the smaller **i3 stainless steel driver** with many of the same performance-enhancing features. New fairway woods were also released in both titanium and steel, as were new lines of junior clubs and golf bags.

John Solheim with the new i3 irons

In 2001, we'll continue to do what we've done every previous year- designing golf clubs to help you play your best.

While all of our products are designed with innovative features to enhance your performance, each is also designed to be fit to you, the individual golfer. Your unique build and swing make you different from the other players in your foursome. That's why we offer so many fitting options for each product in our line. We'd like to suggest that you visit your local club fitter to learn how these fitting options effect your results. Over the past several years, we have brought thousands of golf professionals from around the world, to our factory in Phoenix for in-depth, hands-on training, helping them become better club fitters. After an informative half-hour fitting session, your fitter will be able to recommend club specifications that will help you get the most out of your golf swing. Not only will you ask yourself why you didn't get fit before, the choice of PING will become obvious.

The official home of one of the most recognisable brand names in golf was frankly a little less impressive than we had hoped. They've recently put up a notice to all visitors to say that we can look forward to a new and improved site, but what does Ping Golf have to offer us right now?

Well, the site, as one would expect, focuses on the Ping brand and their equipment. On entering you are welcomed with the latest news

You're encouraged to register any of your Ping products online and, as an incentive, you'll be able to replace equipment with exactly the same ones that you had before – which would be important to most golfers.

There's a good section on fitting, so that you get the best possible clubs to suit you. Follow the steps, and you'll find out which colour coding group you fit. This will allow you to have Ping clubs made to fit.

The site also offers you a behind the scenes tour of the factory and the process of making Ping clubs, as well as some interesting history of the brand.

RATING Refer to pg8 for rating explanations.

Overall Rating	✪✪✪
Ease of Use	✪✪✪✪
Content	✪✪✪✪
Look & Feel	✪✪✪
Customer Service	✪✪✪
Site Speed	✪✪✪
Technical	✪✪✪

MAIN POINTS:

» The definitive place for Ping product information online.

Pinnacle Golf

http://www.pinnaclegolf.com

If you like style as well as substance when it comes to your golfing websites, then here's one you'll enjoy: Pinnacle Golf is a great site for streaming media, with a Flash game to test your expertise... or rather, your expertise with the Pinnacle products.

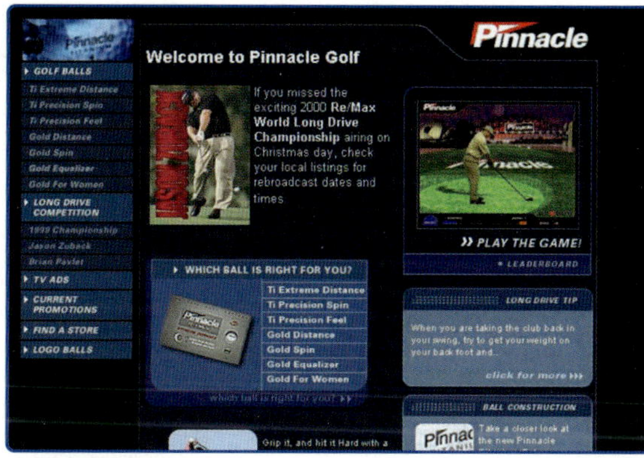

This site is essentially an advertising and display area for Pinnacle golfing equipment. In spite of this, (or perhaps because Pinnacle want it to appeal to as broad an audience as possible) it still manages to go further than the common "advertorial" site. One of the most impressive things about it is the extent to which the product is put in the spotlight, with pop-up windows going into ever greater depth about the Pinnacle range. There is also a page which enables you to find a store from which to buy the product because, after all, the ultimate aim of this page is to encourage you to become a Pinnacle owner.

Above all, though, there is a certain amount of design finesse involved in the site which creates an easy and effective viewing experience. Ironically, some of the most innovative features to be found here manage to simultaneously be a blessing and a curse. The Flash game for one, which is entertaining and a nice distraction, was still painfully slow to download.

We could not find any obvious e-mail address to send queries to.

RATING Refer to pg8 for rating explanations.

Overall Rating	✪✪✪
Ease of Use	✪✪✪✪
Content	✪✪✪
Look & Feel	✪✪✪✪
Customer Service	✪
Site Speed	✪✪✪
Technical	✪✪✪✪✪

MAIN POINTS:

>> Good use of Flash to liven up things up.

ProsPlay.com

http://www.prosplay.com

If you're convinced there's something holding you back from being the best golfer that you can possibly be, if you're sure it's the tools and not the craftsman that is to blame for missing that all important shot, then you'll want to know which equipment is winning the major competitions. ProsPlay is here to tell all.

The main feature of this site is that it tracks what equipment the pros are using, then tallies the points they score and assigns them to the equipment they play with.

The information is gathered by a number of methods including spotters at competitions, taping and viewing hours of recorded TV coverage, and insider info from tour caddies.

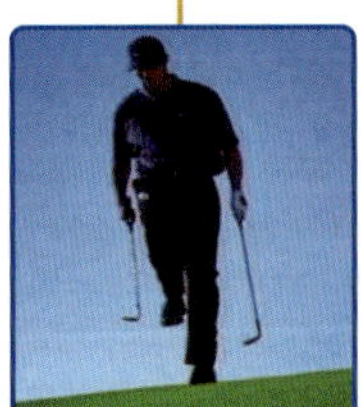

The site is really easy to use and filters down the basic information, presenting it so you can see who the pros are that are responsible for making a particular piece of equipment climb up or down the "charts".

The site also offers a place for you to post your own messages and comments, and strike up discussions with other golfers around the world.

RATING Refer to pg8 for rating explanations.

Overall Rating	✪✪✪✪
Ease of Use	✪✪✪✪
Content	✪✪✪✪
Look & Feel	✪✪✪
Customer Service	✪✪✪✪✪
Site Speed	✪✪✪
Technical	✪✪✪✪

MAIN POINTS:

>> Great info on the equipment that makes a difference in big money tournaments.

Taylormade Golf

http://www.taylormadegolf.com

The official site of Taylor Made golf clubs currently devotes its opening page to their new 300 series of clubs. Strangely, we are immediately presented with a pop-up advertisement for these same clubs. Progress past this stage however, and the site is well worth a visit.

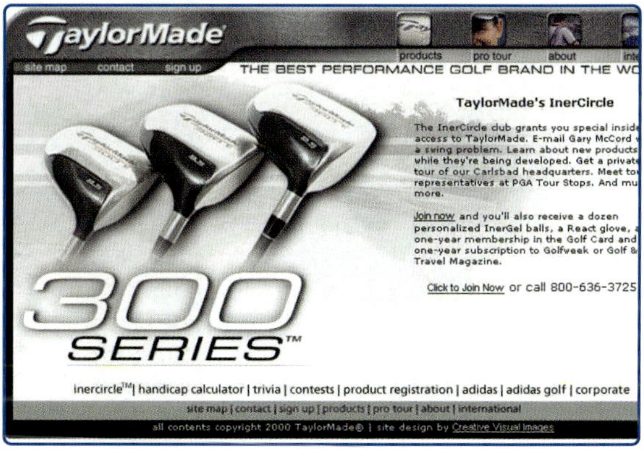

It's certainly very detailed, providing you with all the latest updates and developments regarding the Taylor Made range. Whether its metal woods, irons, women's or kids clubs, you'll find something about each of them here. If you're not based in the United States, you'll find links to sites that are tailored (no pun intended) to your country – a nice touch, that shows they're looking to appeal to a truly worldwide audience.

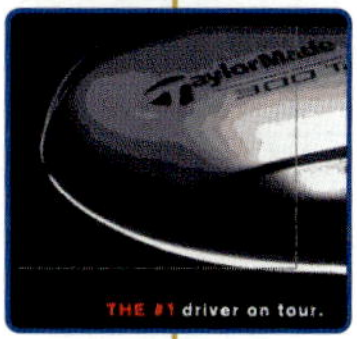

Equally pleasing, in addition to all the advertorial content you'll find, there are plenty of extra features that won't try to sell you a thing (the handicap calculator and trivia contests are some of the most notable) so this site is certainly worth a visit and comes highly recommended.

RATING Refer to pg8 for rating explanations.

Overall Rating	✪✪✪✪
Ease of Use	✪✪✪✪
Content	✪✪✪✪
Look & Feel	✪✪✪✪
Customer Service	✪✪✪
Site Speed	✪✪✪✪
Technical	✪✪✪✪

MAIN POINTS:

>> Attractive and easy to use.

Titleist (UK)

http://www.titleist.co.uk

As you may have guessed from the name, this site focuses on Titleist Golf products, balls and clubs for the UK market.

If you want to find out more information on Titleist equipment, then this is without a doubt the site for you.

They provide more information about a golf ball then we thought was possible. All the product profiles feature a well written and thorough description, with product specification, images, features and benefits. Since not everyone enjoys reading such a great deal of information onscreen, a printer friendly version of most of the profiles is available for offline reading.

Getting exactly the right clubs is essential to having a good game, (so they say) and so you'll find a page detailing all the UK stockists who are able to fit you for a custom set of Titleist clubs. After all, anything that gives you an edge over your opponents has to be worthwhile.

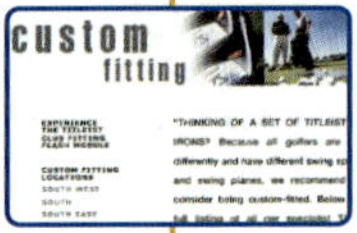

Should you need convincing, the list of professional golfers who use Titleist products will probably do the trick.

RATING Refer to pg8 for rating explanations.

Overall Rating	✪✪✪✪
Ease of Use	✪✪✪✪
Content	✪✪✪
Look & Feel	✪✪✪✪
Customer Service	✪✪✪
Site Speed	✪✪✪
Technical	✪✪✪

MAIN POINTS:

>> If Titleist is your chosen brand, then this is the site for you.

Titleist

http://www.titleist.com

If you're passionate about golf and keep up to date on the biggest names in the game, then you'll inevitably have heard the name Titleist passed around the course. If so, and you're not sure what all your golfing friends are raving about, or you just want to impress them with your encyclopaedic knowledge of the brand, then here's the US site for you.

This is the official home of Titleist on the Internet, and covers every aspect of the innovative golf ball – and we do mean every aspect. You'll find details about everything from the relevance of the material that the balls are made from (which, they stress, is of the very highest quality) to an insight into the technology surrounding their product.

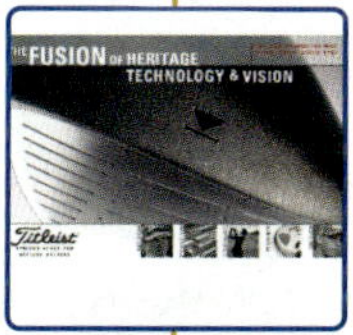

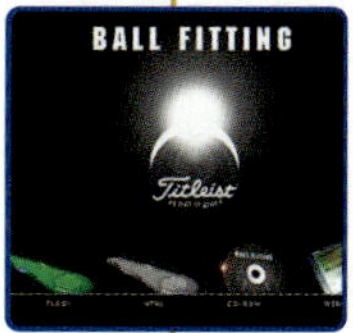

Feedback is encouraged through an online form, whereby complaints and suggestions can be made directly to the manufacturers while an in-house news section deals with appointments and developments within the company. Importantly, the web site does diversify to give background and golf history for a number of the world's top players. There is a section for the UK and one dedicated to the Titleist users of Japan as well as a comprehensive diary of upcoming demonstrations.

RATING Refer to pg8 for rating explanations.

Overall Rating	✪✪✪
Ease of Use	✪✪✪✪
Content	✪✪✪
Look & Feel	✪✪✪
Customer Service	N/A
Site Speed	✪✪✪
Technical	✪✪✪

MAIN POINTS:

>> The site is fast, efficient and well designed.

Topflite Golf

http://www.topflite.com

Topflite.com is the official home of Topflite golfing equipment on the Internet.

In general, its design is very clear, graphically pleasing and uses simple, straightforward navigation while managing to clearly illustrate their products.

From the sidebar one can access the product information pages of their balls and clube, an international dealer locator, warranty and registration pages and a link to the Spalding Sports shop.

The product information pages, as you would expect, provide a wealth of detailed information on the products as well as links to where you can buy.

The site offers a dealer locator with a handy search area for US retailers and lists all international distributors.

A nice touch is their "Hole in One" link which allows you to fill in the details of a hole in one that you've had and they will send you a "hole in one certificate of achievement."

RATING Refer to pg8 for rating explanations.

Overall Rating	✪✪✪
Ease of Use	✪✪✪
Content	✪
Look & Feel	✪✪✪
Customer Service	✪✪✪
Site Speed	✪✪✪✪
Technical	✪✪✪

MAIN POINTS:

>> Good graphics and clear presentation.

Other Equipment Link Listings

Other Equipment related sites reviewed		Page
BestValueGolf.com	http://www.bestvaluegolf.com	184
Chipshot.com	http://www.chipshot.com	187
Designer Golf Gifts	http://www.designergolfgifts.com	106
Global Golf	http://www.globalgolf.com	86
Golf Illustrated	http://www.golfillustrated.com	166
Golf Ladies	http://www.golfladies.com	226
Golf Magic	http://www.golfmagic.com	152
Golf Monitor	http://www.golfmonitor.com	153
GolfBalls.com	http://www.golfballs.com	190
Hallson Golf	http://www.hallsongolf.com	192
Ladies Golf Clubs	http://www.ladiesgolfclubs.com	227
Nike Golf	http://www.nikegolf.com	195
ParGolf.com	http://www.pargolf.com	196
St Andrews Links	http://www.standrews.org.uk	97
The Golf Warehouse	http://www.tgw.com	198
Topflite Golf	http://www.topflite.com	64

Other Equipment related sites

http://www.equip2golf.com
http://www.exdiscountgolf.com
http://www.fanaticgolf.com
http://www.fidogolf.com
http://www.flex-fit.qpg.com
http://www.globalgolfinc.com
http://www.golf4less.com
http://www.golfaficionado.com
http://www.golfamericastores.com
http://www.golfbrothers.it
http://www.golfbyconnie.com
http://www.golfcase.com
http://www.golfcenter.com
http://www.golf-classics.com
http://www.golf-clones.com
http://www.golfclothes.com
http://www.golfclubreview.com
http://www.golfclubsetc.com
http://www.golfclubsplus.com
http://www.golfconcierge.com
http://www.golfcraft.com
http://www.golfcraftersinc.com
http://www.golfday.com
http://www.golfdealz.com
http://www.golfden.com
http://www.golf-direct.co.uk
http://www.golfessentials.com
http://www.golfexchange.com
http://www.golfgarage.com
http://www.golfgod.com
http://www.golfideas.com
http://www.golfinn.com
http://www.golfoutlet.com
http://www.golfpeddler.com
http://www.golfprices.com
http://www.golf-prostore.com

Other Equipment Link Listings

http://caddythis.com
http://champspikes.com
http://clubmaker-online.com
http://freedomgolf.com
http://geocities.com/jerryclubstofit
http://golfextras.com
http://golfteck.com/
http://home.earthlink.net/clarksystems
http://home.infospace.com/dvgolf1
http://home.internetcds.com/rwmcclen
http://jabba.tlh.fdt.net/wgarvin
http://macgregorgolf.com/
http://marksgolf.com
http://stansgolf.com/
http://te-ezz.com
http://thegolfswingpage.com
http://theperfectswingtrainer.com
http://tomgolf.freeyellow.com
http://www.123-golf.com
http://www.123greetings.com/sports/golf
http://www.24ktgolfcraft.com
http://www.4golfing.com/
http://www.aa.net/redbirdsports
http://www.accuprogolf.com
http://www.acegolfcarsplace.com
http://www.adamsgolf.com
http://www.adcouple.com
http://www.adincsportstreasures.com
http://www.adros.com
http://www.advancedgolf.com
http://www.advantagegolfgreens.com
http://www.albiongolfcars.com
http://www.alfamall.com
http://www.atlasgolfonline.com
http://www.back9golf.com/spalding.html
http://www.bagelbuddiesgolf.com
http://www.balatabills.com
http://www.ballfinder.com
http://www.bealegend.com
http://www.benningtongolf.com
http://www.bestsportgifts.com
http://www.bgclubs.com
http://www.bhgolf.com
http://www.bigmoss.com
http://www.birdiepal.com
http://www.birkdale-trophies.co.uk
http://www.blackjag.com
http://www.blackplasma.com
http://www.caddythis.com
http://www.cajunmade.com
http://www.carolinasports.com
http://www.carringtonhall.co.uk
http://www.catalogolf.com
http://www.christianitee.com
http://www.cigardriver.com
http://www.circuit-pro.com
http://www.classicgolfproducts.com
http://www.clevelandgolf.com
http://www.clubmakers.com
http://www.clubquiver.com
http://www.clubs4less.com
http://www.clubsac.com
http://www.clubsbydesign.com
http://www.clubshieldplus.com
http://www.clubstofit.com
http://www.copperstix.com
http://www.corporate-golf.com
http://www.criteriongolf.com
http://www.cubila.com
http://www.customclubs.net
http://www.daiwa.com
http://www.dewgooders.com
http://www.dgigolf.com
http://www.dogleggolf.com
http://www.doglegsportswear.com
http://www.downpatgolf.com
http://www.drewcogolf.com
http://www.drgolf.org
http://www.dwquailgolf.net
http://www.dynacraftgolf.com
http://www.dynamicgolfco.com
http://www.egolf.com
http://www.eltagolf.com
http://www.encore-golf.com

Other Equipment Link Listings

http://www.golfshow.com
http://www.golfsmith.com
http://www.golfsouth2000.com
http://www.golfspecialties.com
http://www.golfsportswear.com
http://www.golfsticks.com
http://www.golfstore4u.com
http://www.golftechcanada.com
http://www.golfteck.com
http://www.golfworks.com
http://www.golfww.com
http://www.gophergolf.com
http://www.hometeamgolf.com
http://www.igogolf.com
http://www.igolfstore.com
http://www.innographite.com
http://www.insideright.com
http://www.janwaygolf.com
http://www.jaworgolf.com
http://www.jegolf.co.uk
http://www.johnsclubs.com
http://www.jrgolfclubs.com
http://www.justgolfonline.com
http://www.kidsgolfstuff.com
http://www.kingbo-golf.com
http://www.koolshirts.com
http://www.lazy-bones.com
http://www.lefthandedgolfer.com
http://www.lincolngolf.com
http://www.littleshafty.com
http://www.macbirdie.com
http://www.macgregorgolf.com
http://www.mammothgolf.com
http://www.modernclassicwoods.com
http://www.mrgolf.com
http://www.mydiscountgolfgear.com
http://www.mygolfpro.com
http://www.ontargetgolf.com
http://www.parabolicgolf.com
http://www.parforthecourse.com
http://www.parplace.com
http://www.parplaygolf.com
http://www.peggputters.com
http://www.personalizedgolfballs.com
http://www.pirategolf.com
http://www.planetgolf.com
http://www.positiveputter.com
http://www.precisionputter.com
http://www.premiergolfwear.com
http://www.proclubgolf.com
http://www.pro-curiogolf.com
http://www.progolf-lansing.com
http://www.prostaffgolf.com
http://www.puttingmat.com
http://www.ramgolf.com
http://www.rangergolf.com
http://www.reidlockhart.com
http://www.rochegolf.com
http://www.rockportgolf.com
http://www.seriousgolf.com
http://www.setfit.com
http://www.sitelinegolf.com
http://www.sologolf.com
http://www.standrewsgolf.co.uk
http://www.targetgolf.com
http://www.tartangolf.com
http://www.tbarryknickers.com
http://www.teedoffgolf.com
http://www.teesbytim.com
http://www.tee-up.com
http://www.tensation.com
http://www.thefullswing.com
http://www.thegolfballoutlet.com
http://www.thegolfballplace.com
http://www.the-golf-centre.co.uk
http://www.theworldofgolf.com
http://www.tommyarmour.com
http://www.tradergolf.com
http://www.traxxgolf.com
http://www.tritongolf.com
http://www.truflexgolf.com
http://www.universalgolf.com
http://www.va-golf.com
http://www.virtual-fairway.com
http://www.wowputter.com
http://www.ziplinegolf.com

EZ Webguides

6th hole - general & miscellaneous

Reviews

Cyber Golf

http://www.cybergolf.com

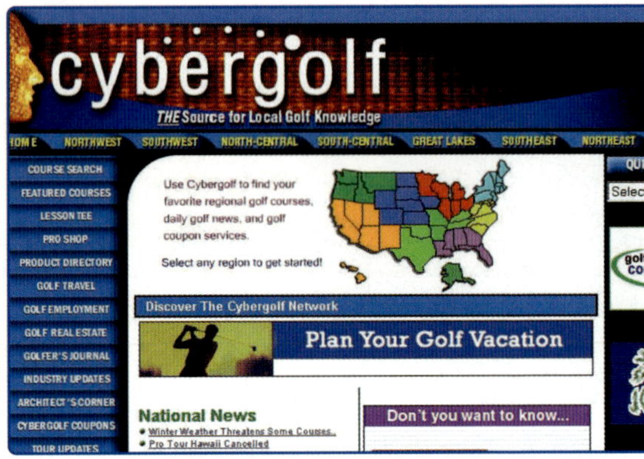

Although it all sounds very hi-tech and virtual reality inspired, Cybergolf isn't anywhere near as futuristic as it sounds. In fact, if you're looking for local golf knowledge in the USA rather than the the virtual world, then this was one of the better sites we could find on the Net.

The front page will offer you a list of regions in the United States, with current golfing news from each state. Then there's a comprehensive list of links to features such as course searches, featured courses, online lessons, pro shops. product directories, golf travel, golf employment, golf schools, golf real estate, a golfers journal, industry updates, an architects corner, tour updates, fitness and nutrition tips and ideas, a gallery of images, golf associations, links to other golfing sites, weather forecasts in the US and more.

Many of the links take you to other pages within Cybergolf itself rather than sending you to other sites on the Internet, so it's a great place to start out.

Unfortunately we didn't receive a response to the contact email we sent, and since there were a couple of broken links on the site too, you're left with the impression that Cybergolf is being a little neglected. This is a genuine shame, because with a little more care and attention Cybergolf has the potential to be a really great site.

RATING Refer to pg8 for rating explanations.

Overall Rating	✪✪✪
Ease of Use	✪✪✪
Content	✪✪✪
Look & Feel	✪✪✪
Customer Service	✪
Site Speed	✪✪✪
Technical	✪✪✪

MAIN POINTS:

>> Good place to start for golf on the Internet.

Free Golf Info.

http://www.freegolfinfo.com

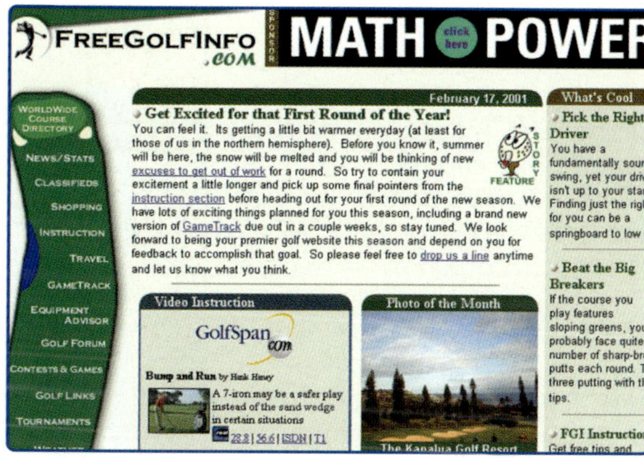

Free Golf Info presents itself as "the largest worldwide golf community" on the Internet. Quite a claim, but how much is public relations hype and how much is true? Does the site manage to live up to the boasts?

Well, there's certainly plenty on offer, and most of the content is theirs. We say most, because one or two sections of the site, including the shopping area, are actually hosted on other sites. In real terms, this means instead of staying within freegolfinfo.com, you'll surf to a completely different site. This can get a bit confusing, being bounced around from one site to another.

The website provides free golf lessons and tips, golf club reviews, handicap tracking and game analysis, golf course info, travel, classifieds, golf jobs and more, all in one place so it's definitely worth a visit.

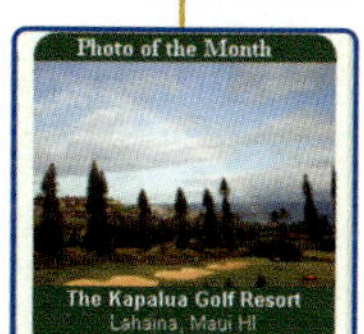

Some of the most notable features of the site include a golf forum where you can interact with golfers from around the world, an excellent game analysis feature and hundreds of free online lessons, perfect for golfers of all skill levels. All features are also highly interactive and there's a distinctly international feeling to the pages. The site design is also pleasant, and easy to use.

RATING Refer to pg8 for rating explanations.

Overall Rating	✪✪✪✪
Ease of Use	✪✪✪
Content	✪✪✪✪
Look & Feel	✪✪✪✪
Customer Service	✪✪✪✪✪
Site Speed	✪✪✪
Technical	✪✪✪

MAIN POINTS:

>> Excellent and engaging content.

Golf Today

http://www.golftoday.co.uk

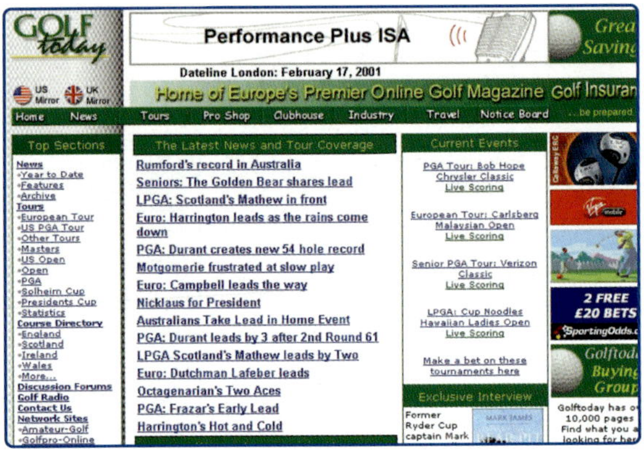

The subtitle for the Golf Today website is "Europe's Premier Online Golf Magazine." Well, it's certainly big enough to serve the whole of Europe, as the Golf Today site is the the hub of the Golf Today Network - a group of six websites containing news and information about every aspect of golf.

Golf Today concentrates on the professional tournaments and general golf news covering all major US, European, Asian and Australian tours. There is also an extensive course directory with over 2,600 golf courses in the UK & Ireland featured. If you like what you find here, then the Golf Today network also operates golfpro-online.com, which focuses on equipment and tuition news, and includes several tuition series including exclusive tips by Ken Venturi, go-golf.net is the travel site, with news of the latest offers as well as links to sites where you can book your holiday online, Golf-industry.com is for those interested or working in the industry, with the latest news, a comprehensive worldwide directory of companies in the golfing business and a notice board for jobs, Amateur-golf.com has everything for the serious amateur, with union/federation news and information as well as the latest amateur event coverage and finally, Golf Ecology focuses on the environmental and ecological aspects of the game.

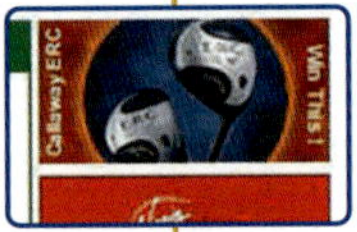

In most of the sites there's a link to a pro shop which in turn takes you to various partner programs.

RATING Refer to pg8 for rating explanations.

Overall Rating	✪✪✪✪
Ease of Use	✪✪✪✪
Content	✪✪✪✪
Look & Feel	✪✪✪
Customer Service	✪✪✪✪✪
Site Speed	✪✪✪
Technical	✪✪✪✪

MAIN POINTS:

>> Great content.

>> Speedy response to our emails.

IGA Golf

http://www.iga-golf.com

We would recommend setting aside at least an hour if you're going to browse International Golf Associates website, because there simply is a huge amount of information here. The depth is truly mind boggling.

In summary:
Sections on fitness, golf insurance, jokes, pro tips, employment, equipment, holidays, golf courses, bookstores, lessons, magazines, stories and a free monthly newsletter

With offices in the US and Switzerland, the site truly is aimed at a worldwide audience.

The most impressive thing we saw was their international course finder which will help you find golf courses in almost any region of any country around the world. It's clear that the database is still building, but it's still the most comprehensive that we've seen online. We would certainly recommend anyone who belongs to a golf club to go along and see if their club is listed. If not, adding it is quick and easy and you'll be doing your club a great service for it's promotion.

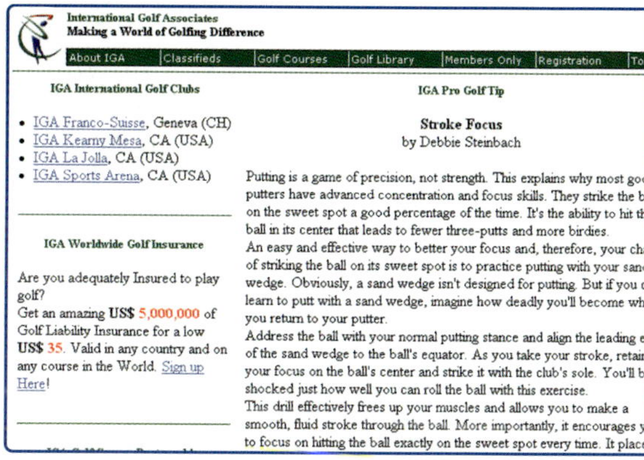

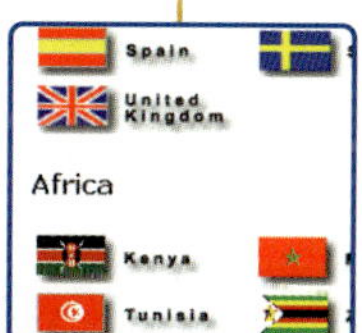

RATING Refer to pg8 for rating explanations.

Overall Rating	✪✪✪✪
Ease of Use	✪✪✪
Content	✪✪✪✪✪
Look & Feel	✪✪✪
Customer Service	✪✪✪
Site Speed	✪✪✪✪
Technical	✪✪✪

MAIN POINTS:
- Stunning depth of information
- Plenty of content to keep you reading.

Little Aussie Golfer

http://www.lag.com.au

With a name like Little Aussie Golfer, you can't help but imagine a small man wandering around a golf course, club in one hand, cold beer in the other, complaining to Dame Edna and Rolf Harris about his Sheila, while a kangaroo hops by and a wallaby watches from under a nearby Eucalyptus tree.

Stereotypes over, what you actually get is both reviews and details of around 1,400 Australian Golf courses, which will prove to be invaluable for golfers living in or planning on visiting Australia. The site also has sections that'll interest a more international audience, with features such as golf instruction articles, question and answer sessions and even reviews of a whole range of golf computer games. The quotes page is packed with words of wisdom from famous and not so famous golfers, who offer gems like "Golf is a game in which you yell Fore, shoot six and write down five" or "I know I'm getting better at golf cos I'm hitting fewer spectators." Genius.

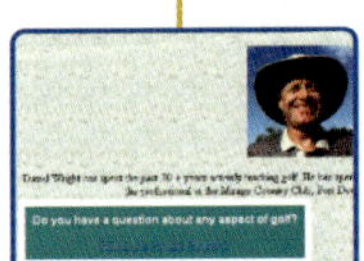

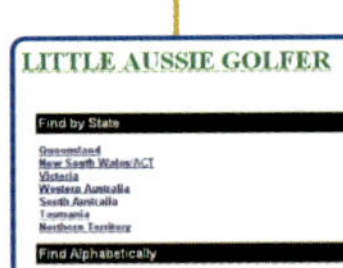

Little Aussie Golfer also features literally hundreds of golf jokes too. Maybe the stereotype about Australians having a good sense of humour is one that we should stick to after all.

RATING Refer to pg8 for rating explanations.

Overall Rating	✪✪✪✪
Ease of Use	✪✪✪
Content	✪✪✪✪
Look & Feel	✪✪✪
Customer Service	✪✪✪✪✪
Site Speed	✪✪✪
Technical	✪✪✪

MAIN POINTS:

>> Clean, clear and easy to use site.

>> Packed with jokes, quotes and words of wisdom.

Shoot59.com

http://www.shoot59.com

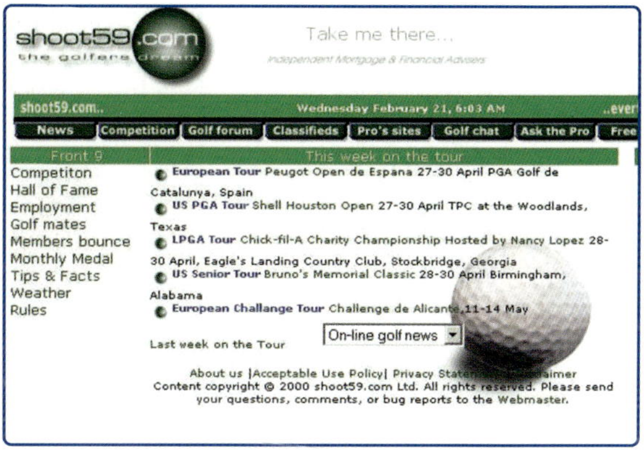

"Shoot59.com," explains the on-site guide "is the ultimate directory for golfers bringing you the golfer 'everything golf on the net'. The Shoot59.com Portal is a dedicated entry-point to the Internet for golfers in the UK. Our aim is to provide golfers in the UK with all the information and Internet services you will ever need, and all no more than a few clicks away."

Quite a mission statement, yet one that they seem determined to live up to. From this site, you'll find a great mix of both original content in the Front 9, features and news stories lifted from other sites on the Internet (they're credited as such, so no plagiarism here) as well as a series of links to other pages, services and online stores in the Back 9 section. Think of it as an online golfing superstore, with everything you need at the one address, and you'll be pretty close to the reality of what Shoot59 is. Interactivity is encouraged, with chat forums where visitors can chat to one another, along with the chance to submit your favourite sites to be including in the links pages. Also, Shoot59 offers a free email address to their subscribers and 25MB of space online, just in case you feel inspired and want to start putting your own golf site on the Internet.

RATING Refer to pg8 for rating explanations.

Overall Rating	✪✪✪
Ease of Use	✪✪✪✪
Content	✪✪✪
Look & Feel	✪✪✪
Customer Service	✪✪✪
Site Speed	✪✪✪✪
Technical	✪✪

MAIN POINTS:

>> Almost perfect blend of original and sourced news and features, with plenty of links.

>> Mainly aimed at UK golfers.

The Golf Portal

http://www.thegolfportal.co.uk

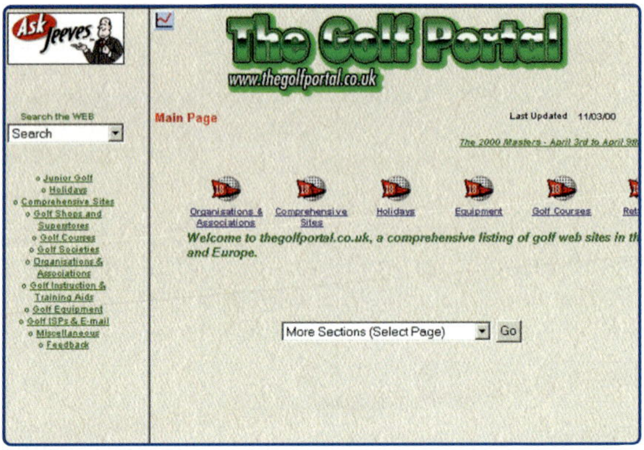

As the name indicates, this is a portal to other golfing sites on the Internet.

You'll find there is a fairly comprehensive listing of suppliers of golfing equipment and clothing, as well as a useful section dedicated to golfing holidays on a global scale.

There is also an interesting link to golf Internet Service Providers (yes, there are such things) and free email. Navigation is via a simple frame based page, and there are no frills or fancy flash animations here. However, some parts of the site are still under construction, which made it difficult to assess their functionality. The site also seemed generally sluggish considering there were very few graphic elements to be found.

Some parts of the site seemed slower than others, so we'll assume this a teething problem that'll be sorted out in time.

Generally the coverage of the many different aspects of golf was fairly comprehensive. Overall, a fairly competent site.

RATING Refer to pg8 for rating explanations.

Overall Rating	✪✪
Ease of Use	✪✪✪
Content	✪✪
Look & Feel	✪✪✪
Customer Service	✪
Site Speed	✪✪
Technical	✪✪✪

MAIN POINTS:

>> Some interesting links.

The Ministry of Golf

http://www.theministryofgolf.com

Hearing someone say: "we don't want your money" can make a refreshing change, especially when it seems that's the only thing websites are after. Yet if that wasn't good enough reason to explore the uniquely titled Ministry Of Golf pages, then the promise to not "shove annoying sales tactics down your throat" will clinch the deal. "We're here to enjoy the game and help you do the same," they promise. As for how they do that, it seems the answer is with tongue firmly in cheek.

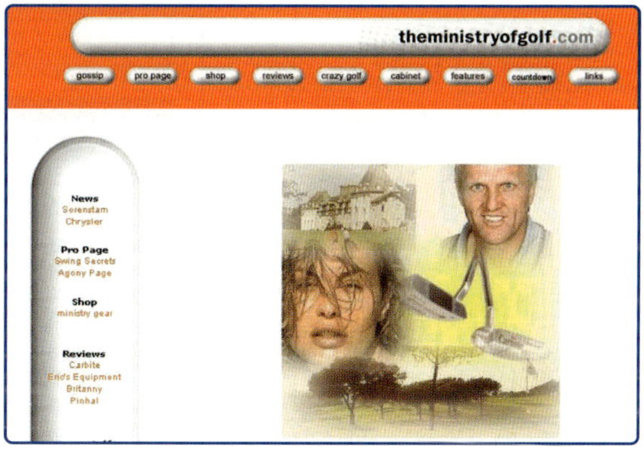

Pop along to the gossip pages and you'll find stories, photographs and jokes submitted by visitors to the site. Try the Crazy Golf pages and you'll be greeted with cartoons parodying golf bores, plus the odd gratuitous picture of semi-nude women. Well, it was only a matter of time before someone used sex to sell the game of golf, wasn't it? Start to explore the features pages

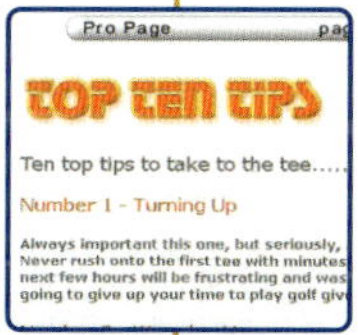

and you'll find, amongst other things, a handy guide to recreating the Masters experience without leaving the comfort of your home, with advice including "sneak down at 7am each morning and put out your folding chair in front of the TV, to make sure you get the best view of the action" and "ask your neighbour if you can park in his driveway for the weekend and give him £50." Parking is free at the Masters, but it gets so busy that people have to leave their cars in the driveways of local residents, for extortionate fees."

RATING Refer to pg8 for rating explanations.

Overall Rating	✪✪✪✪
Ease of Use	✪✪✪✪
Content	✪✪✪
Look & Feel	✪✪
Customer Service	✪✪✪
Site Speed	✪✪✪
Technical	✪✪✪

MAIN POINTS:

>> Genuinely funny and doesn't take itself too seriously.

UK Golf Information Site

http://www.uk-golf.com

This impressive golfing database, while admittedly light on original content, does still provide a great deal of practical information for anyone interested in golf across the British Isles. Indeed, as you can probably guess from the title, UK Golf provides an unashamedly British perspective on the game.

In addition to all the obvious information you'd expect to find on such a site, like guides to golf clubs, courses, country clubs, equipment and so on, you'll also be able to draw upon plenty of unexpected additional information that will nonetheless make playing the game of golf a more enjoyable experience.

Need to find a way of travelling to the course you've always dreamed of playing on? You'll find that here.

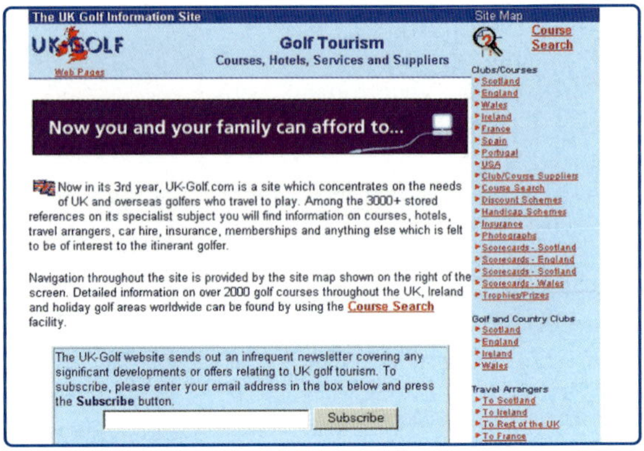

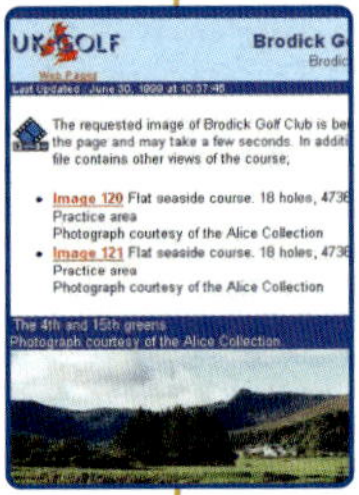

Need somewhere to stay once you get there? UK Golf has that covered too. There are links to literally hundreds of related websites, making UK Golf one of the best starting points for anyone wanting to play in Britain.

The site does lose a couple of credibility points for claiming that golf has become an increasingly "dangerous game over the past few years" but we'll put that down to them being a tad over-cautious.

Either that, or having a particularly bad experience with an impatient caddie...

RATING Refer to pg8 for rating explanations.

Overall Rating	✪✪✪
Ease of Use	✪✪✪
Content	✪
Look & Feel	✪
Customer Service	✪✪✪✪✪
Site Speed	✪✪✪
Technical	✪

MAIN POINTS:

>> Extensive links to hundreds of golfing sites.

Other General & Miscellaneous Link Listings

Other General & Miscellaneous related sites reviewed		Page
American Golf Auction	http://www.americangolfauction.com	46
Bad Golf Monthly	http://www.badgolfmonthly.com	147
CNN Sports Illustrated	http://golf.si.cnn.com	151
Golf and Sporting Occasions	http://www.gso.co.uk	123
Golf Europe	http://www.golfeurope.com	88
Golf Journeys in Ireland	http://www.irishgolf.com	90
Golf Judge	http://www.golfjudge.com	51
Golf.com	http://www.golf.com	154
GolfMonster.com	http://www.golfmonster.com	52
Golfonline	http://www.golfonline.com	53
Hole In One Inc	http://www.holeinoneinc.com	55
Leading Golf Courses of America	http://www.golfmiles.com	217
Liquid Golf	http://www.liquidgolf.com	56
LPGA	http://www.lpga.com	229
PGA of America	http://www.pga.com	157
Places To Golf	http://www.placestogolf.com	218
R&A Golf Club of St. Andrew's	http://www.randa.org	135
Scottish Golf	http://www.scottishgolf.com	96
Sporting Bet	http://www.sportingbet.com	197
US Golf Association	http://www.usga.org	136
World Golf	http://www.worldgolf.com	220

Other General & Miscellaneous related sites

http://americangolfersassoc.com
http://caddythis.com
http://corp2.unisys.com
http://golfclassic.org
http://seniorgolfersamerica.com
http://thegolfersnewsletter.net
http://wiga.org
http://www.19thhole.com
http://www.24hourgolfing.com
http://www.4play.com
http://www.academyofgolf.com
http://www.acegolfcarsplace.com
http://www.advantagegolfgreens.com
http://www.ajga.org
http://www.albiongolfcars.com
http://www.amateurgolf.com
http://www.americangolf.com
http://www.asg.ch
http://www.asga.org
http://www.asgca.org
http://www.asiangolf.com
http://www.awga.org

Link Listings

http://www.azgolf.org
http://www.bamagolf.com
http://www.bcga.org
http://www.bencrenshaw.com
http://www.bettergolf.net
http://www.bigga.co.uk
http://www.bigmoss.com
http://www.birdiepal.com
http://www.birkdale-trophies.co.uk
http://www.cajunmade.com
http://www.carolinasports.com
http://www.carrascogolf.com
http://www.cartpath.com
http://www.celebrityproam.com
http://www.cga.org
http://www.chichi.org.
http://www.clubedge.com
http://www.clubsac.com
http://www.clubshieldplus.com
http://www.coverknits.com
http://www.csgalinks.org
http://www.cypressgolf.com
http://www.donnaandrews.net
http://www.eaglegrip.com
http://www.eaglelinks.com
http://www.easypicker.com
http://www.ecogolf.com
http://www.encore-golf.com
http://www.epgolf.co.za
http://www.fairwaysgreens.com
http://www.fairwaysweekly.com
http://www.familygolf.org
http://www.fargogolfers.com
http://www.fathersongolf.com
http://www.fcwtgolf.com
http://www.fdnygolf.com
http://www.ffg.org
http://www.flextee.net
http://www.foregolfersonly.com
http://www.frbg.be
http://www.fringegolf.com
http://www.fsga.org
http://www.futurestour.com
http://www.gam.org
http://www.gcsaa.org
http://www.ggcc.com
http://www.glassetcher.com
http://www.gocaddie.com
http://www.goforegolf.com
http://www.golfball.com
http://www.golfclassifieds.co.uk
http://www.golfcoffee.com
http://www.golfcollection.com
http://www.golfcritters.com
http://www.golfforms.com
http://www.golfgamearrangers.com
http://www.golf-jokes.co.uk
http://www.golflabels.com
http://www.golflins.com
http://www.golfmarker.com
http://www.golfplaza.com
http://www.golfprices.com
http://www.golfsminitours.com
http://www.golfspecialties.com
http://www.golf-stat.com
http://www.golftrain.com
http://www.golfweb.com
http://www.golfwholesale.com
http://www.gripitandripit.com
http://www.gripping.com
http://www.gsga.org
http://www.harriscollection.com
http://www.hitandsit.com
http://www.husband-wife-golf.com
http://www.ibuygolfclubs.com
http://www.idahogolfassn.org
http://www.igolf.com
http://www.igolf2.com
http://www.ijgt.com
http://www.isgagolf.org
http://www.jdrtool.com
http://www.jgaa.org

Link Listings

http://www.jkgolfpro.com
http://www.jrgolf.com
http://www.juniorgolftournaments.com
http://www.kahmagolf.com
http://www.kangaroogolf.com
http://www.kansasgolf.org
http://www.kgu.or.ke
http://www.kleetkleen2000.com
http://www.knuckleglove.com
http://www.kpga.com
http://www.larrynelson.com
http://www.leftygolf.org
http://www.lookforgolf.com
http://www.lusogolf.org
http://www.luxurycarts.com
http://www.mesga.org
http://www.mgaa.com
http://www.mgalinks.org
http://www.mogolf.org
http://www.muligangolf.com
http://www.mulligantour.com
http://www.mysportsbox.com
http://www.nationwidegolf.com
http://www.ncga.org
http://www.night-magic.com
http://www.njgs.com
http://www.ntga.org
http://www.nysga.org
http://www.oasiswheel.com
http://www.oceancitygolf.com
http://www.ohiogolf.org
http://www.orgolf.org
http://www.outbackgolf.com
http://www.parts4carts.com
http://www.pcma.net
http://www.percisegolf.com
http://www.pgaonline.com
http://www.pgtaa.com
http://www.pgtca.com
http://www.pinhighgreens.com
http://www.powellsequipment.com
http://www.ppgagolf.com
http://www.proamopen.com
http://www.proclubmakers.org
http://www.p-uj.com
http://www.puttingmat.com
http://www.qualityinnovations.com
http://www.realgolf.tv
http://www.relianceintl.com
http://www.rollinggreenservices.com
http://www.rotanet.uk.com
http://www.scga.org
http://www.sharkchallenge.com
http://www.shivas.org
http://www.singlesgolf.com
http://www.snga.org
http://www.statcardgolf.com
http://www.teamgolf.com
http://www.tee2greengolf.com
http://www.themasters.cc
http://www.topgolfer.com
http://www.toucangolf.com
http://www.tpkgolf.com
http://www.trashmasters.com
http://www.triple-s-products.com
http://www.uga.org
http://www.unitedbet.com
http://www.usgtf.com
http://www.vermontpga.com
http://www.vsga.org
http://www.wackygolf.com
http://www.wallyarmstrong.com
http://www.wemingogolf.com
http://www.worldamateur.com
http://www.worldpro-am.com
http://www.worldputtingchamp.com
http://www.worldwidewebofgolf.com
http://www.wpga.co.za
http://www.wpga.org
http://www.yogiberraclassic.org

EZ Webguides

7th hole - golf courses

Reviews

Balmoral Golf

http://www.balmoral-golf-scotland.co.uk

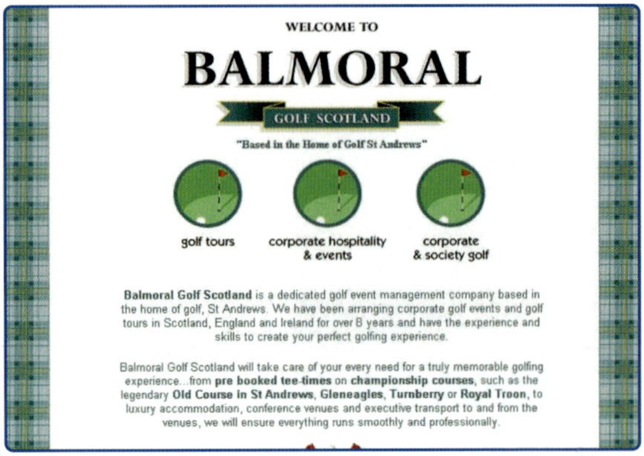

This golfing management company site offers access and information to a number of golf tours and events, which must be good: you've only got to look at their impressive list of clients to see that they must be doing something right.

Indeed, while this is an excellent site in many respects, there are few anomalies that stop it from being a great overall experience.

The first is that while it does offer a link to the courses, there is very little in the way of graphics to give you some idea of what they look like.

Secondly, the navigation system is a bit confusing, making it difficult to return to the homepage without using the back button.

Some of the golf tours feature a lot of detail, while some do not.

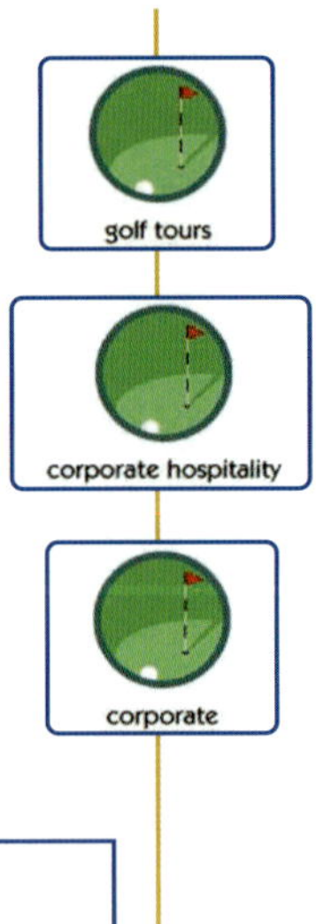

There is also a low level of interactivity, with the exception of the token email form that's provided.

Having said this, it's a credit to the rest of the site that Balmoral Golf still remains worth a visit, providing some interesting and informative golf tour possibilities. The problem lies essentially with the design itself, so if you're prepared to be a bit patient you'll still manage to get the best out of this site.

RATING Refer to pg8 for rating explanations.

Overall Rating	✪✪✪
Ease of Use	✪✪
Content	✪✪✪
Look & Feel	✪✪✪✪
Customer Service	✪✪✪
Site Speed	✪✪✪
Technical	✪✪

MAIN POINTS:

>> Good information and interesting tours.

Eighteen Global

http://www.18global.com

Eighteen Global truly lives up to its name.

On the first page you are given the option of navigating in five different directions, depending on where you wish to golf. Your choices are the USA, South Africa, the United Kingdom, Australia and the Rest of the World.

There are no radical differences between the five sections however, but it's nice that they include little touches to make each page have its own identity.

Once you choose which country you're interested in, the site then offers you a number of other options after you register. You're provided with services such as planning golf vacations, information, links about upcoming golf events and a well stocked Pro

Shop, with country specific shipping available so that you're not stuck with overseas mail charges.

It is true that you can find most of these services available on other sites but, Eighteen Global gives you all these options in a package that is both easy to navigate and fast moving. The site truly does offer a complete package to help meet your golf needs. Be it for the latest news updates or ordering that new nine iron, this site is extremely useful and we highly recommend it.

RATING Refer to pg8 for rating explanations.

Overall Rating	✪✪✪✪
Ease of Use	✪✪✪✪
Content	✪✪✪✪
Look & Feel	✪✪✪
Customer Service	✪✪✪✪
Site Speed	✪✪✪✪
Technical	✪✪✪✪

MAIN POINTS:
>> Great golfing site.

Global Golf

http://www.globalgolf.com

When a website claims to be truly global, you could be forgiven for taking that with a pinch of salt. After all, the world is a big place, and it's an ambitious project to try and cover all golf related goings on in one country, let alone world-wide. Yet that seems to be the goal Global Golf has set itself. As to whether or not they'll achieve it remains to be seen, but they've certainly started heading in the right direction.

Global Golf is one of the few websites online that covers golf courses in Asian countries like Malaysia, Thailand and Singapore in addition to the more traditional and commonly found venues in North America and Europe. Not content with that, the site promises to add New Zealand, Indonesia and the United Arab Emirates to the growing list too. There's an excellent online guide to hotels and B&Bs, which will not only tell you all about the places you can stay, but also makes booking a room as simple as clicking a mouse.

Similarly, the holiday packages available here are excellent and offer great value for money. With the cash you save, you might even want to gamble some of it through the online betting service this site offers or buy a cap bearing the logo of the Bombay Golf and Racing Club in India. Maybe this site really will become truly global after all...

RATING Refer to pg8 for rating explanations.

Overall Rating	✪✪✪✪
Ease of Use	✪✪✪
Content	✪✪✪
Look & Feel	✪✪✪✪
Customer Service	✪✪✪
Site Speed	✪✪✪
Technical	✪✪✪

MAIN POINTS:

>> Some excellent offers on holidays and accomodation.

>> International coverage.

Global Golf Guide

http://www.globalgolfguide.com

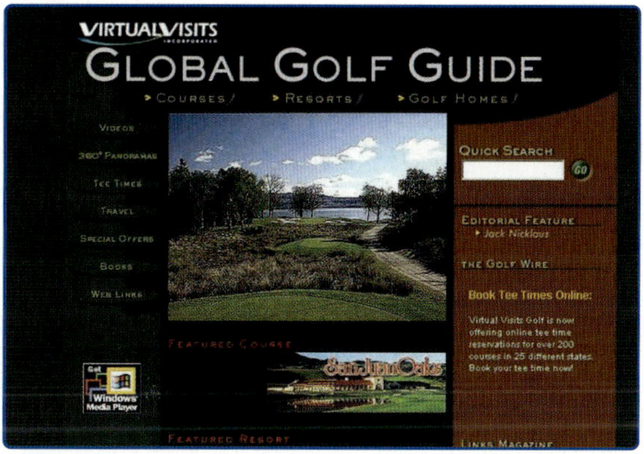

Once in a while, you come across a site that you feel you should make a permanent link to...we think Global Golf Guide is one such site.

It provides an overview of golf courses, resorts and ideal golf vacation spots the world over.

Rather than just tell you about them – albeit in a very descriptive and pleasing way – you'll also find videos too, so you can get a real first hand impression of what it would be like to play at, visit or stay at the highlighted venues. All you'll need to play them is Windows Media Player, which is free to download from the Microsoft website.

The site also boasts a Panoramic view of the courses, but again you'll need to download the required plug in to view it. The one catch is that the videos took a tad too long to open for our liking, but then again this might be due to other factors rather than bad media design. (Often the Internet, just like busy roads, suffers from its own "rush hour" when the sheer volume of people using it makes your connection run more slowly.) Still, the site is certainly one of the most attractive that we have seen - with a clear, glossy presentation and simple navigation.

Highly recom-mended and well worth a visit.

RATING Refer to pg8 for rating explanations.

Overall Rating	★★★★
Ease of Use	★★★
Content	★★★★
Look & Feel	★★★
Customer Service	★★★
Site Speed	★★★
Technical	★★★★

MAIN POINTS:

>> Good interactive use of a range of media.

Golf Europe

http://www.golfeurope.com

Seemingly, the Eurovision song contest isn't the only thing that unites Europeans under a common interest. Now you can add golf to the list too.

Indeed, that's exactly what Golf Europe has done, compiling a comprehensive listing of over 4,000 clubs across Europe and attracting around 90,000 visitors a month.

There's much more than a simple club guide or impressive figures to keep you coming back. You'll find interaction between visitors is encouraged at every step, with lively forums for just about every aspect of golf from equipment, the junior and senior game, tournaments (or tour-namnts as it says on the site) and even architecture. Sure to keep users talking.

There's also a handy guide to golf tips and tuition should you need to polish up your technique, as well as an extensive reference section covering the rules, terminology and biggest names in the sport.

One feature that stands out and is not found on many other sites, is the classified section, continuing Golf Europe's trend of encouraging its users to talk to one another. This is seemingly the busiest part of the site, jam packed with adverts from fellow golfers who are either looking for or selling equipment, tuition, travel or accommodation. Certainly worth a look.

RATING Refer to pg8 for rating explanations.

Overall Rating	✪✪✪✪
Ease of Use	✪✪✪✪
Content	✪✪✪✪
Look & Feel	✪✪✪
Customer Service	✪✪✪✪
Site Speed	✪✪✪✪
Technical	✪✪✪

MAIN POINTS:

>> More than enough content to keep you clicking through the site.

Golf in Europe

http://www.ecs.net/golf

No prizes for even the most observant of you out there that guess this site is, indeed, about golf in Europe.

On entry you're presented with a selection of options focusing on subjects such as golf clubs, publishing, tourism, business, tours and software.

Selecting the golf clubs prompts you to choose a European country, and then proceeds to display a list of all the clubs it has listed. If you've selected one of the larger members of the European community, the list can be pretty overwhelming. Luckily, you can view clubs alphabetically or by region, and you are provided basic details on each club, in addition to contact details where available.

The tourism links give pretty basic details of hotels and restaurants using a similar country by country

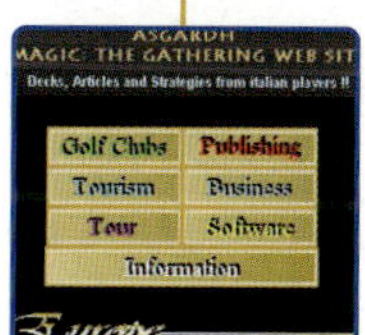

guide. While the business option links you to a page where various golf related companies have provided their contact details. Essentially a message board for people who are after your business and custom. There are all sorts of links in here that could be helpful for finding golfing equipment retailers, holidays and so on throughout Europe.

Finally, the software button will present you with links to downloadable software products including screensavers, golf games, statistics handlers, scoring packages and more. More often than not, these applications are free too, so well worth clicking on.

RATING Refer to pg8 for rating explanations.

Overall Rating	✪✪✪
Ease of Use	✪✪✪
Content	✪✪✪
Look & Feel	✪✪
Customer Service	✪✪✪
Site Speed	✪✪✪
Technical	✪✪✪✪

MAIN POINTS:

>> Reasonable info on golfing in Europe. Lots of nice freebies.

Golf Journeys in Ireland

http://www.irishgolf.com

"Ireland. There is, quite simply, no better place to play golf," announces the home page of this great site dedicated to golfing on the Emerald Isle.

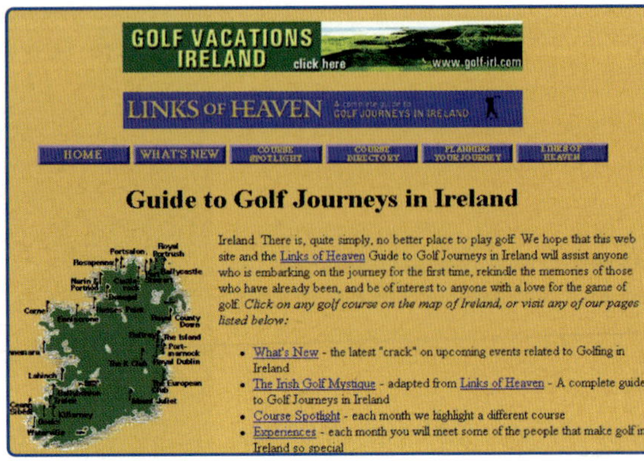

Well, while the makers of webpages like Scottish Golf may take exception to that statement, Irishgolf.com goes a long way to convince us that Ireland may indeed be the best place to experience the game.

When you first visit the site, you can chose to navigate your way around by either clicking the on screen map to jump to a course of your choice, or simply follow the links to take a more leisurely wander through the information packed pages. You'll be able to plan your journey to any one of the 130 courses covered on the site, read personal experiences of fellow golfers who have fallen in love with the game in Ireland, or simply keep up to date with upcoming events to mark on your golfing calendar.

Add to this a suitably respectful tribute to Ireland's own golfing legend Eddie Hackett, and you've got a comprehensive guide to all aspects of the game and its influence on the country.

Just be sure to wear green while you're playing, and enjoy a pint of the black stuff when you're done.

RATING Refer to pg8 for rating explanations.

Overall Rating	✪✪✪✪
Ease of Use	✪✪✪
Content	✪✪✪✪
Look & Feel	✪✪✪
Customer Service	✪✪✪✪
Site Speed	✪✪✪✪
Technical	✪✪✪✪

MAIN POINTS:
>> Perfect if you plan on playing the game in the Emerald Isle.

GolfCaddie.com

http://www.golfcaddie.com

You want courses? We got courses. Golf Caddie.com provides the visitor with comprehensive information on more than 16,000 different courses across the US.

It typifies the term "user friendly" and is ideal for both golfers and vacationers, providing them with updates on course conditions, contact addresses, guides to the cities and states in which the best courses can be found in, along with information on various hotels, motels and guest houses in the surrounding areas. And that's just the ones they gloss over.

If Golf Caddie really likes a course, it really goes to town. In the "Premier" courses, you'll find an intensive, all encompassing level of information regarding everything from the course description, its scoreboards, hole by hole analysis and much more. Obviously compiled by people who know their stuff.

However, it's not all flawless. The Proshop wasn't completed when we visited the site. Also the site features many advertisement promotions and clicking on them will take you to an unrelated website.

Once the site has ironed out a few technicalities it could be very useful to golfers wanting to play in the US. ■

RATING Refer to pg8 for rating explanations.

Overall Rating	✪✪✪
Ease of Use	✪✪✪
Content	✪✪✪✪
Look & Feel	✪✪✪
Customer Service	✪✪✪
Site Speed	✪✪
Technical	✪✪

MAIN POINTS:

>> Intensive information on more than 16,000 US courses.

>> Some technical work still needs to be completed.

Golfcourses.org

http://www.golfcourses.org

This site has a comprehensive list of UK golf courses, with an easy to use search facility.

Users can search by typing in the name of a golf course, entering the name of the nearest town (if there's more than one course in the town you enter, it will list them all) or by narrowing your choices down step by step: first, clicking on a map of the UK, then selecting a county and finally choosing from a list of courses within the area you've zoomed in on. For each result, there are listings of the club (address, phone number, email, location etc), course details, facilities, membership information, nearby hotels and a map of how to get there.

Headlines from around the world are drawn directly from other golfing sites such as pga.com, golfweb.com and golf.com. There is also a live news feed from www.sportlive.net, but this facility was out of action when we visited. Sadly, this is a risk you take when drawing content from another source.

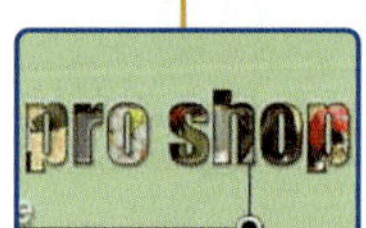

There is a separate review section written by golfers using the site, which by no means covers every course in the UK. However, the list is continually growing as more people visit the site and add their own reviews. Pay a visit yourself, and you could be the first person to literally put your favourite course on the map.

RATING Refer to pg8 for rating explanations.

Overall Rating	★★★
Ease of Use	★★★
Content	★★★★
Look & Feel	★★★
Customer Service	★★★
Site Speed	★★★★
Technical	★★

MAIN POINTS:

>> Thorough course search facility (UK courses only).

GolfGreenFees.com

http://www.golfgreenfees.com

Some may find that the site loading is a bit on the slow side, but otherwise GolfGreenFees.com is a smartly designed site with a lot to offer to any golfer, be they casual or more serious about their game.

They give you cold, hard facts in a well designed format, all from a unique UK and Ireland perspective.

Course finders are divided by region and give you a wide variety of courses for whatever part of the country you wish to try your luck in. They also provide the same service for driving ranges - often seen as the black sheep of the golfing family - which is not something many sites bother with.

Their Golf Shop offers a wide range of golf related products ranging from the obvious (balls, bags, irons) to the less likely choices (books, golf video games for your home computer etc).

However, they don't actually sell all of the products themselves: for some they merely provide links to the product on various shopping oriented sites such as Amazon.

Be forewarned though that, this site does not appear to be secure, so be careful about entering your credit card information on the site. We would still recommend this site as it is easy to use and packed with information.

RATING Refer to pg8 for rating explanations.

Overall Rating	✪✪✪
Ease of Use	✪✪✪✪
Content	✪✪✪✪
Look & Feel	✪✪✪
Customer Service	✪
Site Speed	✪✪✪
Technical	✪✪✪

MAIN POINTS:

- Features one of the few Course Finders that will also locate Driving Ranges.
- UK and Ireland site.

PGA Net

http://www.pganet.net

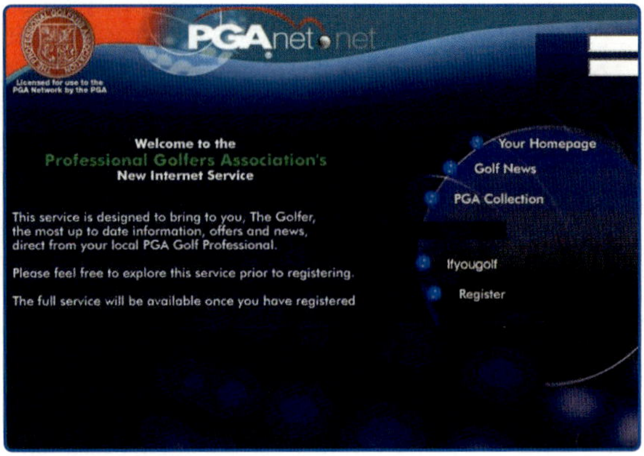

Well designed, informative and up to date: PGAnet is definitely a must visit site.

The design itself is the first thing that really catches your eye here. It's functional and attractive without trying too hard to impress or be flashy for no reason. Right from the front page, choices are presented in an easy to follow manner that won't leave you scratching your head or wondering how you wound up someplace.

News is updated daily and leader boards for ongoing tournaments are easy to find and presented in a clean, easy to read style. If you prefer to have your news delivered to you rather than going to look for it, they offer a free daily newsletter too.

It's worth registering as a member here, as the whole process is simple and, more importantly, free. Once you're registered, you are given even more options and access to members only parts of the site, which should keep you coming back for more.

Special mention must be given to the course finder feature. Looking for a good local or not so local venue for a game? PGAnet offers both a search engine and map on which you can choose the general region that you wish to golf in. But it doesn't stop there: once you choose your general region, you are then given another map of that area which enables you to really pinpoint your venue.

RATING Refer to pg8 for rating explanations.

Overall Rating	✪✪✪✪✪
Ease of Use	✪✪✪✪
Content	✪✪✪✪
Look & Feel	✪✪✪✪
Customer Service	✪✪✪
Site Speed	✪✪✪✪
Technical	✪✪✪✪

MAIN POINTS:

>> A great site that gets even better once you're a registered member.

Scotland's Golf Courses

http://www.scotlands-golf-courses.com

When you consider how many consider Scotland to be the spiritual home of the game of golf, and add into the equation that the scenery and views found there are some of the most stunning in the world, it's a little surprising that there aren't more websites dedicated to it.

Going some way to redressing the balance is the rather unwieldy titled Scotland's Golf Courses which is, as you might expect, the complete guide to golfing in Scotland, the home of golf. It offers a comprehensive review of more than 500 Scottish courses, plus the best in travel, an accommodation directory and those all important tee times. If you want to play at courses like St Andrews, Muirfield, Carnoustie, Troon, Turnberry or Royal Dornoch then you need look no further: this is the site for you.

Even if you prefer to watch rather than partake in the sport, Scotland's Golf Courses will still have something for you. There's a great listing section covering amateur and professional events in Scotland and an online forum where you can share your thoughts on the game,

Open Championship pages, offer the latest golfing news and on-line shopping – perfect if you want to snap up anything from books to golf clubs.

RATING Refer to pg8 for rating explanations.

Overall Rating	✪✪✪
Ease of Use	✪✪✪✪
Content	✪✪✪
Look & Feel	✪✪✪✪
Customer Service	✪
Site Speed	✪✪✪
Technical	✪✪

MAIN POINTS:

>> Great site, combining a love of golf with an equally strong love of Scotland.

Scottish Golf

http://www.scottishgolf.com

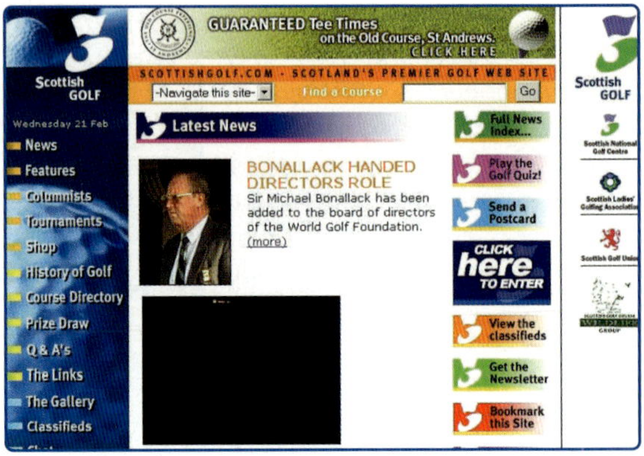

Take regularly updated news, columns and great features, mix in a slick, professional and well designed site and what've you got? The answer, it seems, is Scottish Golf.

This excellent guide to the world of golf is easily one of the best of its kind on the Internet. You'll have a hard time finding a flaw in either the extensive content or with the site itself, which exudes an air of authority, objectivity and style that make it stand out from the crowd.

Whether you're looking for the latest golfing news, or prefer to delve into the history of the game (you'll be able to trace its roots back to the 15th Century with the history pages) then there's guaranteed to be something here for you.

One of the many nice touches is the live Millennium Golf Cam, perched on top of the St Andrews Golf Club and taking in a great view of the 1st and 18th fairways, the world renowned R&A headquarters and even the beaches beyond. This is a brilliant little feature, but remember that if you want to see it, do it in daylight hours GMT.

Overall, an excellent golf site, that goes a long way to setting the standard for what a definitive golfing site should be.

RATING Refer to pg8 for rating explanations.

Overall Rating	✪✪✪✪✪
Ease of Use	✪✪✪✪
Content	✪✪✪✪
Look & Feel	✪✪✪✪
Customer Service	✪✪✪✪✪
Site Speed	✪✪✪✪
Technical	✪✪✪✪✪

MAIN POINTS:

>> Simply one of the best golfing sites online.

>> Features a webcam to view the St Andrews fairways.

St Andrews Links

http://www.standrews.org.uk

When you consider that St Andrews doesn't really need to do any kind of self-promotion, advertising or marketing to ensure its continued success, it's pleasing to find they do have some kind of presence on the Internet. Rather than rest on their laurels and rely on the fact that their name alone is enough to ensure a steady flow of devoted golfers make the pilgrimage there from around the world, they've still made the effort to put a website online - and it's a good site too.

Well presented and with a clear and quick navigational system, it's hard to fault the St. Andrews site.

The history section to these renowned Links courses has to be one of the most impressive features you'll find here, as golf has been played at St Andrews since around 1400 and as a result, the Old Course is renowned throughout the world.

You'll find information about fees and an online booking system on the site, while the courses themselves are well documented with some truly breathtaking images.

We feel happy to recommend this site to any golfer.

RATING Refer to pg8 for rating explanations.

Overall Rating	★★★★
Ease of Use	★★★
Content	★★★★
Look & Feel	★★★★
Customer Service	★★★★
Site Speed	★★★
Technical	★★★

MAIN POINTS:

>> Simple, easy to use and packed with history.

Tailor Made Golf

http://www.tailormadegolf.co.uk

Don't be put off by the length of time this site takes to load. When you click on the site a status bar pops up informing you that a game is loading. Unfortunately this can't be bypassed.

Once it has finished you find it is not a game at all but the site's navigation system. You are presented with the silhouette of a little golfer called Charlie who you drag to one of a number of greens annotated by different worldwide locations. Click on one and Charlie accurately hits the ball into the hole on that green and you are taken to that location on the site - original and great to play with.

This site deals in specialist holidays, and while there is lots of information about accommodation and resorts, an online booking system wasn't apparent.

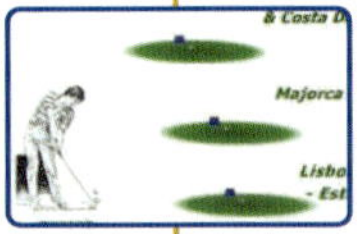

Some of the links on the home page didn't work, but once you get to the golfing resorts themselves there is lots of useful information, with everything from the weather you can expect there to what facilities the resorts have to offer. Added to this are listings of golf courses with relevant information.

Ultimately, if you can put up with the wait while the home page loads, this is a visually impressive site with some good golf resort information.

RATING Refer to pg8 for rating explanations.

Overall Rating	✪✪✪
Ease of Use	✪✪
Content	✪✪
Look & Feel	✪✪✪✪
Customer Service	✪✪✪
Site Speed	✪
Technical	✪

MAIN POINTS:

>> Good information on resorts around the world.

>> Attractive site.

The Open Championship

http://www.opengolf.com

The official home of the Open Golf Championship automatically wins points for originality by being one of the few golfing sites on the Internet not to feature a grassy green background.

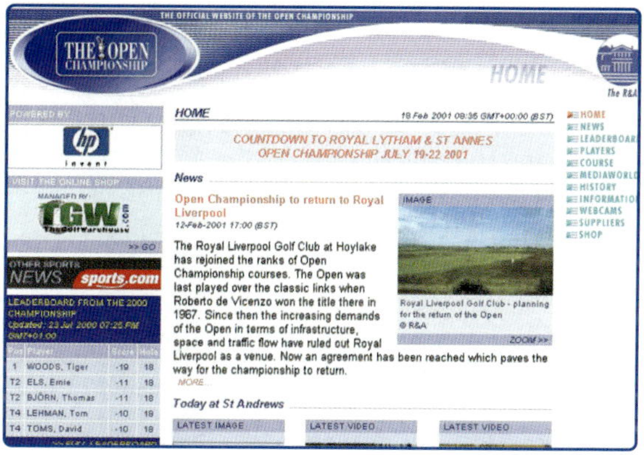

After reviewing so many pages online, anything that is brave enough to break with that particular tradition is OK with us. Luckily, though, there's more to this site than the aesthetics.

Underneath it all is a wealth of information, multimedia elements and historical facts befitting such a prestigious championship. There's certainly plenty of history to draw upon as well, considering the Open can be traced back to 1860.

Quite what Willie Park, the first Open Champion would make of the audio and video interviews, player profiles and live webcams that breathe new life into this site when the Championships themselves are in full swing isn't clear. Chances are he'd find it almost as hard to comprehend as the £500,000 prize money the winner can walk away with. Whatever the case, you won't need quite so much to pay a visit to the great online shop where you can pick up a whole range of memorabilia to mark the event. As you'd have come to expect from such an international event, you can buy easily no matter where you're from. Prices are clearly displayed in both US and UK currency, and shipping and handling charges are clear. The phrase "shop with confidence" could have been invented for this section of the site. Highly recommended.

RATING Refer to pg8 for rating explanations.

Overall Rating	✪✪✪✪
Ease of Use	✪✪✪✪
Content	✪✪✪
Look & Feel	✪✪✪✪
Customer Service	✪✪✪✪
Site Speed	✪✪✪
Technical	✪✪✪✪

MAIN POINTS:

>> An excellent site.

US Open

http://www.usopen.com

As soon as you see the familiar USGA logo you know that this isn't an amateur fan site - we're dealing with the official home of The US Open Championships.

What impresses from the beginning is the graphically intensive and crystal clear navigation that's used to make moving around the site simple and easy. As you might expect, the history section is comprehensive, giving a concise retrospective of the playoffs, past champions, records and previous results. Everything that you need to know about the U.S. Open is clearly displayed, but it's not just historically accurate - there is no lack of content here and you will find everything is completely up to date.

The hospitality section allows you to download comprehensive information on various country clubs, while the only downside to this site is that some of the pages were under construction or awaiting input at the time of this review. We assume that this was because we visited the site some months prior to the championships taking place, and if there was ever a logical time to do such upgrading, it would be as far away from the time when they can expect the most visitors.

We thought it would be a good idea on this site to include some sort of forums or chatrooms, as an event such as the Open is sure to generate lively conversation.

RATING Refer to pg8 for rating explanations.

Overall Rating	★★★★
Ease of Use	★★★★
Content	★★★
Look & Feel	★★★
Customer Service	★★★
Site Speed	★★★★
Technical	★★★

MAIN POINTS:

>> Easy access to comprehensive information.

Other Golf Courses Link Listings

Other Golf Courses related sites reviewed		Page
Cyber Golf	http://www.cybergolf.com	70
Courses of America	http://www.golfmiles.com	217
Golf Art	http://www.golf-art.com	14
Golf Breaks	http://www.golfbreaks.com	214
Golf Illustrated	http://www.golfillustrated.com	166
Golf.co.uk	http://www.golf.co.uk	37
Golfing Ireland	http://www.golfingireland.com	216
Little Aussie Golfer	http://www.lag.com.au	74
Masters2000	http://www.masters.org	156
My Golf Zone	http://www.mygolfzone.com	41
Pepsi Little Peoples Golf	http://www.littlepeoplesgolf.com	143
Places To Golf	http://www.placestogolf.com	218
Titleist Golf	http://www.titleist.com	63
US Senior Open	http://www.ussenioropen.com	160

Other Golf Courses related sites

http://www.1-888-golf-florida.com
http://www.1golf.com
http://www.234golf.com
http://www.abbeysprings.com
http://www.abitagolf.com
http://www.altasierragolf.com
http://www.ancalacc.com
http://www.arrowheadcc.com
http://www.avilabeachresort.com
http://www.ballymeade.com
http://www.battlecreekgc.com
http://www.baygolf.com
http://www.bayhills.com
http://www.bcgolfguide.com
http://www.bcrthenatural.com
http://www.bellinghamgcc.com
http://www.berrycreek.com
http://www.bigcanoe.com
http://www.birkdale.com
http://www.blackcreek.com
http://www.blackstonegolfclub.com
http://www.bluerockgolfcourse.com
http://www.boundaryoak.com
http://www.bridlewoodgolf.com
http://www.brigadoongolf.com
http://www.brookhillgolf.com
http://www.calabogiehighlandsgolf.com
http://www.ccfairfax.org
http://www.centennialgolf.com
http://www.chaletgolf.com
http://www.chascoaks.com
http://www.cherrycreeklinks.com
http://www.chesapeakegolf.com
http://www.chevychasegolf.com
http://www.chxcountryclub.com
http://www.cincoranchgolfclub.com
http://www.claremontgolf.com
http://www.cliftonhollow.com
http://www.coralspringsgolf.com
http://www.coveredbridge.com

Other Golf Courses Link Listings

http://www.cowalgolfclub.co.uk
http://www.cramermountain.com
http://www.cranburygolf.com
http://www.cresthollow.com
http://www.crimsoncreek.com
http://www.crystalspringsgolf.com
http://www.daltonranch.com
http://www.deerislandgolf.com
http://www.deserthorizons.com
http://www.diamondbackgc.com
http://www.eaglesbluff.com
http://www.eastpointe-cc.com
http://www.echosprings1.com
http://www.eelrivergc.com
http://www.eganridge.com
http://www.elkridgegolf.com
http://www.emersongolf.com
http://www.eteetime.com
http://www.falconsfire.com
http://www.fancourt.co.za
http://www.fcg-int.com
http://www.gainesvillegolf.cc
http://www.gatewaynational.com
http://www.genoalakes.com
http://www.glastonburyhills.com
http://www.glendalelakes.com
http://www.glendornoch.com
http://www.goforgolf.com
http://www.goldhillsgolf.com
http://www.golf.th.com
http://www.golf007.com
http://www.golfatlanta.com
http://www.golfball.com
http://www.golfccc.com
http://www.golfclub.org.lb
http://www.golfcourse.com
http://www.golfersweb.com
http://www.golfflorida.net
http://www.golfgreens.com
http://www.golfindiana.com
http://www.golfmirage.ca
http://www.golf-reservations.co.uk
http://www.golfsbestdeals.com
http://www.golf-sempachersee.ch
http://www.golfsw.com
http://www.golfterrebonne.ca
http://www.golf-today.com
http://www.golfuniverse.com
http://www.golfus.com
http://www.golfvacations.com
http://www.golfzone.com.hk
http://www.grayhawk.com
http://www.greathopegolf.com
http://www.greenfieldsgolf.com
http://www.halifaxplantation.com
http://www.hamptonclub.com
http://www.harrisonhills.com
http://www.hartefeldnational.com
http://www.heatherglen.com
http://www.heathlands.com
http://www.heritagehighlands.com
http://www.hickoryhills.com
http://www.hiddenvalleygolf.com
http://www.hlcc.org
http://www.hlgreens.com
http://www.houndears.com
http://www.illini-golf.com
http://www.ironwoodgolf.com
http://www.kentucky-golfer.com
http://www.kissgolf.com
http://www.kolomi.com
http://www.lakearthur.com
http://www.lakewoodgolf.com
http://www.lasvegasgolfres.com
http://www.laurelridgeclub.com
http://www.lochmeregolf.com
http://www.luanahills.com
http://www.macgregordowns.org
http://www.maderagolf.com
http://www.maplehillgc.com
http://www.mediaaccess.com
http://www.millcreekgolfresort.com

Other Golf Courses Link Listings

http://www.millquarter.com
http://www.morgancreekgolf.com
http://www.mygolftime.com
http://www.myrtlewood-golf.com
http://www.nationalgolf.com.au
http://www.northgatecountryclub.com
http://www.nutterscrossing.com
http://www.ocean-city.com
http://www.oceantrails.com
http://www.oldepoint.com
http://www.oldorchardgolf.com
http://www.oldranch.com
http://www.osagenationalgolfclub.com
http://www.ottawagolf.com
http://www.pebblebeach.com
http://www.pilgrimsoak.com
http://www.pioneerhills.golffan.com
http://www.pittmeadowsgolf.com
http://www.prairieviewgc.com
http://www.presidiogolf.com
http://www.providencecc.com
http://www.provogolfclub.com
http://www.publicgolfcourses.com
http://www.pumpkinridge.com
http://www.ramblewoodcc.com
http://www.raspberryfalls.com
http://www.redwoods-golf.com
http://www.riverbendgolf.com
http://www.riverhillsgolf.com
http://www.royaldornoch.com
http://www.royal-liverpool-golf.com
http://www.royalmelbourne.com.au
http://www.royal-westmoreland.com
http://www.sanctuarygc.com
http://www.santaanagolf.com
http://www.saugeengolf.com
http://www.scarborogcc.com
http://www.seattlegolf.com
http://www.sirenglen.com
http://www.southwickgolf.com
http://www.standrewscc.com
http://www.standrewsgolf.com
http://www.stevinsonranch.com
http://www.stluciagolf.com
http://www.successstories.com
http://www.sultansrun.com
http://www.sundancegolf.com
http://www.sunolvalley.com
http://www.swinggolfireland.com
http://www.sycamorehills.com
http://www.tangleridge.com
http://www.taterhill.com
http://www.tcgc.com
http://www.tealbend.com
http://www.teeitup.com
http://www.teematic.com
http://www.teetime.com
http://www.terracedowns.co.nz
http://www.thebayclub.com
http://www.thecarolina.com
http://www.thechallenge.com
http://www.thefalls.bc.ca
http://www.thesawmill.com
http://www.torreypinesgc.com
http://www.trentoncc.com
http://www.tripolicc.com
http://www.troongolf.com
http://www.twinshields.com
http://www.uwharriepoint.com
http://www.vanburengolf.com
http://www.victoriagolf.com
http://www.vieragolf.com
http://www.wakefieldvalley.com
http://www.walnutcreekgolf.com
http://www.watervillegolf.com
http://www.waylandgolf.com
http://www.webfairway.com
http://www.wentworthgolf.com
http://www.wilddunes.com
http://www.wildwoodgreen.com
http://www.willowbrookcountryclub.com
http://www.worldsofgolf.com

Reviews

Designer Golf Gifts

http://www.designergolfgifts.com

Everyone likes stuff that's strange and unique. After all, if we didn't, why would garage sales and flea markets be so popular and widespread! And now, Designer Golf Gifts proves that even golfers are not immune!

With everything from clocks to furniture and lamps to wine holders, all golf themed of course, Designer Golf Gifts definitely offers a wide array of odd products that should make the eyes of any golf nut light up with delight.

They even offer golf ball display cases so that you can keep safe all your special game winning balls.

The site design is plain, yet simple. No flash intros on this one, but you do get nice, clear pictures of all products.

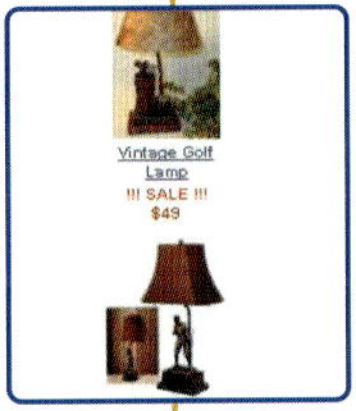

Ordering is via a secure server, but they do not ship outside the US on the order form. However, they do note that if you contact them they are able to provide you with full international shipping information.

Really though, even if you decide not to order anything, this site is must see. Some of the items they sell will intrigue you while some of it will make you laugh in disbelief.

At Designer Golf Gifts, it's all about the game... and how you live it!

RATING Refer to pg8 for rating explanations.

Overall Rating	★★★
Ease of Use	★★★
Content	★★★★
Look & Feel	★★
Customer Service	★★★
Site Speed	★★★
Technical	★★★

MAIN POINTS:

>> Worth a visit for the bizarre golfing gifts you'll find here.

Golfer Gift

http://www.golfergift.com

Golfer Gift is an "entry" page which links back to www.personalizationmall.com, a collection of gift categories in one site.

So although not a "golf only" site we though it would fit well into our gift section because it contains some really worthwhile products.

The look and feel of the site is a little "bright" with orange's, greens and whites, but worth enduring for the products they offer.

You'll find a good range of low to high priced items and definitely "something different" for an avid golfer. The products are offered in a few categories like whimsical apparel, golf accessories, novel keepsake items, executive and desktop items and finally a few

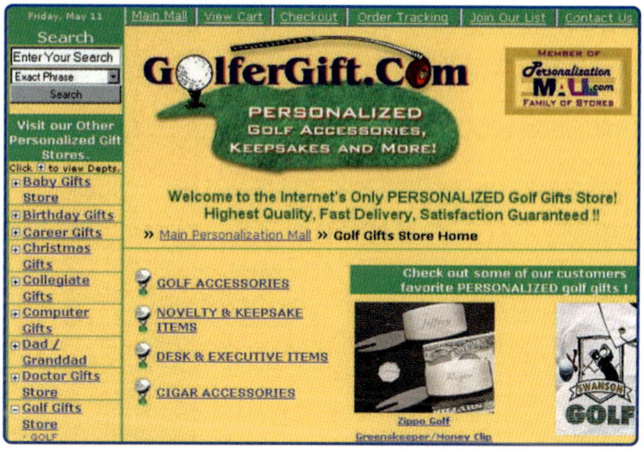

cigar accessories with golf images and markings.

All items can be personalized in one way or another, and the site offers international shipping either to the purchaser, or direct to the person you are buying for.

They claim to personalize and ship within 3-5 days of order, which we thought was fairly quick.

Well worth a visit for something original as a gift to any golfer.

RATING Refer to pg8 for rating explanations.

Overall Rating	✪✪✪✪
Ease of Use	✪✪✪
Content	✪✪✪✪
Look & Feel	✪✪
Customer Service	✪✪✪✪
Site Speed	✪✪✪
Technical	✪✪✪✪

MAIN POINTS:

>> Some great novelty gifts and personalized golfing gadgets.

Golf Shop 2000

http://www.golfersedge.com

If you're looking for a straight forward golf gift shop, then Golf Shop 2000 may be the site for you.

The site currently only ships inside the US. However, they add that, should you live "off shore", they will try to arrange something for you if you email them. It would be a bonus if they catered more comprehensively for the international audience that they recognise is out there.

If you decide to try to order something from the site, you'll find a nice array of products to choose from. Some categories include golf accessories, clubs, furnishings and lamps. But compared to other similar sites, their prices are a bit on the high side. Still, ordering is done on a secure server, so if they have that one can't miss item, you can feel safer giving out your credit card info.

Overall this isn't a bad site and has a reasonable selection of merchandise.

RATING Refer to pg8 for rating explanations.

Overall Rating	✪✪
Ease of Use	✪✪✪
Content	✪✪
Look & Feel	✪✪✪
Customer Service	✪
Site Speed	✪✪✪✪
Technical	✪✪

MAIN POINTS:

>> Orders for a fairly wide range of gifts can be placed securely.

Golfingly Yours

http://www.golfinglyyours.com

According to the web site, Golf Digest magazine once called Golfingly Yours "one of the Internet's best sites".

One of the products they offer on the site caught some of our reviewers attention, as it might for a golfer who has a really hard time out on the course. The "Championship Golf Course Pewter Hip Flask". Now, if you have a bad game, you can drown your sorrows right there on the green, and not have to wait till you get to the 19th hole.

But in all seriousness, the flask in question, and the rest of the items found on this site, appear to be of high quality. In fact, even the site itself is impressively presented, from the splash picture that you're greeted with on the front page onwards. Done in an old style of photography, the picture, though large, loads fast and is a good example of what you'll find in the rest of the site.

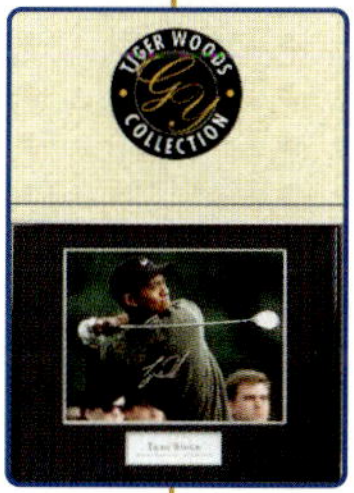

You'll find that the site is well done, with item pictures that are both fast to load and contain a good amount of detail. And yes, thankfully, ordering is done on a secure server.

Overall, this site looks great, as do their products. Definitely check it out. Now if you'll excuse me, I've got to see a man about a flask...

RATING Refer to pg8 for rating explanations.

Overall Rating	✪✪✪✪
Ease of Use	✪✪✪
Content	✪✪✪
Look & Feel	✪✪✪✪
Customer Service	✪✪✪
Site Speed	✪✪✪✪
Technical	✪✪✪

MAIN POINTS:
>> Plenty of images of the products on offer.

Other Golf Gifts Link Listings

Other Golf Gifts related sites reviewed

Other Golf Gifts related sites

http://archie3.hypermart.net/travelhumidors.htm
http://www.adcomarketing.com
http://www.beverlyhillsusa.com/edingolf.html
http://www.caddy.com
http://www.foremostevents.com/golfgift.htm
http://www.golfandgifts.com
http://www.golfballgifts.com
http://www.golfgod.com
http://www.golf-novelties.com
http://www.golfwholesale.com/golf_crp.htm
http://www.jacknicklauscalendar.com
http://www.justadd.com
http://www.macbirdie.com
http://www.macgolf.com
http://www.newgolfgifts.com
http://www.off2golf.com
http://www.osbornegolf.com
http://www.playgolfnow.com
http://www.southernappeal.com
http://www.thegolfpeople.com
http://www.the-green-goddess.com
http://www.vizzit.com/gifts.htm
http://www.weddinghelpers.com/golf.html
http://www.world-presence.com/featured.htm

Reviews

America's Favorite Golf Schools

http://www.afgs.com

America's Favourite Golf Schools operates golf improvement vacations at over 45 locations in the US, France and Morocco.

The look and feel of the site could be improved on, but the basic layout adds to the ease of use and speed of browsing.

The site provides comprehensive information and plenty of images of the schools, full pricing details and contact details if you have any queries or require more information.

Top marks to their customer care team too. We were very impressed with their response to initial email.

Finding locations is easy, by state or through their graphical map

which gives a general idea of their locations throughout the country.

Reservations can be made online or by telephone. There is also a testimonial section with letters from happy customers.

A basic, but effective site that serves its intended purpose.

RATING Refer to pg8 for rating explanations.

Overall Rating	✪✪✪
Ease of Use	✪✪✪✪
Content	✪✪✪✪
Look & Feel	✪✪✪
Customer Service	✪✪✪✪✪
Site Speed	✪✪✪
Technical	✪✪✪

MAIN POINTS:

» Good information and great response to our email.

Arnold Palmer's Golf Academy

http://www.apga.com

There is no doubt that Arnold Palmer is one of the biggest names ever to play the game. For close to five decades, he has been highly successful and clearly made that all important step into the mainstream as someone that non-golfing fans recognize.

As his successes, more of which can be read about on the site, speak for themselves, there's really no question as to why someone would want to learn with the man himself, or at a school that practices Mr. Arnold's beliefs. Which is why, if you're seriously interested in becoming a better golfer, you should make checking out the site for Arnold Palmer's Golf Academy one of the first things that you do.

Located in the US, the school offers a wide array of different programs available to you, including a five day course which involves four hours of instruction a day and covers a variety of topics to help improve your game. Also, all classes are done on a four students to one teacher ratio, thus ensuring you of more personal attention They also offer a small pro shop, but it's really an additional attraction rather than the main appeal of the site.

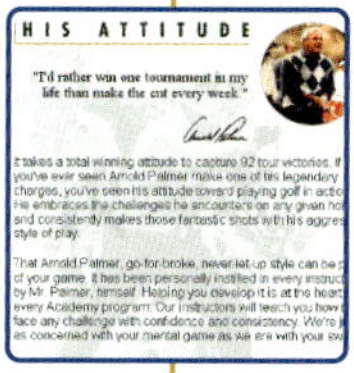

We recommend a visit to the APGA site, if only to give yourself an idea of what you should expect from any great golf school.

RATING Refer to pg8 for rating explanations.

Overall Rating	✪✪✪✪
Ease of Use	✪✪✪
Content	✪✪✪
Look & Feel	✪✪✪
Customer Service	✪✪✪✪
Site Speed	✪✪✪
Technical	✪✪✪

MAIN POINTS:

>> When a site has such big name approval, you know you'll get something good.

Ben Sutton Golf School

http://www.bensuttongolfschool.com

We don't know about you, but we think that holidays were invented so that you could take a break from work. The appeal of time away from whatever you normally do 9 to 5 is that you can switch off, relax and unwind. The Ben Sutton Golf School looks like a great place to take a vacation for anyone who would like to go somewhere to sharpen up their golfing skills.

The site is not complicated at all, due to the fact that it's really just an advert for the school, but there's all the information that you'd need to decide whether it was the holiday destination for you.

The level of instruction here appears to be very high, judging by what we've found on the site, and they provide enough images and background to explain what you can expect during your stay.

You can learn a little about the history of the school, the facilities available, accommodation, their location, 3, 5 and 7 day stays, the type of instruction you'll receive and even the instructors they have.

We were not impressed that they failed to respond to our email, but otherwise a good site.

RATING Refer to pg8 for rating explanations.

Overall Rating	✪✪✪
Ease of Use	✪✪✪
Content	✪✪
Look & Feel	✪✪
Customer Service	✪
Site Speed	✪✪✪
Technical	✪✪✪

MAIN POINTS:

>> Comprehensive information on the school. Well laid out.

>> No response to contact.

Bird Golf

http://www.birdgolf.com

The people behind this site definitely think highly of their service. There it is, right on the home page: The Bird Golf Academy provides "The Ultimate Golf Learning Experience"

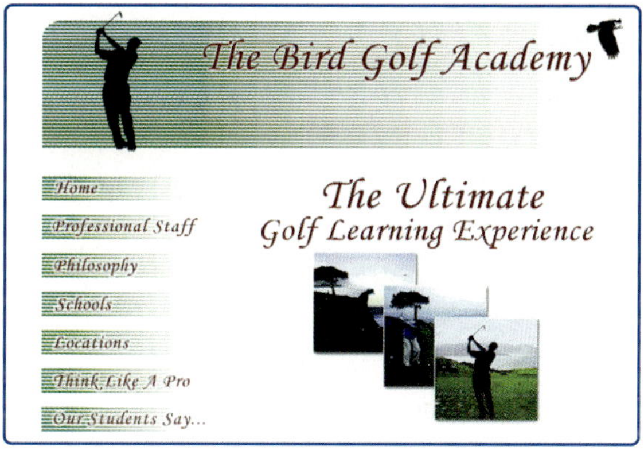

The problem, however, is it's almost impossible to tell just how good they are without attending lessons there yourself, but from looking over the site, I'd say there's at least a small chance that they may be right.

For starters, their instructors include winners of many major golf tournaments around the world and, depending on the package you choose, there are no more than two students for every one teacher. You also get unlimited course time during your stay so that you can immediately try out what you've learned, rather than hoping you remember it all until you get home.

The school has four locations in the US and is mainly aimed at the US market but is open to golfers from elsewhere in the world.

RATING Refer to pg8 for rating explanations.

Overall Rating	✪✪✪
Ease of Use	✪✪✪
Content	✪✪✪✪
Look & Feel	✪✪✪
Customer Service	✪✪✪✪
Site Speed	✪✪✪
Technical	✪✪

MAIN POINTS:

>> Good site that promotes the schools well.

Golf Director

http://www.golfdirector.com

No, this is not an account of what would happen if Alfred Hitchcock, Stanley Kubrick and George Lucas all got together on a Hollywood green for a quick game. Instead, Golf Director presents itself as an "online guide to UK Golf Clubs."

It provides information on over 2,000 golf clubs and hotels across Britain, and allows visitors to search for perfect places to play by using a map, or alternatively by selecting a county of interest.

All fairly straightforward, admittedly, but the site could certainly do with a stronger search engine facility. The results of searches, such as they are, bring up the names, basic details and contact information of the clubs found. If you're lucky, the venue you opt for may be spotlighted in the featured clubs section, which contains more in-depth guides and a pseudo 3D facility for viewing individual holes from each course. This will give you a much better insight into what to expect, and whether or not your journey there would be worthwhile.

When we first visited, not many clubs had been entered in the featured section, but the site was relatively new then, so we'll give them the benefit of the doubt and expect more courses will be added in time.

RATING Refer to pg8 for rating explanations.

Overall Rating	✪✪✪
Ease of Use	✪✪✪✪
Content	✪✪
Look & Feel	✪✪✪
Customer Service	✪✪✪
Site Speed	✪✪✪
Technical	✪✪✪

MAIN POINTS:

>> Promises excellent coverage of UK golf courses.

International Junior Golf Academy

http://www.ijga.com

I f you're a young person who loves golf and wants to play it on any kind of professional level, then the International Junior Golf Academy claims to be the place for you.

Located in the US, they describe themselves as "the golf and academic school designed for students who are interested in pursuing excellence on the golf course, in the classroom and in life." In other words, this place is as close to golf bootcamp as you're likely to get.

Each student is interviewed comprehensively, so that his or her program can be tailored to best meet their needs, while "report cards" will be sent home to the parents keeping the proud mom and dad up to date on their prodigy's progress.

Courses range in length from one day to three-month summer classes. Instructors include a number of PGA and LPGA professionals, so obviously the class of instruction is of the highest level.

The site itself provides the necessary information and presents it in an easy to use way.

If you're interested in sending your child this summer, for intense golf training or even if you want to convince your parents to send you, then give this site a look.

RATING Refer to pg8 for rating explanations.

Overall Rating	✪✪✪
Ease of Use	✪✪✪
Content	✪✪
Look & Feel	✪✪
Customer Service	✪✪
Site Speed	✪✪✪
Technical	✪✪✪

MAIN POINTS:

>> Excellent golfing school, with top quality instruction.

Learning Vacations

http://www.lvgolfschools.com

If you're one of those people who looks for more than just lying in the sun during their breaks away, then Learning Vacations could be the perfect holiday for you.

They offer a choice of seven US destinations, including San diego, Phoenix, Orlando, Catskill Mountains, Niagara Falls, Myrtle Beach and Fort Lauderdale where you can spend three or five days under golf instruction, staying in a nearby hotel. Rest assured, for those five or so days, you'll eat, sleep, think and basically live golf.

The site offers enough information for you to decide whether or not you would be interested, and then offers you the facility to contact them, to make reservations or ask additional questions.

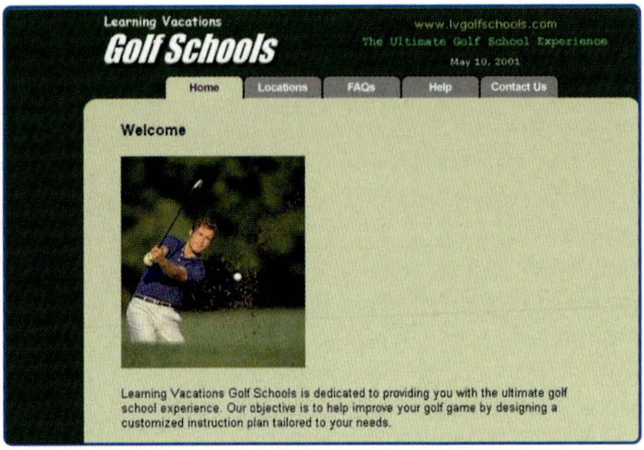

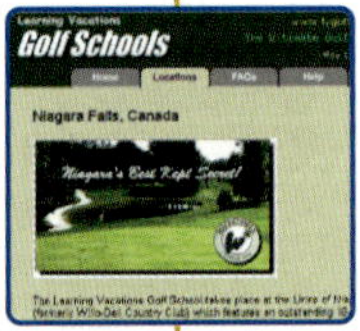

Each of the destinations is presented on a different page, with information on the courses and accommodation offered.

To give you some idea of what to expect from your break, you'll find typical features of each school, a day's schedule, a sample itinerary of either the three or five day stay as well as everything you could want to know about the hotel, online. Booking couldn't be simpler, and you'll find some genuinely great discounts for group bookings – perfect if your golfing friends decide a golfing holiday is in order.

RATING Refer to pg8 for rating explanations.

Overall Rating	✪✪✪✪
Ease of Use	✪✪✪
Content	✪✪✪
Look & Feel	✪✪✪✪
Customer Service	✪✪✪
Site Speed	✪✪
Technical	✪✪✪

MAIN POINTS:

>> Clearly laid out site.

United States Schools of Golf

http://www.ussog.com

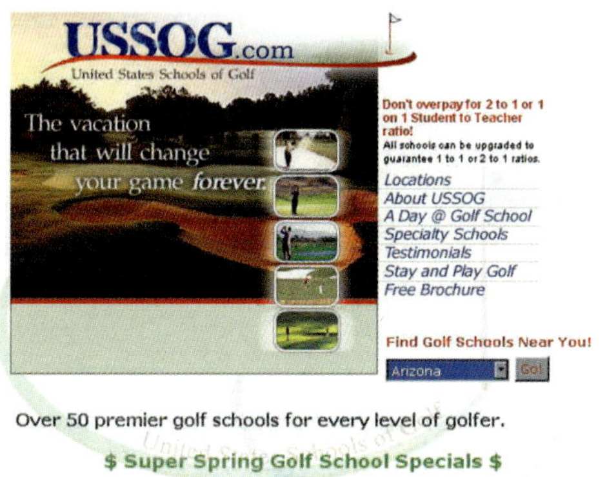

US School's of Golf provides detailed information on over 50 of the top US golf schools across the states.

Each school is presented with clear information and some spectacular images showing you what you can expect.

The site boasts the "top vote" in Quality of Golf Instruction by the Professional Golf Teachers and Coaches of America 1995, 1996, 1997 & 1998 and from the looks of it by their site, are still right up there today.

For each school you are presented with a detailed description of the package including the accommodation, a list of all that is included with regards the lessons, such as video analysis, how many hours a day of lessons, cart and green fees etc, and a clear pricing of the different packages included as well as the costs for taking along non students.

You can take a look at what an average day of lessons will be like, and then once you've decided where you'd like to spend a few days of golfing lessons, they allow you to place a preliminary booking online which rounds things off nicely.

If you need something special rather than group training sessions, then you may also find it here. The site also offers Junior golfing, one to one, two to one and three to one student/coach ratios, and finally corporate golf programs and incentives.

RATING Refer to pg8 for rating explanations.

Overall Rating	✪✪✪✪
Ease of Use	✪✪✪✪✪
Content	✪✪✪✪✪
Look & Feel	✪✪✪✪
Customer Service	✪✪
Site Speed	✪✪✪✪✪
Technical	✪✪✪✪✪

MAIN POINTS:

>> Fast site, easy to navigate and full of useful information.

Other Golf Schools Link Listings

Other Golf Schools related sites reviewed		Page
CityOfGolf	http://www.cityofgolf.com	150
Golf 4 Kids	http://www.golf4kids.co.uk	142
InsideGolf.com	http://www.insidegolf.com	155
Online Golf Lessons	http://www.onlinegolflessons.com	133
PGA Professional	http://www.pgaprofessional.com	134
UK Golf Information Site	http://www.uk-golf.com	78
World Golf Village	http://www.wgv.com	161

Other Golf Schools related sites

http://golfing-hawaii.com
http://golfschoolsetc.com
http://golfstudionyc.com
http://hometown.aol.com/puttmagic
http://ww4.choice.net/davy/home.htm
http://www.agagolf.com
http://www.caligolf.com
http://www.classicswing.com
http://www.czgolfschool.com
http://www.davidglenz.com
http://www.eden-golf.com
http://www.fivestargolfschool.on.ca
http://www.golfacademy.com
http://www.golfadirondacks.com
http://www.golfbreakthroughs.com
http://www.golfenomics.com
http://www.golf-florida.com
http://www.golfschoolsdaytona.com
http://www.golfschoolsinfo.com
http://www.golfstandards.com
http://www.golfuniversity.com
http://www.grassrootsgolf.com
http://www.heartlandgolfschools.com
http://www.illinoisgolfacademy.com
http://www.jrgolfacademy.com
http://www.kostismccordlearning.com
http://www.leadbetter.com
http://www.mjung-golfacademy.com
http://www.montana.com/mtgolf
http://www.net-magic.net/golf
http://www.njgolf.com
http://www.onr.com/user/puett
http://www.pgagolfacademy.com
http://www.pgtaa.com
http://www.rinagolf.com
http://www.schmidbauer-golf.com
http://www.scigolf.com
http://www.shawguides.com/golf
http://www.sonomagolfschool.com
http://www.sorrellgolf.com
http://www.straight-shootin-golf.com
http://www.summitgolfacademy.com
http://www.swingrite.com
http://www.swingsolutions.com
http://www.swingsthething.com
http://www.thegolfschool.com
http://www.ttateengolftour.com
http://www.vipgolfacademy.com
http://www.weteachgolf.com

Reviews

About Golf

http://www.aboutgolf.com

About Golf is an attractive site that acts as an Internet portal for golf games, professional golf instruction and golf travel.

They have extensive online golf lessons, which provide plenty of clear, large images and step-by-step instructions to take you through the tutorials. Some video footage would have been a helpful addition to the site, but nevertheless there is a good range of lessons here.

If you think practicing is too much like hard work and prefer your golf to remain firmly in the virtual world, the site also includes golf games that can be downloaded, with technical support and clear guides on how to get the games up and running. At the time of our visit, World Tours II was available as a free download. The site carries reviews of the game and had included negative as well as positive feedback.

There is also a travel guide section on the site which provides 7 US destinations and gives information on popular courses in these areas.

RATING Refer to pg8 for rating explanations.

Overall Rating	✪✪✪
Ease of Use	✪✪✪
Content	✪✪
Look & Feel	✪✪✪
Customer Service	✪✪✪
Site Speed	✪✪✪✪
Technical	✪✪✪

MAIN POINTS:

>> Good instructional tips

>> Golf game with free download

Golf and Sporting Occasions

http://www.gso.co.uk

Golf and Sporting Occasions, is geared towards organising "Golf Days" for groups and companies...so what's it doing in this chapter?

We felt that this site (or rather the service they offer) deserved a place in the guide, and since they offer to provide instruction time in their packages as an "extra", this was the best place we could find to put it.

So, if you and a group, or your company are interested in planning a day (or a few) of golf, then this would be a good place to start looking.

The site boasts of clients such as Heinz, Fujifilm and General Motors and all have good things to say about it, so obviously this company knows what they are doing.

During the cold winter months, they also offer winter sports getaways. Even a hint as to prices is missing from the site however, so you may want to contact them before presenting any ideas to your boss.

The site itself is utilitarian as few pictures are used and information is provided in plain text. Don't look for cool design and functionality on this one.

The lack of such glitz however, also ensures that things load fast. and navigation retains this speed and is easy to do.

RATING Refer to pg8 for rating explanations.

Overall Rating	✪✪✪
Ease of Use	✪✪✪
Content	✪✪✪
Look & Feel	✪✪✪
Customer Service	✪✪✪
Site Speed	✪✪✪✪
Technical	✪✪

MAIN POINTS:

>> Offers golf themed corporate entertainment.

Golf Span

http://www.golfspan.com

GolfSpan is one of the best places on the Internet for any golfer hoping to receive tuition, advice or instruction. The site requires you to register, but once in, you have a wealth of knowledge at your finger tips.

They have a large number of what appear to be very qualified instructors on hand, ready to offer words of wisdom to fellow golfers.

You can choose from any of the instructors on their list, which displays a photo as well as a summary of their experience as teachers. Click on a name, and you are introduced to each one with a welcoming streamed video. The clips keep coming, with loads of streaming video instructions on just about any subject you care to mention. You needn't concern yourself about whether or not your internet connection will handle the streaming as there are options for users of any speed from a 28K modem and up. The streaming quality is very good even on our 56K modem connection we use for testing, yet for those who may have problems streaming, they also offer the option to download the file for saving on your hard drive and viewing later. Both Real and Windows media formats are supported. Golfspan is also affiliated with customgolf.com (an online golf store) and golfingedge .com (swing analysis), also reviewed in this edition of the guide.

RATING Refer to pg8 for rating explanations.

Overall Rating	✪✪✪✪✪
Ease of Use	✪✪✪✪✪
Content	✪✪✪✪
Look & Feel	✪✪✪✪
Customer Service	✪✪✪✪✪
Site Speed	✪✪✪✪✪
Technical	✪✪✪✪✪

MAIN POINTS:

>> 'Wealth of information from top class teachers'. Great video instruction.

Golf Teaching Pro

http://www.golfteachingpro.com

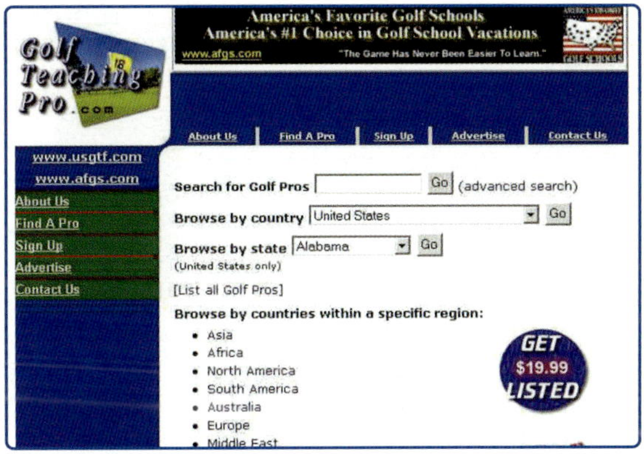

"Functional" is the word that springs to mind when first visiting the Golf Teaching Pro website. Rather than go all out with visually impressive animation or audio, you get a very simple, virtually image free site. One obvious advantage of this is that the site itself is quick loading, no matter what your Internet connection.

What we have here is an online directory of qualified golf professionals and trained instructors. Assuming you're looking for such tuition, you're encouraged to browse by country (and state, if you're in the US) to find a golf pro that lives close to you.

If geography isn't an issue, you can also perform a detailed search for golf pros that match a specific criteria, such as tourn-ament finishes and types of certifications. You're then free to contact the pro directly via the web site: no more having to write down telephone numbers to call later or even memorise an e-mail address.

Within five minutes, you're sure to find a qualified golf pro within travelling distance, ready, willing and able to help you improve your game. If, of course, the price is right.

RATING Refer to pg8 for rating explanations.

Overall Rating	✪✪✪
Ease of Use	✪✪✪✪
Content	✪✪
Look & Feel	✪✪
Customer Service	✪✪✪✪✪
Site Speed	✪✪✪✪
Technical	✪✪

MAIN POINTS:

>> Enables you to find a golf pro quickly.

GolfCircuit.com

http://www.golfcircuit.com

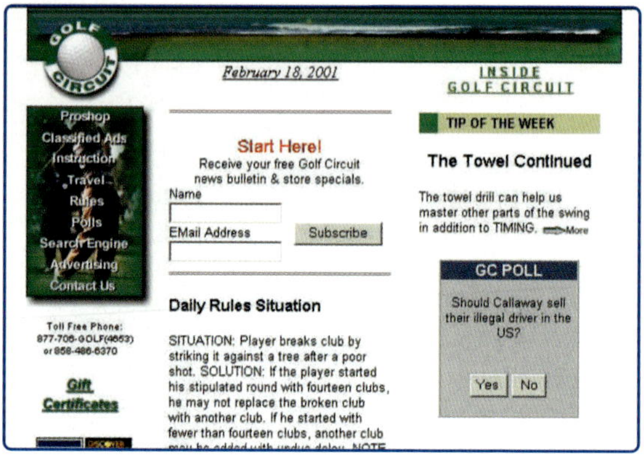

At first glance, you'd be forgiven for thinking that there really wasn't all that much content to be found at GolfCircuitcom.

The home page is fairly minimalist, with lots of clean white space, and is not at all cluttered. Do a bit of digging, and you'll find there's more to this one that meets the eye.

Start clicking on the links and you'll find fairly packed pages devoted to subjects such as classified ads, polls, rules, travel, a pro shop and so on. You'll start to think maybe your first impression was wrong.

One of the most impressive features of this site is the instructional area, with tips and dozens of golfing tutorials filled with advice that should help to improve any game.

There is also a clickable map of the United States that can direct you to various resorts. A little more care could have been taken over this, however. It may have been a better idea to limit the map, as many areas seem to be without resorts.

The Instruction site however makes a vist well worthwhile.

RATING Refer to pg8 for rating explanations.

Overall Rating	✪✪✪
Ease of Use	✪✪✪
Content	✪✪
Look & Feel	✪✪✪
Customer Service	✪✪
Site Speed	✪✪✪✪
Technical	✪✪✪

MAIN POINTS:

>> Good instructional tips.

Golfing Edge

http://www.golfingedge.com

Golfing Edge looks like a great place to get some good golfing advice, making the most of the Internet to send video clips around the world.

The site offers annual membership at a rate of US$19.95. For this fee, you're allowed to submit video footage of your swing, using any club you wish to hone your technique on. If you have the technology, you can submit videos digitally for the advisors to view. Failing that, you can simply post a VHS cassette to them and they'll convert it for you.

Once uploaded, you and an instructor can go over the tiniest details of your swing, and he will offer expert advice on how to improve. You can compare your swing to other players, as the instructor is able to draw upon a library of pre-recorded examples while you are both online to clearly illustrate what he is talking about or the kind of technique you should try to employ.

The site uses Shockwave to allow you and the instructor to watch your video clips together, and the initial load of this can take some time, but once it's there you'll see it was worth the wait.

We thought the site was really great and the concept way up there with the best, but were disappointed that nobody was home to answer our emails.

RATING Refer to pg8 for rating explanations.

Overall Rating	✪✪✪
Ease of Use	✪✪✪✪
Content	✪✪✪✪
Look & Feel	✪✪✪✪
Customer Service	✪
Site Speed	✪✪✪
Technical	✪✪✪✪✪

MAIN POINTS:

» Innovative, with excellent use of cutting edge technology.

GolfServ

http://www.golfserv.com

Golfserv.com offers players a place to track handicaps online, book tee times, review course information and scorecards, check out equipment reviews and even take lessons. Best of all, though - It's all free!

Signing up for an account is quick and easy, with just a couple of boxes to fill in, which is a nice change compared with some free sites. They do ask for more information once you've registered, but it's entirely optional whether you give it or not.

Currently, the site only covers the US, Canada and Mexico but we understand that international expansion is on the cards, making Golfserv.com one to keep an eye on if you're international. Until then, there are still plenty of services that any international visitor can make use of.

The Before you Play section provides in-depth information on courses, as well as tips on the type of warm up exercise you should do as a part of your pre-game preparation. After playing a round, you can enter your scores online and keep track of your personal game statistics.

As it stands now, Golfserv.com still manages to hold its own amongst strong competition. Once the international expansion is completed, however, few will come close to this one.

RATING Refer to pg8 for rating explanations.

Category	Stars
Overall Rating	4
Ease of Use	4
Content	4
Look & Feel	5
Customer Service	3
Site Speed	4
Technical	4

MAIN POINTS:

>> Good training service, with a great personal game tracking tool.

HealthyGolf.org

http://www.healthygolf.org

All sports, even low impact ones like golf, can have both beneficial and detrimental effects to your health, according to how you play them. With that in mind, learning how to play the game well and put the minimum amount of stress on your body has got to be a good idea.

That's where Healthy Golf comes in. This is an excellent site for golfers concerned about taking care of themselves, both on and off the course.

The site explores health issues related to golf in an easily digestible format. Everything is covered here, from diet and exercise to injuries and sensible diets. Literally every aspect of health is catered for: there's even a section on correct postures and stances to help you figure out if

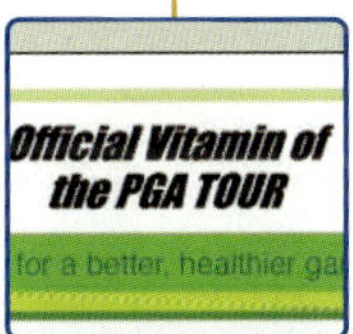

that pain in the back might be caused by the position you take over the tee.

Overall, the health section is very informative with well-presented sections (the self help pages, with clear step-by-step illustrations to aid golf fitness deserve a special mention) while the questions and answers page adds to the comprehensive feel of this site.

In addition, you'll find a newsroom where you can sign up for an email newsletter, while an archive gives the final touch to this neat and attractive site.

RATING Refer to pg8 for rating explanations.

Overall Rating	★★★★
Ease of Use	★★★★
Content	★★★
Look & Feel	★★★★
Customer Service	★★★
Site Speed	★★★★
Technical	★★★★

MAIN POINTS:

>> One of the most important golf sites you could ever visit.

Keepers Of The Game

http://www.keepersofthegame.org

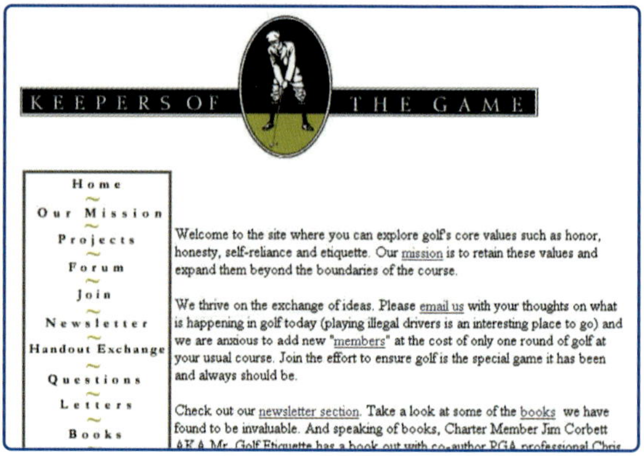

Keepers of the Game deals with the etiquette and previously unwritten codes of behaviour in golf. As with any competitive sport, golf players are governed by rules and regulations. What else would you expect from the sport of gentlemen?

There are various projects listed which not only keep a strict watch on the ethics of golf, but also monitor certain aspects of the game to enhance and elevate the sport to a new level. Ambitious stuff.

Membership, which enables you to become a Keeper of the Game, offers prestigious status but also warns that sacrifices will have to be made for the good of golf. The site does well to accomplish a renewed awareness amongst golfers and non-golfers about the wonderful benefits of playing the game according to the old standards of honesty and courtesy. You're reminded that whatever it takes, you must ensure these standards are continued, and even have an impact beyond golf. The "olde worlde" look of the site hammers home the message that modern golfers must never forget the traditions of the game.

The section dealing with letters is informative and gives the opportunity to express opinions and make suggestions, while the Books section is essentially a reference guide with reviews, but without the option of shopping online.

Overall, the site is easy to navigate, with a handy contents page listing email, phone, fax and a mailing address.

RATING Refer to pg8 for rating explanations.

Category	Stars
Overall Rating	4
Ease of Use	4
Content	4
Look & Feel	5
Customer Service	4
Site Speed	4
Technical	4

MAIN POINTS:

>> Content is concise, to the point and aptly related to the subject.

National Golf Foundation

http://www.ngf.org

This site means what it says in its opening blurb: "The mission of the National Golf Foundation is to foster the growth and economic vitality of golf. We accomplish this by providing golf business research, information and consulting services to people, companies and organizations throughout the world involved in the business of golf."

Or, in plain English, this site is specifically aimed at the growth of the golf industry.

The information available here is extensive, from an appraisal of golf courses to tax related issues. There is also an enormously detailed golf directory, which deals with information on, amongst other things, advertising and marketing, working with the media, event planning and much more.

The range of informational services is also impressive with helpful facts on almost any economic or industry topic. If you feel like reading up on the subject, links to publications on the business as a whole can be added to a handy shopping basket for purchase. The navigation is well organized and workmanlike. The only way to take full advantage of the site is through becoming a member.

This site is a must for anyone interested in finding out how things work within the golf industry.

RATING Refer to pg8 for rating explanations.

Overall Rating	★★★★
Ease of Use	★★★★
Content	★★★★★
Look & Feel	★★★
Customer Service	★★
Site Speed	★★★★
Technical	★★★

MAIN POINTS:

>> Good, unique content, with slick presentation.

>> Need to become a member for optimum use of this site.

Online Golf Lessons

http://www.onlinegolflessons.com

Now this site is something special. If you're determined to improve your game, but can't spare the time or the money to have tuition in the real world, Online Golf Lessons may be just what you're looking for.

Hosted by PGA Pro Matt Kluck, this great site can take you step by step from the basics of the game, through to advanced techniques to refine your performance and even work on your conditioning.

The 15 stage course starts with the grip, and leads you at your own pace through backswing, downswing and impact, eventually finishing with pitching, putting and chipping.

The lessons themselves feature large, easy to see images to guide you along the way, along with video clips and narration.

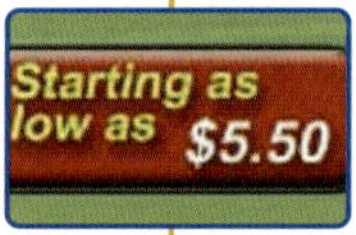

It's probably not advisable to be swinging your club very close to your monitor, it's still a very useful guide to becoming a better golfer.

You do have to pay if you chose to undertake the course (subscription starts at around $5.50 US), but there is a free lesson to give you a taste of what to expect from the rest of the tutorials. This is a great way of checking out if this kind of online learning is for you before you part with your hard earned cash. Now if you'll excuse me, I've got a lesson to get back to...

RATING Refer to pg8 for rating explanations.

Overall Rating	✪✪✪
Ease of Use	✪✪✪✪
Content	✪✪✪✪
Look & Feel	✪✪✪✪
Customer Service	✪✪✪
Site Speed	✪✪✪
Technical	✪✪✪✪✪

MAIN POINTS:

>> An innovative way of learning the game.

PGA Professional

http://www.pgaprofessional.com

"Anyone can improve if they're systematic about it", promises the PGA Professional site.

While we're all for the power of mind over matter and positive thinking, using some of their numerous tips couldn't hurt either.

This site is attractively laid out and covers every aspect of golf instruction. It allows you to submit video footage of yourself out on the course for one of their golfing experts to analyse and offer words of advice upon (but check that the video tape you send is NTSC compatible). Alternatively you can stick to the more traditional method of emailing a question about your form or technique, which will be deliberated over by the golfing gurus that run the site.

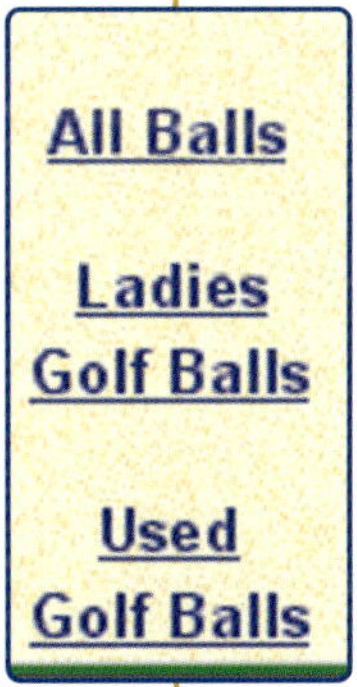

This site is very approachable and it feels like your friendly local club (which just happens to have members popping in from all over the world).

It has a Pro Shop with secure server, lots of links and an entertainment section with jokes and cartoons.

It even has a virtual lounge with oak panelling and golf pictures hanging on the walls.

RATING Refer to pg8 for rating explanations.

Overall Rating	✪✪✪
Ease of Use	✪✪✪
Content	✪✪✪
Look & Feel	✪✪
Customer Service	✪✪✪
Site Speed	✪✪✪
Technical	✪✪

MAIN POINTS:

>> Several ways of getting professional advice on your game.

Royal and Ancient Golf Club of St. Andrew's

http://www.randa.org

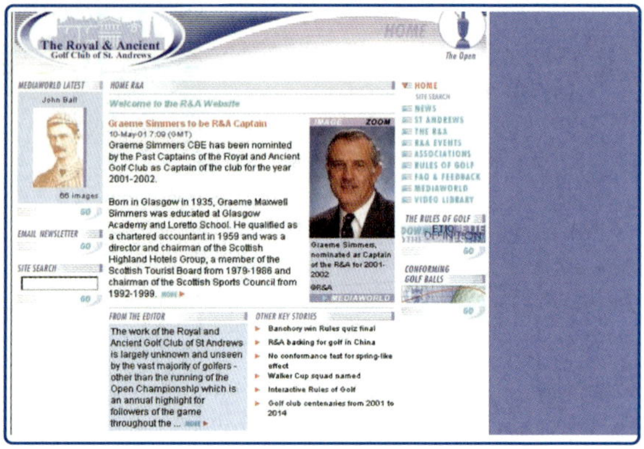

The Royal and Ancient Golf Club of St. Andrews (R&A) is, along with the United States Golf Association, the official worldwide administrator of the rules of golf.

Established in 1754, the club is seen as a leading authority on all matters concerning the game, and also hosts the Open Championships.

As you might expect, much of this site is devoted to the rules of golf covering etiquette, definitions and difficult decisions. There are video clips to accompany the rules and illustrate their points clearly. They have every aspect of the rules of golf covered, and even run a competition on the rules for other clubs to enter. If you only visit one page on the site, have a look at the section on funny moments in on-course decision making (a golfer in Africa killed a snake with his club as he swung - did it count as a shot?).

There's plenty more to be found here, though, such as an interesting history section and a some great multimedia pages with audio and video clips of news events. The R&A have a major programme for junior golfers too, and this is well covered on the site.

All in all, you'll find the official home of the R&A very easy to navigate, gentle on the eye and at the cutting edge of current technology. Unconditionally recommended.

RATING Refer to pg8 for rating explanations.

Overall Rating	✪✪✪✪
Ease of Use	✪✪✪✪
Content	✪✪✪✪
Look & Feel	✪✪✪
Customer Service	✪✪✪✪
Site Speed	✪✪✪
Technical	✪✪✪✪

MAIN POINTS:

>> The leading authority on the rules of golf.

United States Golf Association

http://www.usga.org

When it comes to powerful organisations within the world of golf, you won't find many with more influence than the USGA.

It's the United States Golf Association that write, interpret and maintain the rules of golf along with the R&A at St. Andrews. They are a non-profit making organisation, run by golfers for golfers, whose motto is "for the good of the game".

Their site, while not as sophisticated as the R&A site, still displays the rules in a straightforward and clear format.

The USGA pages give users online access to all the groups' activities, which tie into everything from the US National Champ-ionships to providing a turf advisory service.

They also run workshops on the rules of the game and keep the history of the sport alive by maintaining an impressive museum, which traces the organisation back to the late 1800s.

If you're looking for souvenirs or special golfing gifts, then you'll find plenty of ideas on the site, and the fact that their shop ships internationally means that wherever you are, you'll still be able to splash out on some of their golfing merchandise. ■

RATING Refer to pg8 for rating explanations.

Overall Rating	✪✪✪✪
Ease of Use	✪✪✪✪
Content	✪✪✪✪
Look & Feel	✪✪
Customer Service	✪✪✪✪
Site Speed	✪✪✪
Technical	✪✪

MAIN POINTS:

>> Clearly laid out home page, with an international online shop.

Other Instruction Link Listings

Other Instruction related sites reviewed		Page
Americas Favorite Golf Schools	http://www.afgs.com	112
BunkerShot.com	http://www.bunkershot.com	149
CityOfGolf	http://www.cityofgolf.com	150
Cyber Golf	http://www.cybergolf.com	70
Free Golf Info.	http://www.freegolfinfo.com	71
Golf 4 Kids	http://www.golf4kids.co.uk	140
Golf Digest	http://www.golfdigest.com	164
Golf Help	http://www.golfhelp.com	35
Golf Illustrated	http://www.golfillustrated.com	166
Golf Review	http://www.golfreview.com	36
Golf.com	http://www.golf.com	154
Little Aussie Golfer	http://www.lag.com.au	74
ProsPlay.com	http://www.prosplay.com	60
St Andrews Links	http://www.standrews.org.uk	97
Taylormade Golf	http://www.taylormadegolf.com	61
World Golf Village	http://www.wgv.com	161

Other Instruction related sites

http://www.1877alesson.com
http://www.4bettergolf.com
http://www.academyofgolf.com
http://www.americangolfcollege.com
http://www.aproch.com
http://www.askthepro.com
http://www.cegolf.com
http://www.compusport.com
http://www.copperhillgolf.com
http://www.doubleeagle.com
http://www.drbee.com
http://www.dreamswing.com
http://www.drheadcoach.com
http://www.fitgolf.com
http://www.galvanogolf.com
http://www.golf101.com
http://www.golfadirondacks.com
http://www.golfbobmann.com
http://www.golfika.com
http://www.golfingmastery.com
http://www.golfinsight.net
http://www.golflearning.com

Other Instruction Link Listings

http://www.golflesson.com
http://www.golflogic.com
http://www.golfsupport.com
http://www.golftesting.com
http://www.golf-trainer.com
http://www.heartlandgolfschools.com
http://www.keytogolf.com
http://www.learnaboutgolf.co.uk
http://www.learninglinks.org
http://www.lessontime.com
http://www.lezionidigolf.com
http://www.lpgagirlsgolfclub.org
http://www.mcgetrickgolf.com
http://www.mentalkeys.com
http://www.mikehebron.com
http://www.nectargolf.com
http://www.noslice.com
http://www.offensedefensegolf.com
http://www.onlinegolfclinic.com
http://www.peaksports.com
http://www.pgapros.com
http://www.pgtaa.com
http://www.pineviewresort.com
http://www.practiceswing.com
http://www.progolfschool.com
http://www.prohealthcenters.com
http://www.ricksmith.com
http://www.sonomagolfschool.com
http://www.sportfit.com
http://www.sportscad.com
http://www.staffordgolf.com
http://www.summitgolfacademy.com
http://www.swingfactory.com
http://www.swingreaction.com
http://www.swingsolutions.com
http://www.thegolfschool.com
http://www.thegolfswingpage.com
http://www.theperfectswingtrainer.com
http://www.train4golf.com
http://www.trevorparkinson.com
http://www.vipgolfacademy.com
http://www.vivid-visions.com
http://www.welzgolf.com
http://www.weteachgolf.com
http://www.winningoffers.com

Reviews

Golf 4 Kids

http://www.golf4kids.co.uk

Enthusiasm is the key to success when it comes to golf, according to Golf 4 Kids. While this may be true, a few words of advice from experienced players couldn't hurt either. That's where this site created especially for junior golfers comes in.

There's a page of sensible advice for kids who are taking their first steps in golf, as well as content that will keep the more seasoned player looking over their youngster's shoulder too.

The black and white cartoon caricatures scattered through the site, with names like Horace Hole and Danny Divot, will probably appeal more to the parents who recognise some of their own characteristics in them rather than the kids themselves, but they still break up the information nicely.

site sponsored by
TPM
TOUR PRO MANAGEMENT LIMITED

The main focus of this site, however, is on the golf camps, tournaments and championships that children between the ages of 6 to 11 can participate in, on both sides of the Atlantic. Perfect if you take your golf seriously.

Unfortunately, at the time of writing this review, the website hadn't been updated in quite a while. As a result, some of the information may not be as up to date as it could be, but this site is still certainly worth a look if you have got a little Tiger Woods wannabe in your family.

RATING Refer to pg8 for rating explanations.

Overall Rating	✪✪✪
Ease of Use	✪✪✪✪
Content	✪✪
Look & Feel	✪✪✪
Customer Service	✪
Site Speed	✪✪✪✪✪
Technical	✪✪✪

MAIN POINTS:

>> Fast to load and easy to navigate, ideal for a site aimed at kids.

Junior Golf World

http://www.juniorgolfworld.com

When you visit this site you are confronted with a pop up window that covers much of the opening screen. Once this is removed and you have settled into the site's "unique" (and occasionally awkward) navigation system there is plenty of interesting content for young golfers.

The site hosts an online picture gallery to which you can upload your own pictures and some good flash games are featured.

There is a java chatroom which opens as a separate window, but takes a while to download. There is also a news section with links to other news sites such as the BBC.

There is comprehensive UK golf course finder with clickable maps to narrow down your search.

This site is to be re-launched shortly, which should iron out some of the design weaknesses, but most importantly it provides useful and entertaining content for the junior golfer.

RATING Refer to pg8 for rating explanations.

Overall Rating	✪✪✪
Ease of Use	✪✪
Content	✪✪✪✪
Look & Feel	✪✪✪
Customer Service	✪✪✪
Site Speed	✪✪
Technical	✪✪

MAIN POINTS:
>> Some good content and fun games for young golfers.

Junior Golfers

http://www.juniorgolfers.com

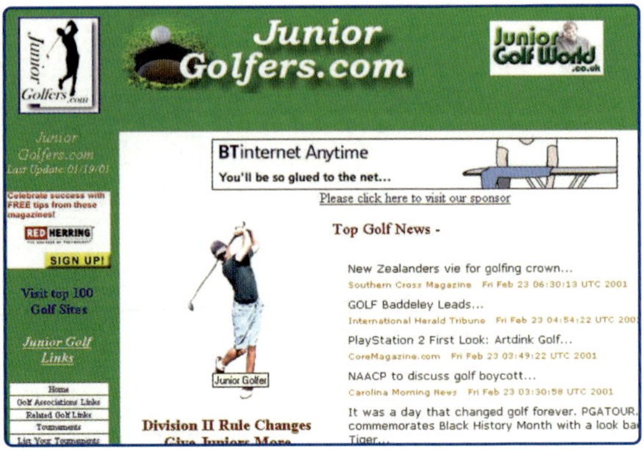

The Junior Golfers site provides informative links and news items that will be of interest to young golf players and their parents.

There is a useful amount of content including a well written "rules of the game" section as well as a current schedule of tournaments.

A fantasy golf challenge game, which requires online registration, adds entertaining interactivity to the site: after all, what kid doesn't enjoy computer games?

One decided advantage to the site is the great section including a clear guide to Junior Golf Associations pages, that can be accessed by US state.

This site was started by a dad when his son took up golf three years ago. At the time of this review he was planning to "retire", but was very much hoping that someone would come along and take the site on and progress it to the "next level".

The site is mainly a set of links, but has enough original content to make it worth a visit for young golfers.

RATING Refer to pg8 for rating explanations.

Overall Rating	✪✪✪
Ease of Use	✪✪
Content	✪✪✪✪
Look & Feel	✪✪✪
Customer Service	✪✪✪
Site Speed	✪✪
Technical	✪✪

MAIN POINTS:

>> Good information and a great fantasy challenge game.

Pepsi Little Peoples Golf

http://www.littlepeoplesgolf.com

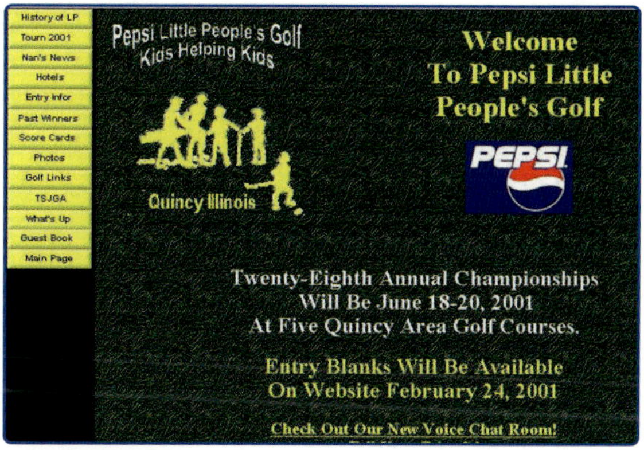

The Pepsi Little Peoples Golf Championship site is linked to one of the biggest brand names in the world, it somehow doesn't look anywhere near as slick as you'd first expect.

The main page, with its green grass background and difficult to read yellow text can be off-putting, and there's little consistency to the overall look and feel of the site. This is a shame, because if you ignore the design, you'll find plenty of content tucked away here.

There's all the information you'd need to get involved with the US based championship, now in its 28th year, including an online application form if you don't want to wait for the mail.

You'll find an extensive history of the championships and details of previous winners, as well as photos from last years event – perfect if you want to get some idea of what to expect.

If you're going to the Championships and need to find somewhere to stay, the site has details and links to help you arrange accommodation. Don't worry if you can't make the event in person, you still won't feel left out: Visitors to the site are encouraged to interact with one another, through the guestbook and live online chat room too, so there's plenty of opportunity to talk to fellow golf enthusiasts.

RATING Refer to pg8 for rating explanations.

Overall Rating	✪✪
Ease of Use	✪✪✪
Content	✪✪✪
Look & Feel	✪
Customer Service	✪✪✪✪
Site Speed	✪✪✪✪
Technical	✪✪

MAIN POINTS:

>> Plenty of content and information.

Other Junior Golfing Link Listings

Other Junior Golf related sites reviewed		Page
Golf Europe	http://www.golfeurope.com	88
Golfweek.com	http://www.golfweek.com	167
InsideGolf.com	http://www.insidegolf.com	155
Liquid Golf	http://www.liquidgolf.com	56
R&A Club St. Andrew's	http://www.randa.org	134

Other Junior Golf related sites

http://www.ajga.org

http://www.golfweb.com/juniors

http://www.golfclubs4kids.com

http://www.igolf.com/beginners/direct/forkids.html

http://www.ijgt.com

http://www.jrgolftour.net

http://www.juniorgolf.com

http://www.juniorworldgolf.com

http://www.kidsgolf.com

http://www.pikelake.com

http://www.taylormadekids.com

http://www.uskidsgolf.com

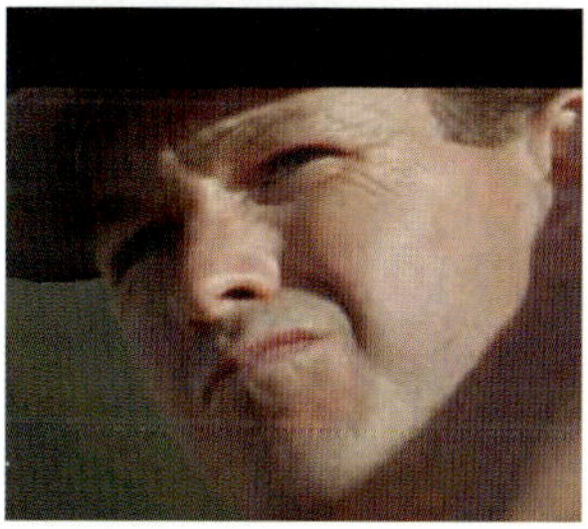

Reviews

Amateur Golf

http://www.amateur-golf.com

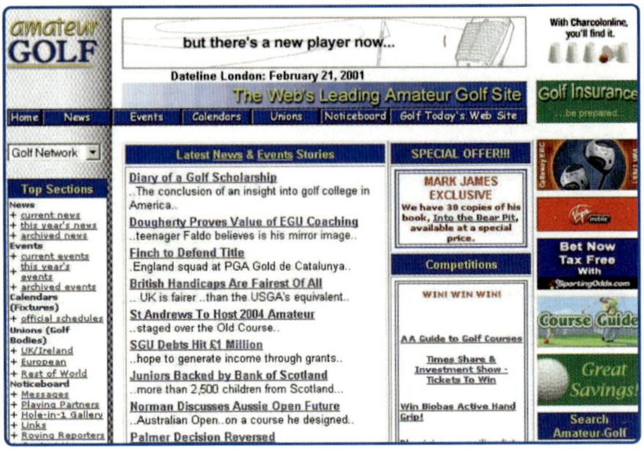

This impressive UK based golfing news site is aimed firmly at the amateur.

It has a fairly comprehensive coverage of breaking stories, as well as archives that are broken down into this week's, this year's, or previous year's news. Great if you're trying to pin-point a story from some time in the recent past.

There are a number of minor irritations, such as pop-up window ads, but most of the information that the amateur golfer needs is available here.

You'll also come across a handy calendar of events, along with a listing of unions that you may want to join. It's links such as these, rather than the obligatory connection to a shopping page,

which add to the overall comprehensive feel of the site. Things are rounded off nicely with a mailing list and good, lively notice board.

In spite of some problems, Amateur Golf still acts as a good springboard for general golfing information and news.

RATING Refer to pg8 for rating explanations.

Overall Rating	✪✪✪
Ease of Use	✪✪✪
Content	✪✪✪✪
Look & Feel	✪✪
Customer Service	✪✪
Site Speed	✪✪✪
Technical	✪✪✪

MAIN POINTS:

>> Good array of news, features and information.

Bad Golf Monthly

http://www.badgolfmonthly.com

No, Bad Golf Monthly isn't the home for those of us who are more likely to get a hole in 101 than in hole in one.

In fact, this is an excellent site with humorous and insightful articles, as well as advice too.

You'll find links to a massive amount of information and other golfing pages, along with products reviews, PGA features... the list goes on and on. You could easily spend a few days on this site and not get bored.

On the downside, some links to other golfing pages seemed to be dead.

You'll find the pages load quickly and efficiently, that the presentation and graphics are presentable and well designed, while the content is well written, entertaining and engaging to read.

An excellent starting place to visit when exploring golf online.

The site for the golfer who really sucks

RATING Refer to pg8 for rating explanations.

Overall Rating	✪✪✪
Ease of Use	✪✪✪
Content	✪✪✪✪
Look & Feel	✪✪✪
Customer Service	✪✪✪
Site Speed	✪✪✪
Technical	✪✪✪

MAIN POINTS:

>> Great content, excellent sense of humour and fun to visit.

BBC Sport

http://www.bbc.co.uk/sport/hi/english/golf

What can we say about the BBC that hasn't already been said? The BBC is internationally renowned for consistently good, high quality and unbiased journalism.

Their brand name is recognised and respected around the world, which goes a long way to explaining why this site covers golf news from across the globe: if you're going to cater to an international audience, then you can't leave anyone out.

If you've visited any of the many BBC sites online, then you'll be familiar with the overall look and feel of their sports section. Its style, design and approach is consistent with the rest of the BBC's impressive stable of sites, further reinforcing their already strong brand and identity. It is solely a news site, but this is no bad thing when done so well.

It features around twenty stories at any given time from the world of golf, as well as a searchable archive of past stories. It lists the official rankings in the golfing world, as well as all the forthcoming fixtures and a results section which covers all of the major tournaments.

Links to other sports and BBC services are always visible on the left of the page, while the site itself is quick, reliable and kept right up to date. Quite simply essential.

RATING Refer to pg8 for rating explanations.

Overall Rating	✪✪✪✪✪
Ease of Use	✪✪✪✪
Content	✪✪✪✪✪
Look & Feel	✪✪✪✪
Customer Service	✪✪✪✪
Site Speed	✪✪✪
Technical	✪✪✪✪

MAIN POINTS:

>> Excellent up to date news reports. Quick and easy to use.

BunkerShot.com

http://www.bunkershot.com

"BSG is a grass roots site for golfers from around the world," announces BunkerShot.com Golf, in what we're assuming is a "pun intended" kind of mission statement. If it's not, and they're serious, it wouldn't be the only example of their site being easily misinterpreted.

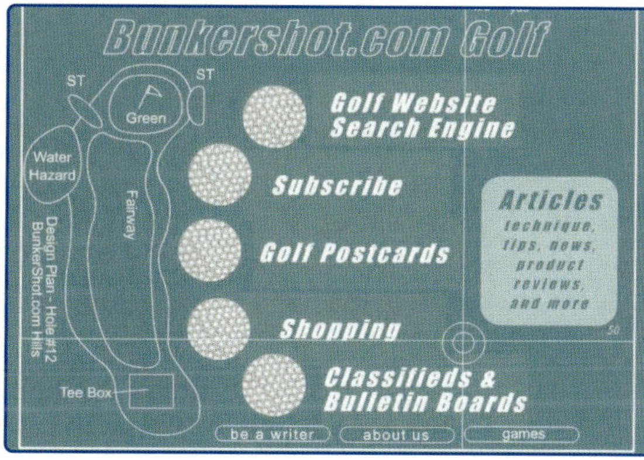

As the home page loads up (incredibly quickly) and a military style blueprint animation begins to play, you can't help but wonder if the bunker in question is a bomb-shelter, and the shot is from a gun. It doesn't help matters when your cursor changes into a gun-sight style crosshair, and the links turn red when you roll over them.

Still, rest assured that for all the military connotations we can come up with, BunkerShot.com is indeed a golfing website, and a rather good one at that. Boasting a dedicated golf only search engine, virtual postcards that you can send to friends via email, golfing games you can play online and plenty of classifieds and bulletin boards, there's no shortage of content here. You can even download golf themed screen-savers, so you can show your allegiance to the game, even when you step away from your computer.

Unfortunately, it appears that the site is being kept alive by its visitors, rather than the people who created it. At the time of writing, the last article from Bunkershot staff was three months prior, while the last submission from a reader was two days old. Redress that balance, and the site would score even higher.

RATING Refer to pg8 for rating explanations.

Overall Rating	✪✪✪
Ease of Use	✪✪✪
Content	✪✪✪
Look & Feel	✪✪✪✪
Customer Service	✪✪✪
Site Speed	✪✪✪✪✪
Technical	✪✪✪✪

MAIN POINTS:

>> Great golfing site with rabid supporters.

CityOfGolf

http://www.cityofgolf.com

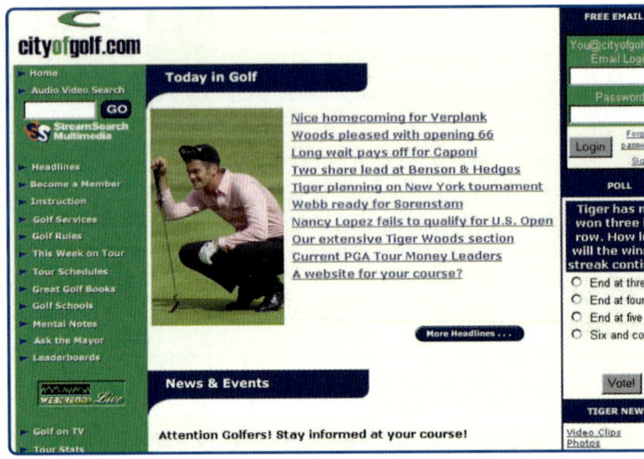

Links to the latest golfing news are the first things that will catch your eye once the City of Golf front page has finished loading. Even the smallest news item is listed and each piece opens in a separate window, so you don't have to worry about losing your place or surfing back to the main site.

Once you get past the news though, there is a wealth of other information that while not necessarily full of hard facts, will still be beneficial - especially to those looking to better their game. They offer links to sites that are, in their opinion, the top 18 golf schools that you can attend.

They also have a great monthly column written by Dr. Bee Epstein-Shepherd who gives you tips on playing your game in the right mental frame of mind. Other compelling features include a service which tracks all your game stats for you, the (somewhat obligatory) tour schedule and a section devoted to Tiger Woods. Did you know his real name is Eldrick and that two year old Tiger appeared on The Michael Douglas show putting with Bob Hope? They do. You can even view Tiger's new swing, frame by frame.

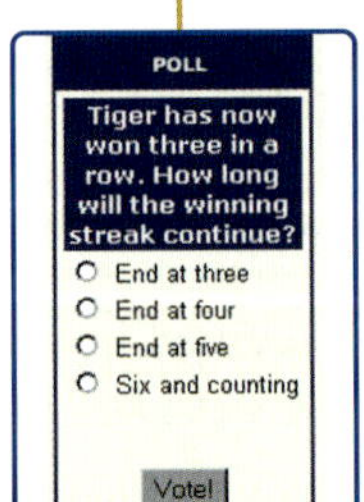

And whatever this site doesn't have, there's a good chance that they'll have links to it. Worth checking out.

RATING Refer to pg8 for rating explanations.

Overall Rating	✪✪✪✪
Ease of Use	✪✪
Content	✪✪✪
Look & Feel	✪✪✪
Customer Service	✪✪
Site Speed	✪✪
Technical	✪✪✪

MAIN POINTS:

>> Great news and features from regular columnists.

CNN Sports Illustrated

http://golf.si.cnn.com

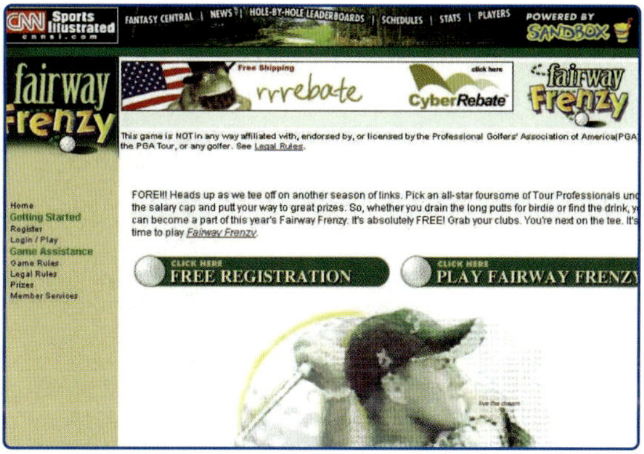

When a website is linked to a well known brand name, you can usually be pretty sure that it's worth a visit. Like the NBC related Golf.com site, the CNN Sports Illustrated Golf pages maintain the high standards that the news network has spent years establishing.

The site opens with a "Fairway Frenzy" feature, and initially it's not very clear as to what it's all about. However with some digging, you'll find that it's a competition where you choose players from the various tours, and then earn points for how well they do in competitions. Essentially, Fantasy Golf. We couldn't figure out what you get at the end of it all, but it's still a great way to "back your favourite players" in the tours. As with the difficulty in finding out what Fairway Frenzy was about, we found navigating the site a little difficult, but once there found a wealth of information.

There are comprehensive sections dedi-cated to news, schedules, hole by hole leader-boards, stats and players too. We never did receive any response to our email, which dragged our overall rating down a little. Understandable, though, when you consider this must be one of the most frequently viewed golfing sites on the Internet.

If you don't need to ask them anything, then CNN Sports Illustrated is great.

RATING Refer to pg8 for rating explanations.

Overall Rating	✪✪✪✪
Ease of Use	✪✪✪✪
Content	✪✪✪✪✪
Look & Feel	✪✪✪✪
Customer Service	✪✪
Site Speed	✪✪✪
Technical	✪✪✪✪

MAIN POINTS:
>> Comprehensive information.

Golf Magic

http://www.golfmagic.com

In spite of the name, Golf Magic doesn't feature caddies being pulled out of a hat or golf balls doing a disappearing act (they can manage that just fine on their own out on the course).

Instead what you'll find here is a fantastic golfing site, packed with both professional and amateur news, reviews, features, player profiles, leaderboards and chat forums.

Whatever section you explore, you'll find the standard of writing is consistently high. There's such a high level of care and attention going into every aspect of Golf Magic, it's clear that the people who maintain it are passionate about the game. When this is so obvious, you can't help but have a little bit of that feeling rub off on you while you're there.

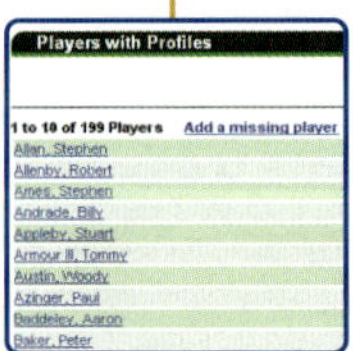

And If the energetic writing style doesn't convince you that the site was created with golfers in mind, then there's another nice touch which we think might, the option to personalise the site, getting news and information that is relevant to your area and filtering out anything that you might not be interested in. Pleasingly, it's incredibly simple to do, and you can customise the site to your heart's content in no time.

RATING Refer to pg8 for rating explanations.

Overall Rating	✪✪✪✪
Ease of Use	✪✪✪✪
Content	✪✪✪✪✪
Look & Feel	✪✪✪✪
Customer Service	✪✪✪✪
Site Speed	✪✪✪✪
Technical	✪✪✪

MAIN POINTS:

>> Customisable to match your interests or local area.

Golf Monitor

http://www.golfmonitor.com

US based site Golf Monitor seems to pride itself on keeping a consistently high standard of content online and clearly takes the business of keeping their pages up and running very seriously. When the first thing you see on a site is an apology that it hasn't been updated in a week or so, then a lengthy explanation why, you know the people maintaining it have a real passion for the game. That, after all, is what it's all about.

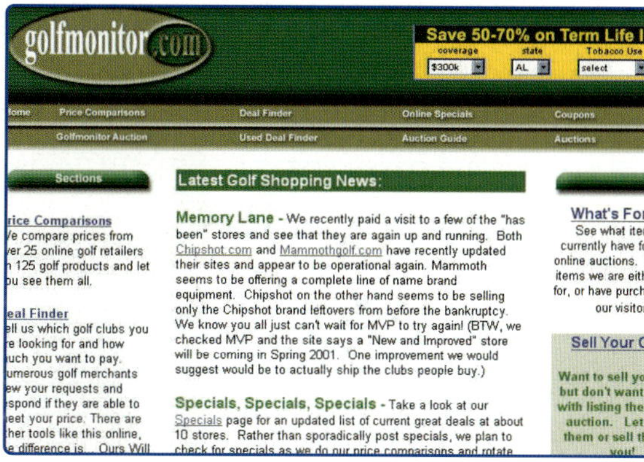

Golf Monitor's creators scour the web to collect the most relevant stories, features and competitions and showcase them all under one roof. "Just the good ones!" they proudly state. Well, you can't argue with the facts. Everything you'll find here, having already been through their vetting process, is likely to be something you'll want to read. All of the reviews, whether it's for brand new state of the art golfing equipment or for the more affordable used clubs, feature the same enthusiastic yet honest tone. Would I buy a used club from these men? After reading their hype free appraisals, combined with the objective stand the site takes as a whole, I probably would.

After all, it's easy to see when people really have a passion about what they're doing, and that shines through on golfmonitor.com. By golf fans, for golf fans. Highly recommended.

RATING Refer to pg8 for rating explanations.

Overall Rating	★★★★
Ease of Use	★★★★
Content	★★★★
Look & Feel	★★★
Customer Service	★★★★
Site Speed	★★★★
Technical	★★★★

MAIN POINTS:

>> Lively, engaging and entertaining.

Golf.com
http://www.golf.com

If you're casually searching for golf related sites on the Internet, chances are this is the one you'll stumble across first.

Bearing the highly sought after www.golf.com, there's a good chance it could get by with the number of visitors who speculatively type in the address.

Fortunately for anyone who does take the chance, they'll find a fantastic site, with all the latest golf news feeds from around the world, special features where they elaborate on some of the current hot topics, including players, competitions and more. You'd expect nothing less from a website owned by NBC, one of the biggest TV networks in the US.

There's a schedules section, with the latest information on all the major tours, both nationally and internationally, as well as a players section where you can find biographies on all the leading names in golf. The instruction section of the site offers you good tips and learning aids for various aspects of the game, while the statistics pages cover topics such as tour stats, leading money makers and more for the PGA, LPGA and SPGA. They have a women's section too.

As you would probably expect from an NBC affiliated site, everything here is presented flawlessly.

Combine this with excellent content, and you'll find this site is more than deserving of the golf.com name.

RATING Refer to pg8 for rating explanations.

Overall Rating	✪✪✪✪
Ease of Use	✪✪✪✪
Content	✪✪✪✪✪
Look & Feel	✪✪✪✪✪
Customer Service	✪
Site Speed	✪✪✪✪
Technical	✪✪✪✪✪

MAIN POINTS:

>> Great content and excellent design equals a brilliant site.

InsideGolf.com

http://www.insidegolf.com

Printed books and magazines are all well and good but let's face it: they can, by their very nature, be a little bit on the two dimensional side. That's what makes the Internet such a great way of reaching a whole new audience. It's worldwide, can be read by anyone at anytime, and most importantly for Insidegolf.com, can feature a range of all singing, all dancing multimedia elements.

They've certainly pulled out all the stops here, because whether it's video footage, animation or audio clips, it's on InsideGolf.com.

The first thing you'll notice is that there's a special focus on streaming video interviews direct from the professional golf tours. You'll see and hear top players, direct from the media centres at the PGA, LPGA, Senior PGA and other professional tournaments talking about their performance in the competitions. There are also streaming videos featuring course overviews and behind the scenes chats with tournament directors and chairpersons. Even the travel section, essential if you need help or advice in planning your golfing trips, features plenty of video footage so you can see and read about where you could be staying. Continuing the multimedia theme, the chatroom uses live audio to allow visitors to talk to one another.

All you need to get the most out of these features is a reasonably powerful computer with a decent connection speed.

RATING Refer to pg8 for rating explanations.

Overall Rating	✪✪✪✪
Ease of Use	✪✪✪
Content	✪✪✪
Look & Feel	✪✪✪
Customer Service	✪✪✪✪✪
Site Speed	✪✪✪
Technical	✪✪✪✪✪

MAIN POINTS:

>> Media intensive site, which is great if you've got a fast connection or are very patient.

Masters2001

http://www.masters.org

This is the official site of the Masters Tournament, and offers all the information about the event that you could ever need. For those lucky enough to be attending, details of transport to and from the tournament are provided, accommodation options are offered, weather forecasts and warnings are given as well as the latest ticket information. For those of us enjoying the tournament from home, the full TV schedule is provided too.

The full history of the tournament is extensively detailed on the site, with results listed from 1934 until the present, including records and statistics. The site provides history of each individual hole at the Augusta National Course, as well as commentary on each hole by Jack Nicklaus. There's even a walking tour of the course, from the clubhouse, through various holes, right to the champions' locker room! The

Leaderboard Section is most informative, with viewing options including the full leaderboard, international leaderboard, eagles summary, hole by hole summary of performance as well as cumulative statistics by hole and by round. A golf addict's dream. Excellent information on all your favourite players is offered, from individual profiles and scoring history at the tournament, to news, photographs and video interviews with the top golfers are also on the site. Finally, course cameras will enable you to view live images from holes 10 to 18.

RATING Refer to pg8 for rating explanations.

Overall Rating	✪✪✪
Ease of Use	✪✪✪
Content	✪✪✪✪
Look & Feel	✪✪✪
Customer Service	✪✪✪
Site Speed	✪✪
Technical	✪✪

MAIN POINTS:

>> Comprehensive site, worthy of a prestigious tournament.

>> Can be demanding, and make less powerful home computers struggle.

PGA of America

http://www.pga.com

This is the official website of the PGA of America. That sentence alone is probably enough reason to visit the site, but we found plenty of others.

As you would no doubt expect from such a prestigious name, the PGA website doesn't let the side down. When it comes to news and features, this one is at the top of its game.

The home page can be a little overpowering with the sheer wealth of information they provide, but if you take the time to go through carefully you'll find the site is jam packed with up to date top level articles and features in the world of golf.

Our advice to visitors would be to use their handy "site map" feature which breaks the information down into a more user friendly, list of links which makes a good platform from which to operate.

The site itself concentrates on the four major tournaments of the PGA tour, covering statistics and the history of professional golf in America, along with worldwide news coverage, special sections for women golfers and juniors, and a great regularly updated kids' quiz.

There are videos to download covering aspects of golfing technique, while visitors to the site can play the addictive IBM Virtual Golf.

You'll also find a wealth of instructional material on the site all provided courtesy of the PGA and with tips from pro's and top level teachers.

Well worth the visit, and a credit to the name.

RATING Refer to pg8 for rating explanations.

Overall Rating	✪✪✪✪✪
Ease of Use	✪✪✪✪
Content	✪✪✪✪✪
Look & Feel	✪✪✪✪
Customer Service	✪✪✪✪
Site Speed	✪✪✪✪
Technical	✪✪✪✪✪

MAIN POINTS:

>> Wealth of news and instructional information presented in a profes sional site.

PGA Tour

http://www.pgatour.com

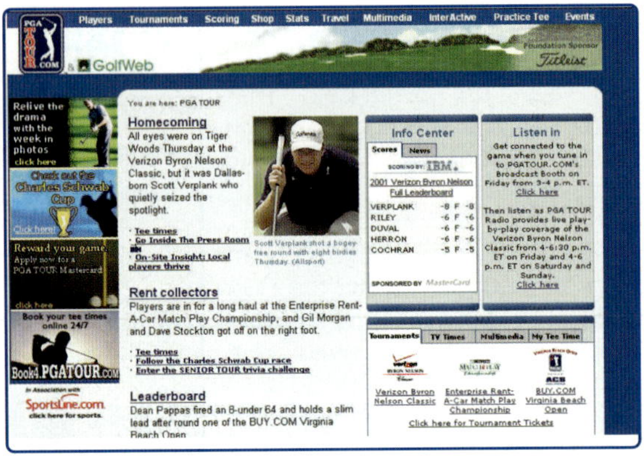

This site is dedicated to the PGA Tour all over the world and is a great place to keep up with current golfing news and events.

The home page features live scores on any PGA Tour game currently being played and it also links to a page with live scoring of the PGA, SPGA, LPGA and European Tour. Comprehensive stuff.

The Tour Schedule section offers a wealth of information, which is thankfully kept up to date. You can view the schedules of a large number of tour-related competitions and events, with the option to see a week back and a week forward of all the big name championships. Great for planning ahead, or checking if you missed something. The Players section offers a wide range of information (biographies, stats, results) on just about any golfer you care to mention (and quite a few you've probably never heard of too).

The site also offers a link to a shop which was "closed for maintenance" during our visit.

Unfortunately, contacting someone proved a little difficult. The contact details are a little "hidden" at the bottom of the page, and both of the emails we sent came back "undeliverable".

RATING Refer to pg8 for rating explanations.

Overall Rating	✪✪✪
Ease of Use	✪✪✪
Content	✪✪
Look & Feel	✪✪✪
Customer Service	✪
Site Speed	✪✪✪
Technical	✪✪

MAIN POINTS:

» Quick, live scores on competition days, covering many tour games.

The Golf Channel

http://www.thegolfchannel.com

The Golf Channel is an absolutely packed site, that offers visitors a lot of detailed content focusing on tour news, information and player profiles, along with plenty of additional good quality content.

Other features of the site include a "what's on" section, with video footage and events that can be found both online and on traditional television channels. There's also a video vault section where you can view interviews and other archived footage. The tours section is filled with excellent content on all the major events, and includes detailed biographies of the key players on each tour. The academy contains a number of areas where you can get tips and other instructional information to help improve your game while the mall link offers you the inevitable access to a pro shop, where you can buy Golf Channel merchandise. While we're in a shopping vein, you'll also find links to The Golf Warehouse online superstore with a huge range of golfing products.

There's also a chat area on the site that allows you to talk to other golfers online and on occasion you might even get to chat to a well known personality when they attend to share his or her thoughts on all manner of golfing subjects.

RATING Refer to pg8 for rating explanations.

Overall Rating	✪✪✪
Ease of Use	✪✪✪✪
Content	✪✪✪✪
Look & Feel	✪✪✪
Customer Service	✪✪✪
Site Speed	✪✪✪
Technical	✪✪✪✪

MAIN POINTS:

>> Technically impressive and content heavy site.

>> May end up "Chatting" to celebrity.

US Senior Open

http://www.usseniooropen.com

If you're looking for cold, hard facts about the US Senior Open, then this is where you'll find them.

The site presents straight information about many aspects of the Senior Open, including past winners, this years players and some of the history. What information they don't have on the site they provide links to, which open in new windows so that you don't have to worry about leaving the site. This can get a little confusing sometimes, but once you get used to it, it's not all bad.

The site itself has a very plain, look about it. With the exception of the drop down menu selections, the most visually stimulating things you can expect are a few black and white pictures.

Bruce Fleisher

Tom Kite

The information itself is usually just plain black text on a white background, which admittedly makes for easy reading.

Overall, if you have any interest in the Senior Open, then this site is worth a quick visit.

RATING Refer to pg8 for rating explanations.

Overall Rating	✪✪✪
Ease of Use	✪✪✪
Content	✪✪✪
Look & Feel	✪
Customer Service	✪✪✪
Site Speed	✪✪✪
Technical	✪✪

MAIN POINTS:

>> Straight forward information on the US open.

World Golf Village

http://www.wgv.com

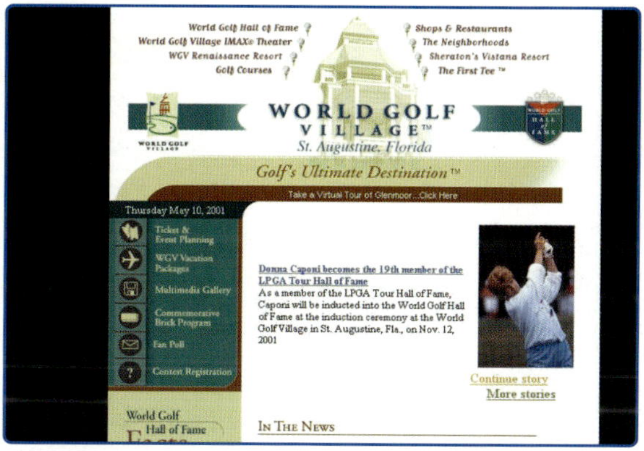

The World Golf Village has just about everything that a golfer might look for. It boasts a golfing hall of fame, an IMAX theatre, links to resorts, golf courses and shops and restaurants too.

The content is impressive, with a range of interesting, informative articles and points of view from the golfing world. Particularly impressive is the multimedia gallery with a range of audio and video clips, as well as a library of golf images. The video inserts are presented in Real Player format, and tailored for different connection speeds. It's within this multimedia section of the site that you'll find some well researched and presented profiles about some of the best know golfing legends of our time.

The site has a top stories section, which is kept up-to-date with major news on golfing events and personalities. There's much more here to read, watch, listen to or download, with information on every aspect of the game you care to mention.

The celebration of the open of the World Golf Village started with a bang!!

The speed and navigation of the site was also impressive, particularly when it came to video downloads.

Unfortunately we couldn't find any email or contact information, but overall, this is clearly an extensive site and one that the golfing enthusiast could easily spend quite some time on. This is definitely a site that deserves a return visit.

RATING Refer to pg8 for rating explanations.

Overall Rating	✪✪✪✪
Ease of Use	✪✪✪✪
Content	✪✪✪✪✪
Look & Feel	✪✪✪✪
Customer Service	✪✪
Site Speed	✪✪✪✪
Technical	✪✪✪✪

MAIN POINTS:

>> Fast site, rich in content. Speedy downloads of multimedia elements.

Other News Link Listings

Other News related sites reviewed		Page
American Golf Auction	http://www.americangolfauction.com	46
Global Golf	http://www.globalgolf.com	86
Golf Illustrated	http://www.golfillustrated.com	166
Golf Today	http://www.golftoday.co.uk	72
Golfweek.com	http://www.golfweek.com	167
Junior Golfers	http://www.juniorgolfers.com	142
KeepersOfTheGame	http://www.keepersofthegame.org	130
LPGA	http://www.lpga.com	229
Maximum Golf	http://www.maximumgolf.com	169
My Golf Zone	http://www.mygolfzone.com	41
PGA Net	http://www.pganet.net	94
Scottish Golf	http://www.scottishgolf.com	96
Titleist Golf	http://www.titleist.com	63
UK Golf Information Site	http://www.uk-golf.com	78
The Open Championship	http://www.opengolf.com	99

Other News related sites

http://sports.yahoo.com/pga

http://www.hole-19.com

http://www.golfers.net

http://www.majorschampion.com

http://www.sportsline.com/u/golf

http://www.thegolfersnetwork.com

Reviews

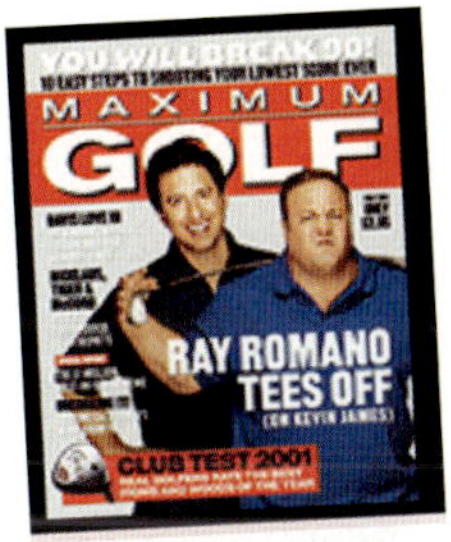
MAXIMUM
GOLF
RAY ROMANO
TEES OFF
CLUB TEST 2001

GOLF
PUTT
LIKE
TIGER

Golf Digest

http://www.golfdigest.com

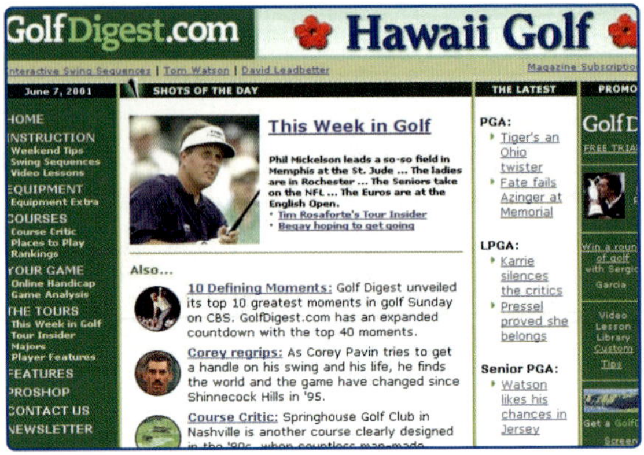

As you might expect from the name, Golf Digest strives to be a guide to all things golf related. If you were looking for golfing instruction, guides to courses and almost anything else relating to the golfing world, then this would be the place to visit, right?

The answer is an emphatic yes. This is a mammoth site with everything from interactive swing sequences to different forms of online instruction. A very current news section that is updated on a daily basis adds immediacy to the site. In-depth coverage of the latest golfing events will mean you'll call back again and again to the site, just to make sure you don't miss any breaking stories. The navigation is a pleasure to use, with clear and attractive links while the feature articles are very impressive. They go far beyond the usual mediocre fare one finds on some sites. Altogether an impressive site - except for a few niggling problems. At the time of testing, some of the pages seemed to be unreachable. This was possibly due to a database problem and should not detract from the overall assessment of the site (unless of course the problem isn't fixed in the immediate future).

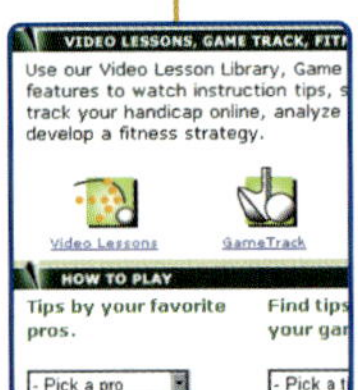

The access speed over a 56k modem seemed a little sluggish for a site of this calibre. However, the response time to our e-mail queries was good, at just over an hour.

RATING Refer to pg8 for rating explanations.

Overall Rating	★★★★
Ease of Use	★★★★
Content	★★★★★
Look & Feel	★★★★
Customer Service	★★★★
Site Speed	★★★
Technical	★★★

MAIN POINTS:

>> Great content, with impressive layout and graphics.

Golf World

http://www.golfworld.com

Golf world is a sister magazine to Golf Digest (but printed weekly rather than monthly) both of which are owned by the New York Times. Others in the stable include Golf World Business and Golf World Women. The content part of the Website is at GolfDigest.com but the rest relates to articles found in the magazine and its back issues.

They offer a tracking system which, once you sign up for it, will help you monitor your golf scores to see if you're improving or not. In addition, for those specifically looking to improve their game, they also have a weekly "Weekend Tips" column, as well as video lessons, which you are able to download or stream directly. One particularly nice feature is the course review and rankings. Each week, their expert reviews a different course and grades it out of ten. A newsletter is also available for those who like their news delivered to their virtual mailbox, while if you're interested in ordering something to be delivered to your real mailbox, they make it fast and easy for those with credit cards. The site itself has a nice, stylized look to it and is easy to move around although it may take a little digging to unearth some of the better features.

RATING Refer to pg8 for rating explanations.

Overall Rating	★★★★
Ease of Use	★★
Content	★★★★★
Look & Feel	★★★
Customer Service	★★★★
Site Speed	★★★
Technical	★★★

MAIN POINTS:

>> Impressive depth of information, with some great and extremely useful features.

Golf Illustrated

http://www.golfillustrated.com

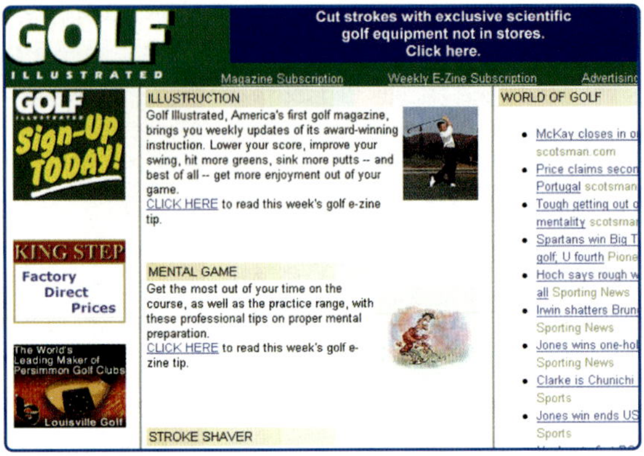

Well, where do we begin with this one? Golf Illustrated is more than just an online golfing magazine. You'll find much more than just golf here. If anything, it's a general purpose lifestyle guide, albeit with a heavy dose of golf.

Golf Illustrated offers, amongst other things, a visually impressive instruction guide to various golfing techniques, strokes and hot tips as well as up to the minute information on golfing equipment. The site covers both the physical and mental aspects of the game, considering how you can help yourself to improve your game with a little bit of training. For the enthusiastic golfer, Golf Illustrated also delves into breaking golf news and the status of the top players and their positions in various tournaments. An added bonus (although slightly unexpected and a little out of place) is a section on the stock market and financial news around the world. Top golf stories from around the globe are also featured in this section, while visitors can be gently reminded that there is more than their favourite game in the world, with scores and results across a range of sports. There is a useful section on weather and course conditions in the United States, with the option of selecting the same information for other countries.

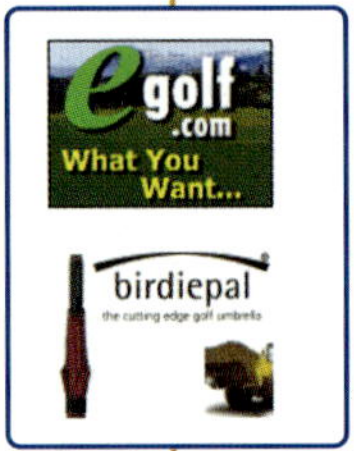

Golf Illustrated also diversifies into reports on local pollen forecasts, scenic drives, and even gardening weather.

RATING Refer to pg8 for rating explanations.

Overall Rating	✪✪✪✪
Ease of Use	✪✪✪✪✪
Content	✪✪✪✪
Look & Feel	✪✪✪
Customer Service	✪✪✪✪
Site Speed	✪✪
Technical	✪✪✪

MAIN POINTS:

>> The site is a one-stop information centre for golfers.

>> Impressive graphics can result in slow loading time.

Golfweek

http://www.golfweek.com

A statistic fan's dream, this is an excellent site if you are after the latest news regarding current golfing tournaments. Whether you're searching for information on the pros or amateurs, these guys are sure to have what you need. You'll find the latest rankings, scores, stats, schedules and results of the ongoing events on the pro tour along with loads of information on smaller American college championships. With a quick click of the mouse you can call up the latest US mens, womens, girls, boys and other major amateur results and rankings from around the world. Nothing like being thorough, is there?

There's a section called Opinion which contains just that: loads of editorials from various columnists (some more eccentric than others) and letters from other contributors. Unlike many other golf sites, Golfweek.com features heavily on business news that relates directly to the golf world. In addition, you'll find coverage on everything from the rules of the game to reviews of golf related videos and books.

Golfweek.com doesn't sell any products related to golf, but instead links to another large online golf store which makes it quick and easy to buy something that you like after reading the review.

RATING Refer to pg8 for rating explanations.

Overall Rating	✪✪✪
Ease of Use	✪✪✪
Content	✪✪✪
Look & Feel	✪✪✪
Customer Service	✪✪✪
Site Speed	✪
Technical	✪✪✪

MAIN POINTS:

>> Really well designed. Easy to navigate, with plenty of information.

Links Magazine

http://www.linksmagazine.com

One thing that you usually have to put up with when it comes to online magazines is an almost unbearable amount of pop-up ads, banners and the like. Yet while Links Magazine Online does inevitably feature its fair share of ads, they are nowhere near as annoying and oppressive as they are on some other sites. Even subscription ads for their print magazine. A subtle ad for subscriptions is the only evidence we could find that there even was a print magazine to accompany this "net version" – and we really liked it.

You can't help but be impressed by the amount of news pieces, reviews and columns you can read here. Every item also includes buttons which take you to a printable version of that story, or allow you to email the story to a friend that you think will find it interesting.

The pieces are usually accompanied by high quality images as well, most of which load quickly and expand should you wish to see it in more detail.

The site itself is also really well done and of high quality, yet still manages to load at a speedy pace.

Links Magazine Online is a site that you simply must visit. Highly recommended.

RATING Refer to pg8 for rating explanations.

Overall Rating	✪✪✪✪✪
Ease of Use	✪✪✪
Content	✪✪✪✪✪
Look & Feel	✪✪✪✪
Customer Service	✪✪✪
Site Speed	✪✪✪
Technical	✪✪✪✪

MAIN POINTS:

>> Excellent online golfing magazine, packed with news, information and features.

Maximum Golf

http://www.maximumgolf.com

Unfortunately the first thing we encountered when entering this site was a massive subscription advert.

If you'd prefer not to take the subscription, you can click on the logo and be transported to the Fox Sports golfing section that has plenty of content on the international game. The site offers plenty of current golf news as well as some good feature stories. There's a leaderboard section where you can keep up to date on whoever is at the forefront of the various PGA tours. The ranking section allows you to see all sorts of interesting statistics on how the various players are performing (there's also an option to see the rankings by "money earned" which was an interesting one).

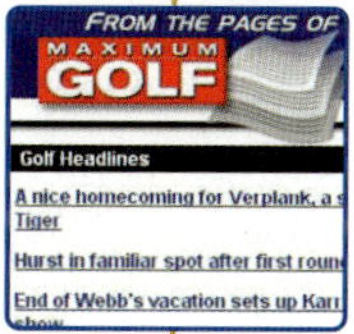

The site also offers a schedule section, which will keep you in the know about what's coming up on the golfing calendar, whoever the defending champions are and what the winning purse is for all the major competitions.

RATING Refer to pg8 for rating explanations.

Overall Rating	✪✪✪✪
Ease of Use	✪✪✪✪
Content	✪✪✪✪✪
Look & Feel	✪✪✪✪
Customer Service	✪✪
Site Speed	✪✪✪
Technical	✪✪✪✪

MAIN POINTS:

>> Plenty of good quality, regularly updated news.

T & L Golf Magazine

http://www.tlgolf.com

When a publishing house puts an online version of one of their titles on the Internet, it simply has to be good. By the direct association with their on the shelf publication, the official website can either help to boost sales and raise the profile of a title, or give potential readers the impression that the magazine isn't worth their time or money. With this in mind, you can't help but imagine the people behind this online version of TLGolf magazine must be feeling quite pleased with themselves.

This excellent site has a host of great articles, features, columns and interviews with celebrities, as well as hints, travel tips and much more.

The golf destinations section is particularly informative, with a useful interactive world map to find most of the golfing destinations on the planet.

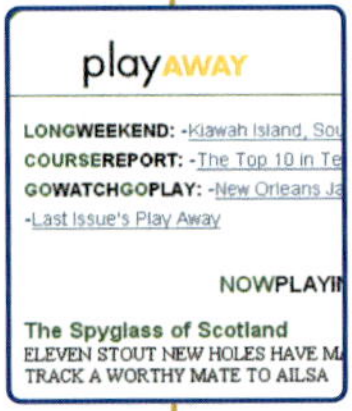

So while it's true there are a host of features on this site, including a great marketplace section for shopping, it's the quality of the articles and consistently high standard of writing that impresses most.

Overall, TLGolf is a fast and slick site, with an easy navigational interface and fantastic articles.

Highly recommended.

RATING Refer to pg8 for rating explanations.

Category	Stars
Overall Rating	5
Ease of Use	4
Content	5
Look & Feel	4
Customer Service	4
Site Speed	4
Technical	4

MAIN POINTS:

>> Informative, well written and entertaining content.

Other Publications Link Listings

Other Publications related sites reviewed		**Page**
My Golf Zone	http://www.mygolfzone.com	41

Other Publications related sites

http://19thhole.com

http://alabamagolfclub.com

http://clubmaker-online.com

http://golfamerica.com

http://michigangolfer.com

http://www.daytongolf.com

http://www.doubleeagle-golfmag.com

http://www.fairwaysgreens.com

http://www.flagstick.com

http://www.golf4u.com

http://www.golfclubreview.com

http://www.golfhouston.com

http://www.golfindia.com

http://www.golfmag.com

http://www.golfnutz.net

http://www.golfweb.com

http://www.golfworldmagazine.com

http://www.igolf.com

http://www.insidethetour.com

http://www.metroteetimes.com

http://www.northeastgolf.com

http://www.nwgolfmap.com

http://www.portman.uk.com

http://www.puremagazine.com

http://www.scoregolf.com

http://www.seniorgolfer.com

http://www.southerngolf.com

http://www.swingweight.com

http://www.teetime-mag.com

http://www.thewgm.com

http://www.totalgolfer.com

http://www.traditionsgolf.com

http://www.triadgolf.com

Reviews

PGA WEST

GOLF LIFESTYLES

Golf Home Realtors
Select one...
International

Golf Apppraisers

http://www.golfappraisers.org

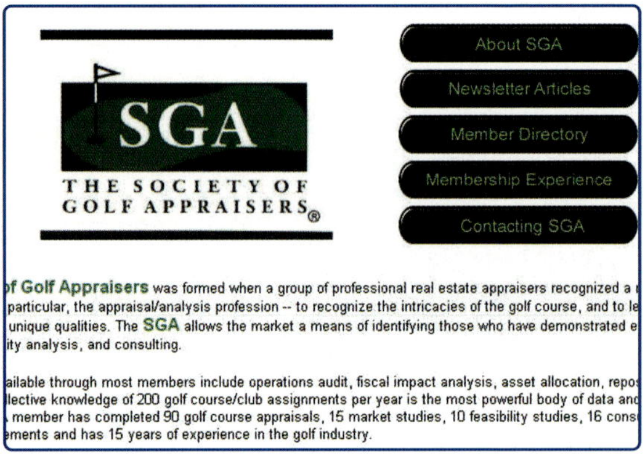

"The Society of Golf Appraisers was formed when a group of professional real estate appraisers recognized a need for the real estate industry - and in particular, the appraisal/ analysis profession - to recognize the intricacies of the golf course, and to learn and understand the golf course industry's unique qualities" explains the homepage of the SGA.

This US based organisation, which has performed golf course appraisals, feasibility studies and market analyses in every state from Alabama to Wisconsin clearly has a great deal of experience and expertise behind it. In real terms, though, just how useful is that kind of knowledge to the average golfer? Frankly, not all that much. In fact, a cursory glance would reveal little or nothing that would be of interest to the visitor.

Nothing, that is, unless you click on the newsletter articles archive. In there, you'll find a whole host of thought provoking studies, reports and features on how golf clubs or courses can improve their standing, increase their profits and continue to grow and develop in the 21st century. Certainly worth looking at, printing out and perhaps slipping to the manager of your favourite course.

There's plenty of statistics that suggest golf is undergoing something of a boom period, so perhaps now is the time to buy shares in your club...

RATING Refer to pg8 for rating explanations.

Overall Rating	✪✪✪
Ease of Use	✪✪
Content	✪✪✪
Look & Feel	✪✪✪
Customer Service	✪✪
Site Speed	✪✪✪
Technical	✪✪

MAIN POINTS:

>> Offers specialist skills that you'd be hard pressed to find elsewhere.

Golf Course Home

http://www.golfcoursehome.net

So you've worked hard all your life. You've taken care of your money, watched the bank balance carefully and always kept a little something aside for your retirement. Now it's time to start enjoying those years of savings,but where do you enjoy your free time (and money) now that work is a thing of the past? Well, the answer could conceivably be found at Golf Course Home.net.

For this is a site that focuses on retirement homes and secure country club communities, ideal if your idea of paradise is spending your retirement in a golf-centric environment. You'll find a host of different communities placed in the spotlight, with a well written review of the lifestyle you'll find there accompanied by plenty of good quality pictures. You'll have no problem figuring out if the lifestyle is for you.

Dig a little deeper into the site and you'll find an archive of previously reviewed golfing communities - just in case any of the featured residences found on the main page don't appeal to you. You can share your plans of settling down in such a location with other like-minded people via the online message board, or simply click on a link and take in the virtual view.

The site is affiliated with Amazon.com (which you'll find reviewed in the books and videos chapter of this guide).

RATING Refer to pg8 for rating explanations.

Overall Rating	✪✪✪✪
Ease of Use	✪✪✪
Content	✪✪✪✪
Look & Feel	✪✪✪
Customer Service	✪✪✪✪
Site Speed	✪✪✪
Technical	✪✪✪✪

MAIN POINTS:

>> Chat forums and virtual tours showcase the interactivity of this site.

Golf Homes

http://golfhomes.com

Have you ever thought how much easier life would be if you had your very own golf course in the grounds of your house?

Sounds like a dream, doesn't it? For most of us, it always will be. For a select few, however, it's a dream that can become a reality – with a little help from Golf Homes.com.

This is the site you need if you're looking for a property with the ultimate golfing accessory as standard, but be warned that such indulgences don't come cheap.

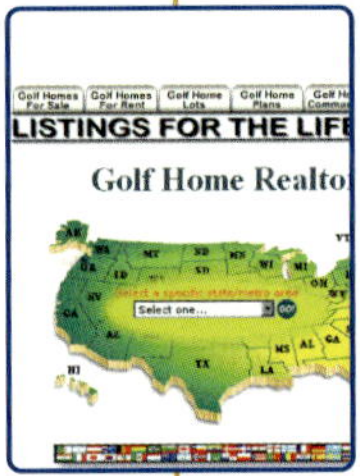

The most desirable residence we found during our review of the site was a pretty impressive Las Vegas home, located on the Vegas Country Club course itself. Oh, and the price? A real bargain at only $3,500,000.

There's plenty more where that came from, with some truly stunning homes around the world for you to feast your eyes upon.

OK, so it may only be a chance to view how the other half live, but there's nothing wrong with dreaming about waking up in one of the palatial homes, strolling out into your "back yard" and playing a quick round before brunch.

RATING Refer to pg8 for rating explanations.

Overall Rating	✪✪
Ease of Use	✪✪✪
Content	✪✪✪
Look & Feel	✪✪✪✪
Customer Service	✪✪✪
Site Speed	✪✪✪
Technical	✪✪

MAIN POINTS:

>> Dream homes, which all can admire and some can buy.

Golf Lifestyles

http://www.golflifestyles.com

If you've paid a visit to www.golfcoursehome.net, which is reviewed on page 185 in this guide, and then pop along to Golf Lifestyles.com, you could be forgiven for thinking you've ended up at the same site. The design, look and feel of both of these golf real estate sites are very similar.

As far as content is concerned, there's very little to separate them. They both feature comprehensive guides to golfing resorts, communities and real estate properties.

They both feature plenty of snapshots of the real estate too – more than enough to make you feel green with envy towards anyone who does live in such a great residence.

Yet it's in the use of technology where Golf Lifestyles just edges ahead of its competitor, because you'll find, amongst other nifty features, a really good virtual tour of some of the properties featured on site.

You'll need to subscribe to the site to get access to all the really good features, but the questions they ask are basic, you shouldn't find yourself inundated with junk email as a result of signing up and you can become a member in a matter of minutes. Well worth it for the chance to wander around a palatial golfing home – even if it is just a virtual stroll.

RATING Refer to pg8 for rating explanations.

Overall Rating	✪✪✪✪
Ease of Use	✪✪✪
Content	✪✪✪✪
Look & Feel	✪✪✪
Customer Service	✪✪✪
Site Speed	✪✪✪✪
Technical	✪✪✪✪✪

MAIN POINTS:

>> Virtual tours. Great photographs of the golfing homes themselves.

Golf Property Analysts

http://www.golfprop.com

T Golf Property Analysts is a well rounded and complete website which presents all that one would need as an introduction to this company.

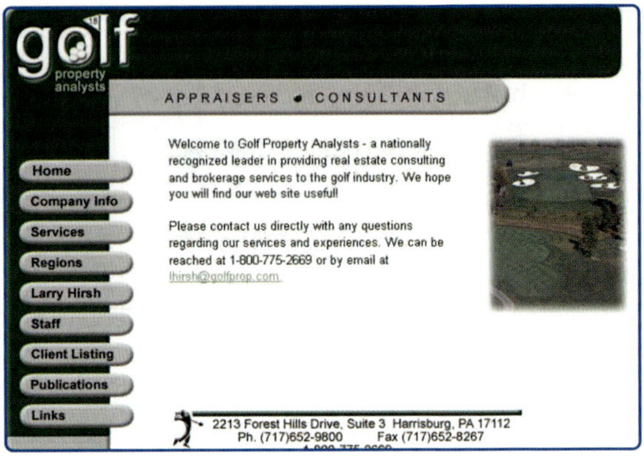

The company operates in a very specialised market providing services that include Appraisals/Valuations, Feasibility Analysis, Litigation Support, Tax Reviews, Sales & Acquisition Services, Advisory & Consulting Services. These services all relate to golfing real estate.

The site gives you some background into the company, with an overview of their chief and introductions to the other staff employed.

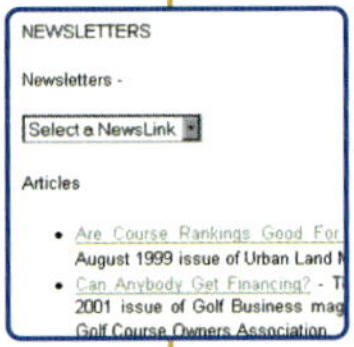

There's a long list highlighting the areas that the company has operated, which covers most of the US. They also present visitors with a long list of impressive clients with whom they have worked.

A List of links presents a visitor with other sites that have reference to this specialised field.

For anyone requiring specialised Golf property related services, this appears to be an all rounded, professional team with plenty of experience.

RATING Refer to pg8 for rating explanations.

Overall Rating	✪✪
Ease of Use	✪✪✪
Content	✪✪
Look & Feel	✪✪
Customer Service	✪✪✪
Site Speed	✪✪✪
Technical	✪✪

MAIN POINTS:

>> Information presented in logical order.

Gulf and Golf Properties

http://www.golfrealtors.net

The site opens with a huge pair of binoculars providing a gateway to two areas of operation. Different, but clean and easy to use...maybe they use the binoculars since most of us can only admire these properties from a distance?

The first area will take you to their information on Gulf Coast homes and investment properties which at the time of our visit was under construction. The second, and of more interest to us, takes you to their section which provides you with "exclusive private and semi-private Florida golf course property information".

If you're looking for a second home, vacation home or somewhere to retire, then where better to find it than somewhere in the sun.

Once you get inside, you may feel a little put off by the design, but there's more to it than this. You have the opportunity of searching by County or City, and filter results for private or semi-private golf courses.

Each result, had a "view" button which takes you to the information page of the course. It would make a major improvement if the images on the site were improved, but we found that their customer service was reasonable and they are happy to send images if requested.

Information pages offer a descriptive write up of the properties as well as a course rating but could certainly do with linking to actual golf course sites to provide visitors with an easy click through to the specific courses.

RATING Refer to pg8 for rating explanations.

Overall Rating	✪✪✪
Ease of Use	✪✪
Content	✪✪✪
Look & Feel	✪✪✪
Customer Service	✪✪✪
Site Speed	✪✪✪✪
Technical	✪✪

MAIN POINTS:

>> Provides golf course property information in Florida.

North American Golf Directory

http://www.golfdirect.com

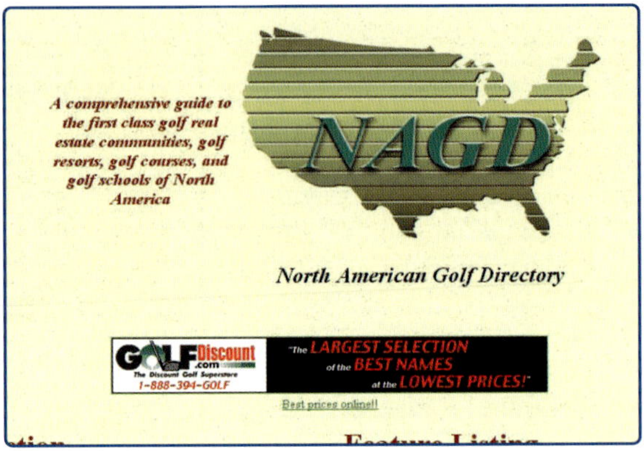

If there was a jack of all trades when it comes to golfing real estate sites, then the North American Golf Directory would have to be it.

Whether it be golf real estate communities, golf resorts, golf courses or even golf schools you're after – assuming they're North American, of course – then this could be a useful site for you.

The overall look and feel of the site is basic, at best. It's logo, a rather kitsch 1970s style metallic map of the US complete with the NAGD initials emblazoned across it. It's design problems could have you leaving the site without even realizing it too, as links to affiliated sites are placed directly along text based links to other sections of the NAGD site.

Overcome this problem and you'll find a fairly comprehensive selection of links

Everything is divided up in fairly logical and intuitive subsections, so you'll be able to avoid anything that doesn't interest you and quickly find the links you're after.

RATING Refer to pg8 for rating explanations.

Overall Rating	✪✪
Ease of Use	✪✪
Content	✪
Look & Feel	✪
Customer Service	✪✪✪
Site Speed	✪✪✪
Technical	✪✪

MAIN POINTS:

>> Plenty of links. Sensible division of topics.

Vacation Homes Unlimited

http://www.vacation-homes.com

Many of us would like to experience living in, and indeed playing golf in other countries, but doing so inevitably means a great deal of expense.

For that reason, it's often an unattainable dream to jet off to another part of the world to experience what life would be like if you lived elsewhere – not as a tourist, but as a local.

Well, that's where Vacation Homes Unlimited Home Exchange comes in. They offer visitors the chance to take a golfing break either within your own country, or at a foreign destination, by undertaking a temporary home swap with another family. This way, the site explains, you can: "experience the local lifestyle in a way package tourists just can't do. When you home exchange, you "live like a local!"

Established in 1986, Vacation Homes Unlimited is one of the longest running companies of its kind. To further ease any concerns you might have about experiencing a home-swap, they're also one of the founding members of the First Home Exchange Alliance - a governing body of home exchange groups. This is clearly a well established company.

If you do have any questions, the site has an extensive Q&A section that will tell you everything you need to know, including average prices. "There's no place like someone else's home" they proudly announce. We can't argue with that.

RATING Refer to pg8 for rating explanations.

Overall Rating	✪✪✪✪
Ease of Use	✪✪✪✪
Content	✪✪✪
Look & Feel	✪✪✪✪
Customer Service	✪✪✪
Site Speed	✪✪✪
Technical	✪✪✪

MAIN POINTS:

>> Great site to support a fantastic home swapping idea.

Other Real Estate Link Listings

Other Real Estate related sites reviewed

Other Real Estate related sites reviewed		Page
Global Golf Guide	http://www.globalgolfguide.com	87
Golfing Ireland	http://www.golfingireland.com	216

Other Real Estate related sites

http://www.arborsprings.com
http://www.bighorngolf.com
http://www.blackdiamondranch.com
http://www.briarridgecc.com
http://www.bridlewoodev.com
http://www.callawassieisland.com
http://www.canterwood.com
http://www.cortijosromero.com
http://www.crookedcreek.com
http://www.crosscreekgolf.com
http://www.daltonranch.com
http://www.debary-cc.com
http://www.garlandusa.com
http://www.golfriverside.com
http://www.gulf-harbour.co.nz
http://www.heritageclub.com
http://www.jeffersonlanding.com
http://www.kingwoodonline.com
http://www.laurel-springs.com
http://www.locusthillhomes.com
http://www.montreuxgolf.com
http://www.oldebeau.net
http://www.pawpawgolf.com
http://www.pganational.com
http://www.pgawest.com
http://www.registryone.com
http://www.reynoldsgolf.com
http://www.ridgesrealty.com
http://www.riverrungolf.com
http://www.sabinosprings.com
http://www.silvercreekplantation.com
http://www.stillwaters.com
http://www.sunrivers.com
http://www.thepowderhorn.com
http://www.thesawmill.com
http://www.thevirginian.com
http://www.tide-water.com
http://www.vineyardsrealty.com
http://www.visitwoodbridge.com
http://www.waldenlake.com
http://www.whitneyoaks.com
http://www.woodcreekgolf.com

EZ Webguides
15th hole - shopping

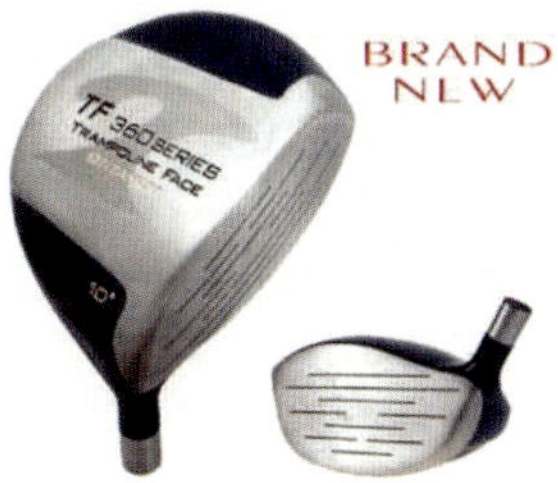

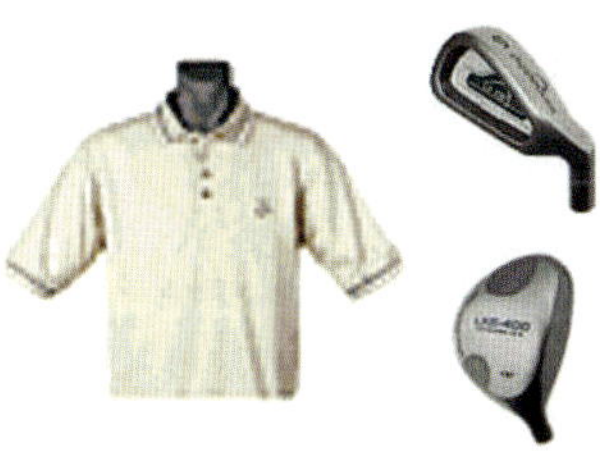

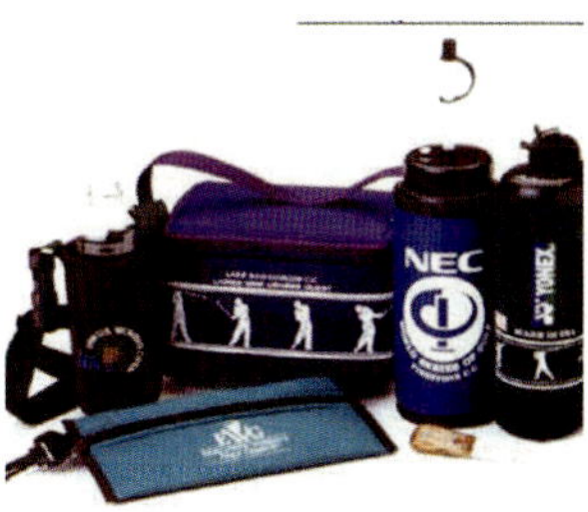

Reviews

BestValueGolf.com

http://www.bestvaluegolf.com

A shopping delight for all golfers. This is easy to use online shopping at it's best.

Not only can you jump directly to any brand of golfing equipment, but there is an excellent search facility which enables the shopper to select anything that might not be listed on the main page.

Chances are, you'll find what you're looking for as the range is truly vast, from familiar brand names such as Wilson, Strata and Callaway Golf, through to Nike, Top Flite and more. The access to these pages, prices, details and the facility to purchase online is lightning quick, even on a standard 56k modem connection. Quite a feat, considering the high level of detail you'll find here.

If you prefer to browse for a specific club rather than by brand, users can explore further categories dealing specifically with irons, putters, clubs for left handers, special deals that are on offer, and a whole list of related sporting equipment.

A comprehensive section on courier services that handle the delivery of purchased goods is also available. If you have any questions about shopping online, you'll find the answers here. The site is technically sound and fast speeds encourage easy movement from section to section.

While the site is not pretty, it's extremely functional.

RATING Refer to pg8 for rating explanations.

Overall Rating	✪✪✪✪
Ease of Use	✪✪✪✪✪
Content	✪✪✪✪✪
Look & Feel	✪✪✪
Customer Service	✪✪✪✪
Site Speed	✪✪✪✪✪
Technical	✪✪✪✪

MAIN POINTS:

>> Extremely quick, easy to use and comprehensive shopping site.

Bird Of Prey

http://www.birdofprey.com

Australia based company Birds of Prey specializes in making high quality golf shirts, which leave more room under the arms so that your swing will be less restricted, larger necks and a longer than average body length.

All shirts are also one hundred percent Australian made, so as you'd expect from a country that is so aware of the dangers of over-exposure to the sun, are designed to help protect you from harmful UV rays.

They boast well over two dozen different designs as well as accessories such as vests, caps and towels, all of which can be customized with your name - for a nominal fee, of course.

One painfully obvious thing is that they clearly don't update their website often. When we visited, the offer on the opening page of the site was a month old.

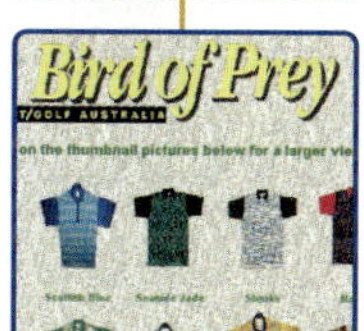

The rest of the site is functional, although there's nothing about it that really stands out or draws your eye to it.

The nicest touch would have to be the bird logo that they use as their backdrop. Its simple and loads fast, yet compliments the site name very well.

RATING Refer to pg8 for rating explanations.

Overall Rating	✪✪
Ease of Use	✪✪✪
Content	✪✪
Look & Feel	✪✪✪
Customer Service	✪
Site Speed	✪✪✪
Technical	✪✪

MAIN POINTS:

>> Extremely quick, easy to use and comprehensive shopping site.

>> Not updated regularly.

Blue Chip Socks

http://www.bluechipsocks.com

If there's one thing sites don't do anywhere near enough of, it's trying to stroke the ego. Which is why, for some strange reason, I really like the fact that the first words on the Blue Chip Socks website are "Welcome, smart person." Nice.

Once you enter the site and click on the "Why Buy?" link, you're given this as one of the reasons to buy their socks: "You become part of an exclusive club: only smart people wear Blue Chip Socks." I swear I can't make stuff like this up - although it is nice to know they have such a high opinion of their customers.

As for the socks though, they promise that they contain a "special fiber that'll help keep foot odor under control" for longer and also help to control the fungus that leads to athlete's foot during those long golf games.

They also offer large discounts off the retail prices of these socks – you're looking at up to fifty percent off, depending on the volume that you buy at once.

So if you're feet are important to you, you may want to give these ones a try

RATING Refer to pg8 for rating explanations.

Overall Rating	✪✪✪
Ease of Use	✪✪✪
Content	✪✪✪
Look & Feel	✪✪✪
Customer Service	✪✪✪✪
Site Speed	✪✪✪
Technical	✪✪

MAIN POINTS:

>> Extremely quick, easy to use shopping site.

Chipshot.com

http://www.chipshot.com

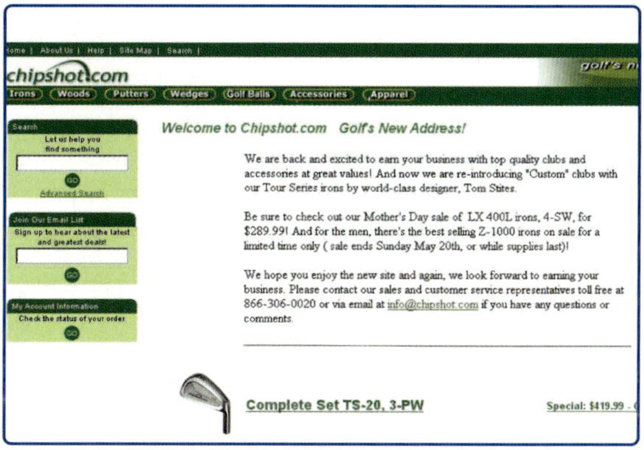

Chipshot.com is an online store with a huge selection of all sorts of golf equipment and offer international delivery to almost any place on the globe in 3-7 working days.

There's a shipping cost calculation option which is easy to find in their "help" section, which saves you a great deal of time looking at something that you may not go through with ordering because of unexpected shipping costs. The site is very easy to use. with a handy search option or a one click listing down the left hand side. This menu covers almost any requirement in the various sections. For example, there's "quickpicks" (here you'll find their most popular and bargain items), gifts and gift certificates, brands, custom made clubs, men, women, juniors, beginners, lefties and experts. There's also an advanced search function that allows searching any combination of the above. We particularly enjoyed the gift finder in the gifts section, which allows you to ask for a recommended gift by choosing from the player type, their skill or by the amount you wish to spend. This makes it easy to see if there is something available to suit your pocket, as well as the person you are buying the gift for. The My Game section is short and sweet - offering 26 lessons and tips on important areas of the game. We were most impressed with a system called Perfect Fit, where you are given the opportunity of creating your ideal set of clubs. This is something that any golfer will benefit from, and it's easy to use too. An excellent idea.

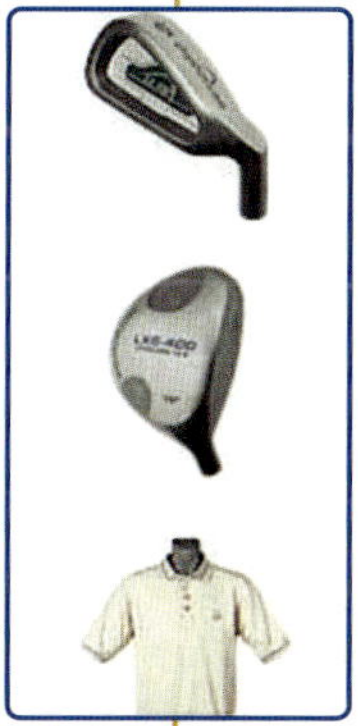

RATING Refer to pg8 for rating explanations.

Overall Rating	✪✪✪✪✪
Ease of Use	✪✪✪✪
Content	✪✪✪✪
Look & Feel	✪✪✪✪
Customer Service	✪✪✪✪✪
Site Speed	✪✪✪✪
Technical	✪✪✪✪✪

MAIN POINTS:

>> Good, clean layout. Simple to use, with a great international shop.

Golf'un

http://www.golfun.net

As the title would suggest, the main focus here is on Golfing Gags, and they have quite a few which you can securely order online, to be shipped anywhere in the world.

The site's design and look and feel is geared toward the gag side of things but still allows you to navigate with ease.

The gags include some really novel golf balls with descriptive names like "the floater", "the fireball", "the exploder", "triple trouble", "hot shots", "survival kit" and the shooter. Each has it's own special features, and they look like they would be great fun on the golf course.

The site doesn't only offer golfing gags, but also has a selection of novel gifts, a section with executive golf gifts (with a putter that would make an excellent gift). There's also a section of unique golf prints worth checking out, and you'll also find a selection of usefull golfing accessories..

The site also has a few books on golf humour for sale, sure to give you laugh and keep you in jokes while on the tee box.

You have the option of buying online, or by phone/fax and a 30 day money back guarantee is offered on all purchases.

All in all, a well rounded site with a small but complete set of specialized golfing merchandise.

RATING Refer to pg8 for rating explanations.

Overall Rating	✪✪✪✪
Ease of Use	✪✪✪✪
Content	✪✪✪✪
Look & Feel	✪✪✪✪
Customer Service	✪✪
Site Speed	✪✪✪✪
Technical	✪✪✪

MAIN POINTS:

>> Great Collection of gags mixed with some worthwhile gifts.

Golf Megadeals

http://www.golfmegadeals.com

It's not often that you come across a great shopping site that make's it easy to navigate.

GolfMegadeals.com is one such site. When you first arrive, you might feel like there isn't much there. The reason, is that they show you their "Best Buys" on the home page after welcoming you, and then provide a drop down menu at the top of the page which will take you quickly to any area of interest.

This is a shopping site, and that's what they concentrate on - presenting you with their products and allowing you to purchase them quickly and easily either securely online or by phone/fax.

International shipping is available so you can buy from anywhere in the world.

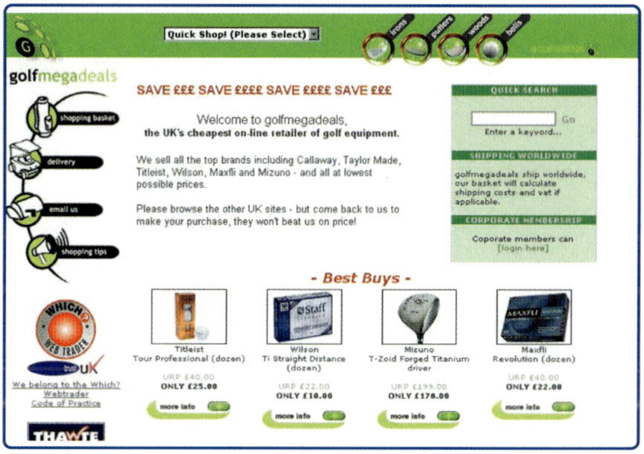

The only thing that we thought could have been improved was the content and range of products on offer. They have top brand names, but are also missing a few. They have putters listed on their menu of items, but didn't have any for sale when we visited, possibly just out of stock?

All in all, a good place to go for "no hassle" shopping for the basics, woods, irons and balls.

RATING Refer to pg8 for rating explanations.

Overall Rating	✪✪✪✪
Ease of Use	✪✪✪✪✪
Content	✪✪✪
Look & Feel	✪✪✪✪✪
Customer Service	✪✪✪✪✪
Site Speed	✪✪✪✪✪
Technical	✪✪✪✪✪

MAIN POINTS:

- Speedy response to our email enquiries.
- Easy to navigate.

GolfBalls.com

http://www.golfballs.com

If you're looking for somewhere to buy golf balls, and we mean ANY type of golf balls, then a visit to Golfballs.com is a must. The site, as you would expect it to, offers golf balls for sale. Nothing more, nothing less. You can buy balls from pretty much any big name manufacturer, used balls by name, quality and quantity, or you can have them produce custom balls with either a logo or another personalised image. Golfballs.com also offer you a selection of trick balls which you can use on your friends for a laugh.

The site is well designed with a fresh look and feel, with a navigation system that makes it easy to find what you're looking for. They offer "live" customer service online, where you can talk to someone on the site who should be able to answer any queries you might have. Good idea, in theory. In practice, each time we tried it, we received a "no operators are available" message and we received no response to our attempt to contact them by email either.

We did however find the site full of information and it supplied answers to all the questions we could think of.

RATING Refer to pg8 for rating explanations.

Overall Rating	★★★
Ease of Use	★★★★
Content	★★★
Look & Feel	★★★
Customer Service	★
Site Speed	★★★★
Technical	★★★

MAIN POINTS:

>> Great look and feel, with some innovative ideas.

>> Lots of information and answers to common questions.

>> No response to enquiries.

GolfDiscount.com

http://www.golfdiscount.com

If longevity is a sign of success on the Internet – and let's face it, with so many famous .com companies going bankrupt, having a long online life is quite an achievement – then GolfDiscount.com must be doing something right. This golf equipment retailer says that it's been selling clubs, balls, bags and accessories to golfers online since 1995.

With the massive array of products for sale this site truly lives up to its claim to be a golfing discount supersite. While the range of items is certainly good, what is even more impressive is the comprehensive and all-inclusive feel of this site.

There are additional elements like a news section and, more importantly, a very useful helpdesk where various problems can be sorted out. The items for sale have good graphic representation as well as full product information if you're interested in buying.

There's a pop-up "tip of the day" page which adds to a generally pleasing atmosphere and makes this site more than just an online store.

There is also the facility to download a full catalogue of the items offered for browsing through offline.

RATING Refer to pg8 for rating explanations.

Overall Rating	✪✪✪✪
Ease of Use	✪✪✪✪
Content	✪✪✪✪
Look & Feel	✪✪✪
Customer Service	✪✪✪
Site Speed	✪✪✪
Technical	✪✪✪

MAIN POINTS:

>> A vast range of golfing products, well presented.

Hallson Golf

http://www.hallsongolf.com

Hallson golf makes and sells custom clubs, produced to your exact specifications.

From the outset, the sheer size of the full range, their specifications and other information given about the products can't fail to impress.

You can select the exact specifications for each club, and quickly add it to the shopping cart for purchasing. We found the process very simple as the site also gives clear instructions on how to order, as well as documented details on the other important aspects of the selection and purchasing process. It's obvious that the designers have thought through the entire selection very carefully, and as a result the purchasing process makes for a faultless and smooth online experience.

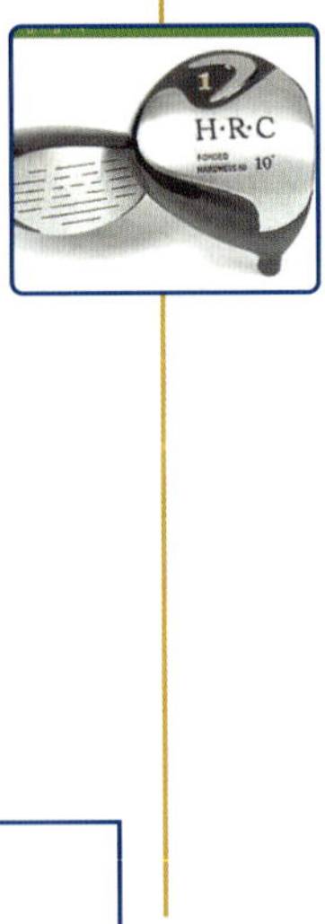

There are also some added extras to draw you in, including a golf news section - which unfortunately seemed a bit lacking in content. There are also links to golf magazines to enhance the look and feel of the site.

The main focus of Hallson, however, is clearly its ability to present and sell customized clubs. As such, it does this very well. Certainly worth a visit.

RATING Refer to pg8 for rating explanations.

Overall Rating	✪✪✪✪
Ease of Use	✪✪✪
Content	✪✪✪✪
Look & Feel	✪✪✪
Customer Service	✪✪
Site Speed	✪✪✪✪
Technical	✪✪✪✪

MAIN POINTS:

>> Well thought out design and good club specifications.

Hip Action

http://www.hipaction.com

Hip Action's online shop offers golf equipment at very competitive prices and free delivery for orders over a certain amount.

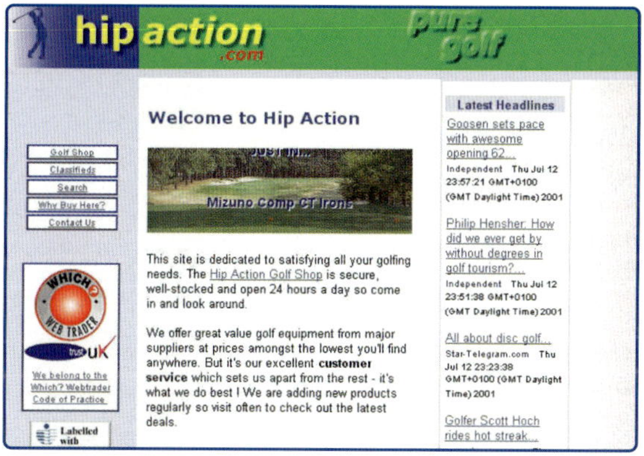

The site also runs a classified section that is split into different categories from clubs and other equipment to tuition services, although since this is a fairly new site, some categories have no entries yet.

There is a page of testimonies from satisfied customers and we would have to agree with these about Hip Action's extraordinary customer service as they replied to our email in four minutes (and that was at 11pm). Their personal and cheery replies to our queries made us warm to the site. Friendly and helpful interactivity on a site lends it personality and makes it more than just an Internet mail-order catalogue. Although the shop is the main feature of the site, there is also an email advice line and a news section with links to golfing news stories on other sites such as the BBC. The site is obviously kept bang up to date; all the news links are changed at least daily.

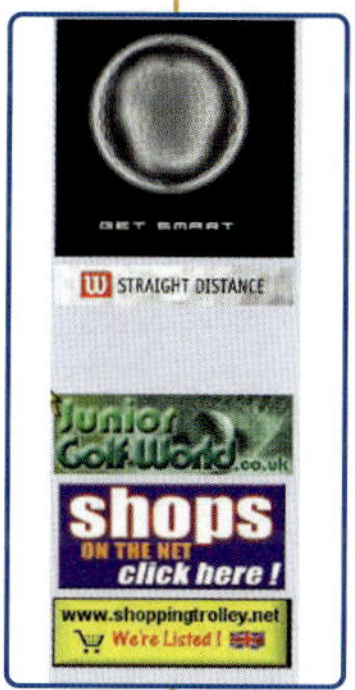

The site does lack a home button when you are visiting the shop pages and currently only delivers within the UK, but is well worth visiting if you want great prices and efficient service with a virtual smile.

RATING Refer to pg8 for rating explanations

Overall Rating	✪✪✪✪
Ease of Use	✪✪✪
Content	✪✪✪
Look & Feel	✪✪✪
Customer Service	✪✪✪✪✪
Site Speed	✪✪✪
Technical	✪✪✪

MAIN POINTS:

>> Competitively priced equipment

>> Excellent Customer Service

Links Worldwide

http://www.linksworldwide.com

Every business starts somewhere, and Links Worldwide hopes you start yours with them. In their own words, they were "created to provide any golfer, amateur or Pro, a way to have their own home-based golf business which entitles them to take advantage of tax subsidies granted to all small businesses by Congress". This site is US based, but you may be able to gain some insight from Links Worldwide if you are planning to start your own golf based business outside of the United States.

If you're not interested in business tips, there is another reason to visit the site: the Pro Shop. Simply put, Links Worldwide has an extensive, well maintained online store that allows you to move about surprisingly quickly, considering the size and quality of the product shots, which give you a clear idea exactly what you are ordering.

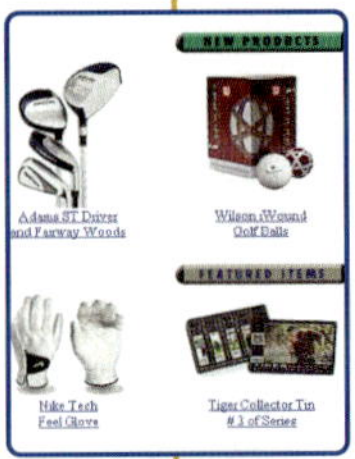

In addition, all ordering is done on a secure server, so you can feel safe entering your credit card and personal information.

RATING Refer to pg8 for rating explanations.

Overall Rating	✪✪
Ease of Use	✪✪✪
Content	✪✪
Look & Feel	✪✪
Customer Service	✪✪
Site Speed	✪✪✪
Technical	✪✪

MAIN POINTS:

>> Good shopping site with additional features and information.

Nike Golf

http://www.nikegolf.com

If you're looking for a site that screams professionalism, looks slick and is well polished, then you won't find much better than Nike Golf. Packed with the most recognisable faces from the game (prepare to be greeted by Tiger Woods at every turn).

The official Nike Golf site does has a heavy focus on the sales side of the game. Essentially, the primary purpose of this site is to promote the range of Nike products: quite a range it is, too.

You'll find footwear, clothing, golf balls, equipment and merchandising, all emblazoned with the Nike logo.

Yet even though they could have quite easily gotten away with simply selling the range and not bothering with any optional extras, there are still plenty of reasons to visit, even if your credit card is going to stay firmly tucked away. You'll find tons of downloadable Nike ads featuring Mr Woods, as well as a fantastic screensaver that will, as the site says "take you away from your office, desk, cubicle, or work space onto some of the most beautiful courses in the world." Anything that manages to do that can't be a bad thing. It's free too.

Explore the site and you'll find plenty of other flashy animations, features and games to keep you entertained.

RATING Refer to pg8 for rating explanations.

Overall Rating	★★★★★
Ease of Use	★★★★
Content	★★★★
Look & Feel	★★★★★
Customer Service	★★★★
Site Speed	★★★
Technical	★★★★★

MAIN POINTS:

>> Gorgeous. Nike clearly invested a lot of money in this site - and it's paid off in style.

ParGolf.com

http://www.pargolf.com

Almost every golf web site offers some kind of golfing equipment for sale. Be it putters, balls or a new nine iron, it's pretty easy to find those essential golf supplies. But what about those less than essential supplies? The little luxuries. You know, the ones that you don't technically need, but just look cool, odd or just plain tempting that you've got to have them? Well, that's where Par Golf Supply, Inc. comes in. Cigar cutters, Golf Tee Matchbooks and you can even get a wedding themed golf ball for that lucky someone in your life.

Online purchase is facilitated by a single form where you need to type in all the details of a products you want to purchase and makes facility to add logos and personalisation information. The site itself is well designed without being to flashy.

For the most part it's very plain, but this means it loads quickly. You will, however, find yourself having to wait a few extra seconds for the product pictures to load, but it's worth it because it gives you a clear picture of exactly what it is you're considering buying.

RATING Refer to pg8 for rating explanations.

Overall Rating	✪✪
Ease of Use	✪✪✪
Content	✪✪✪
Look & Feel	✪✪
Customer Service	✪✪✪
Site Speed	✪✪✪
Technical	✪✪

MAIN POINTS:

>> You'll find some unique and tempting golfing merchandise here.

Sporting Bet

http://www.sportingbet.com

We're not exactly sure if this is the right place for this one, but we thought it needed to be covered somewhere, and since it's going to require you to take out your credit card...it ended up in the "shopping" chapter.

If you're looking for a place where you can place online bets on the outcome of major golfing events – as well as practically every other sport you care to mention – and more importantly you want your winnings it to be tax free, then www.sportingbet.com is for you.

Once you've registered as a member by filling out a simple online form, you're free to place bets on any event you choose. The odds are clearly shown, and even an inexperienced user will find it easy to place a bet in a matter of minutes. As they say on TV, all major credit cards are accepted.

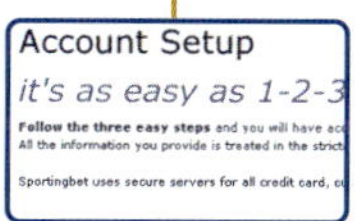

Whether or not you win anything is another matter of course and as the old adage goes, the real winners are always the bookmakers themselves.

However, if you're curious and fancy a flutter, or simply can't face the walk to the betting shop, Sporting Bet is worth a visit.

RATING Refer to pg8 for rating explanations.

Overall Rating	✪✪✪
Ease of Use	✪✪✪✪
Content	✪
Look & Feel	✪✪✪
Customer Service	✪✪✪
Site Speed	✪✪✪✪
Technical	✪✪✪

MAIN POINTS:

>> Easy - almost too easy - to use.

The Golf Warehouse

http://www.tgw.com

Paying a visit to the Golf Warehouse can be very much like visiting a warehouse in the real world. When you arrive at the site, you'll be immediately hit with just how massive their range of golfing equipment, apparel, teaching aids, memorabilia and art really is.

Just like in a real warehouse, it will inevitably seem a little daunting trying to find something you're looking for, especially when the home page you're greeted with is packed with pictures of all sorts of golfing merchandise. If it's top brands you're after, then this is the place to go. From Adidas and Ashworth, via Firestone and Florsheim through to Zevo Golf, all the names are here.

Golf Warehouse has made more than adequate provision for its overseas customers.

If you don't mind converting the currency yourself, there's nothing stopping you from placing an order.

The site, situated in the US offers a special worldwide service, with two day delivery to major European cities and resonable delivery times to other countries.

Very impressive.

RATING Refer to pg8 for rating explanations.

Overall Rating	✪✪✪✪
Ease of Use	✪✪✪✪
Content	✪✪✪✪
Look & Feel	✪✪✪
Customer Service	✪✪✪✪✪
Site Speed	✪✪✪
Technical	✪✪✪

MAIN POINTS:

» Super fast world wide delivery.

» Huge range of good prices.

Other Shopping Link Listings

Other Shopping related sites reviewed		Page
About Golf	http://www.aboutgolf.com	122
American Golf Auction	http://www.americangolfauction.com	46
Barnes & Noble	http://www.bn.com	23
Books On Golf	http://www.booksongolf.com	24
Callaway Golf	http://www.callawaygolf.com	47
Clubfinders Golf	http://www.clubfindersgolf.com	48
Dandy Golf	http://www.dandygolf.com	49
Designer Golf Gifts	http://www.designergolfgifts.com	106
Drop Putters	http://www.drop-putters.com	50
Eighteen Global	http://www.18global.com	85
Global Golf	http://www.globalgolf.com	86
Golf.co.uk	http://www.golf.co.uk	37
Golf Art	http://www.golf-art.com	14
GolfGreenfees.com	http://www.golfgreenfees.com	93
Golfingly Yours	http://www.golfinglyyours.com	109
Golf Judge	http://www.golfjudge.com	51
Golf Ladies	http://www.golfladies.com	226
Golf Magic	http://www.golfmagic.com	152
Golf Monitor	http://www.golfmonitor.com	153
GolfMonster.com	http://www.golfmonster.com	52
Golfonline	http://www.golfonline.com	53
Golfshoes Plus	http://www.golfshoesplus.com	29
Golf Shop 2000	http://www.golfersedge.com	108
Golfspan Pro Shop	http://www.customgolf.com	54
Golfweek.com	http://www.golfweek.com	167
InsideGolf.com	http://www.insidegolf.com	155
Ladies Golf Clubs	http://www.ladiesgolfclubs.com	227
Lady Classic	http://www.ladyclassic.com	228
Liquid Golf	http://www.liquidgolf.com	56
My Golf Zone	http://www.mygolfzone.com	41

Other Shopping Link Listings

Online Golf Lessons	http://www.onlinegolflessons.com	132
PGA Professional	http://www.pgaprofessional.com	133
PGA Tour	http://www.pgatour.com	158
Scotlands Golf Courses	http://www.scotlands-golf-courses.com	95
She Golfs	http://www.shegolfs.com	230
Silver Stone Publishing	http://www.silverstoneart.com	17
St Andrews Golf	http://www.stagolf.co.uk	30
St Andrews Links	http://www.standrews.org.uk	97
Titliest Golf	http://www.titleist.com	63
US Golf Association	http://www.usga.org	135
The Open Championship	http://www.opengolf.com	97
Wee Generation	http://www.weegeneration.com	31

Other Shopping related sites

http://thegolf-shop.com
http://www.allansgolfshop.com
http://www.bobsgolf.co.uk
http://www.bobmartinsgolf.com
http://www.bulldoggolfclubs.com
http://www.caddieshackgolf.com
http://www.cajungolf.com
http://www.clearvisiongolf.com
http://www.clubshield.com
http://www.clubcraft.com
http://www.coolgolf.com
http://www.clubproshops.com
http://www.cyberproshop.com
http://www.golf4less.com
http://www.golfbox.com
http://www.golfbymail.com
http://www.golfcrazy.com
http://www.golfshoponline.com
http://www.proamgolfshop.com
http://www.shopecosse.com
http://www.thegolfproshop.com
http://www.thewomensproshop.com
http://www.usgolfshop.com
http://www.yourgolfproshop.com

Reviews

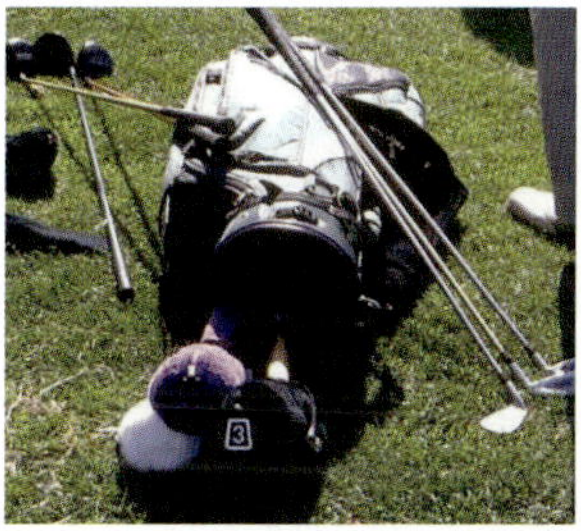

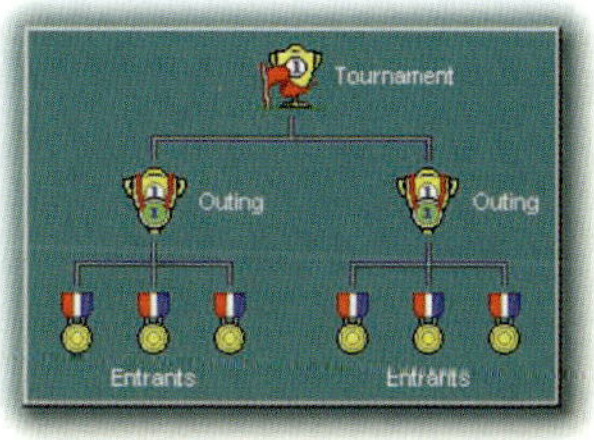

Baron Modular Solutions

http://www.baron.co.uk

When it comes to golf, you'll basically find three kinds of software devoted to it. The first, and probably the one most people are aware of, is the video game version, where you're free to wander a virtual course or two, and take every shot from your keyboard or mouse. Then there are the various handicap calculators, score monitors and golfing aids that help to keep track of your performance on real world courses. Then, probably the least well known, is the software devoted to people within the golfing industry.

The Baron Modular Solution enables any venue where golf is played, be it courses, golf clubs, hotels or leisure resorts to make the most of technology and ensure they're getting the most out of their facilities. Under the overall Baron banner, you'll find software that can help membership or booking management, international golf competition management, online booking or even food and beverage sales or bar work. Quite comprehensive stuff.

Everything seems to run flawlessly in Windows, while each of the modules works well with the other, doing away with unnecessary duplication of information and eliminating any modules that aren't applicable to your business.

RATING Refer to pg8 for rating explanations.

Overall Rating	★★★
Ease of Use	★★★★
Content	★★★
Look & Feel	★★★
Customer Service	★★★
Site Speed	★★★
Technical	★★★

MAIN POINTS:

>> Running a golf course, club or tournament just got a lot easier.

Focus 2000

http://www.focus2k.com

Focus 2000 produces software for golfers that includes custom handicap calculators, golf tournament managers, golf trip planners, and even a program that combines all of the above elements to calculate match results from golf trips. Talk about being spoilt for choice.

The site is constructed in a straightforward way with clear navigation and instructions.

The news section is reasonably comprehensive and gives updates on products, but seemed somewhat out of date (the last news item was posted one month prior to this review). The software is clearly displayed with plenty of details and a screen shot of the specific module. We would have liked to have seen a few more images from the products, and possibly some way of interacting with a demo of the software itself.

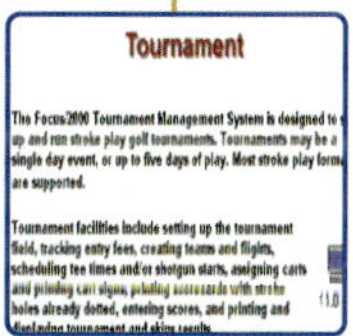

In a similar vein, there were some areas that had no graphics at all and only textual information. The lack of design on the site combined with a few small technical problems we came across, doesn't do justice to what appears to be a really good piece of software.

RATING Refer to pg8 for rating explanations.

Overall Rating	✪✪✪
Ease of Use	✪✪✪
Content	✪✪✪
Look & Feel	✪✪
Customer Service	✪
Site Speed	✪✪✪
Technical	✪✪

MAIN POINTS:

>> Detailed descriptions of the software.

Golf Technology

http://www.golftechnology.com

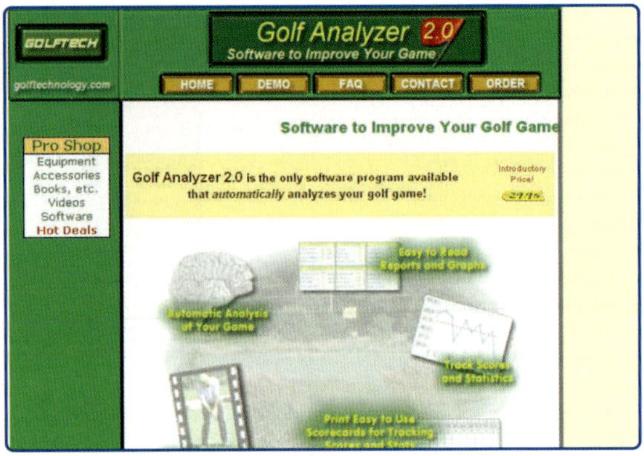

Golftechnology basically offers one product of their own. It's called Golf Analyser and thats exactly what it appears to do.

With the Analyser, you can create and print clear, information packed charts, graphs and reports, all generated from the basic information that you enter about your game.

Similarly, you can track much more in depth facts about your game, from driving distances, fairways hit, greens hit, penalty strokes and sand saves.

Clearly the creator of this software knows his stuff when it comes to golf. The option to print your own scorecards is a welcome bonus too.

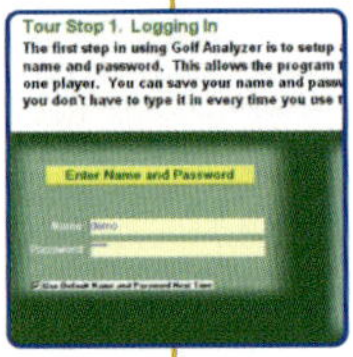

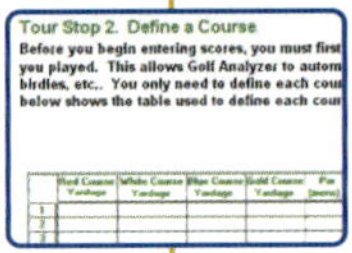

The instructional videos included within the game help to make it a great overall package, and one that any golfer looking to track and analyse their game would find useful.

The site has a cool little side menu that follows your scrolling movement which links to other shopping sites, so be aware that if you purchase from this menu, it'll be through another site.

The site design is simple and the content is good describing the software they offer in plenty of detail on the product.

RATING Refer to pg8 for rating explanations.

Overall Rating	✪✪✪
Ease of Use	✪✪✪✪✪
Content	✪✪✪✪✪
Look & Feel	✪✪✪
Customer Service	✪✪
Site Speed	✪✪✪
Technical	✪✪✪✪

MAIN POINTS:

>> Fantastic piece of software, filled with features.

Handicalc

http://www.handicalc.com

Handicalc.com offers a range of golf software products for individuals, leagues, clubs, associations and golf tournament sponsors.

Each product is described in detail with features, and plenty of screenshots to give visitors a good idea of what the software can do. As well as this, demo versions of each piece of software are available for download, which allows you to "try before you buy".

The site design is simple, and so is quick and easy to navigate.

Ordering is facilitated through digitalriver.com, one of the worlds largest online software stores for downloads and so you are assured of a professional service and secure online transaction.

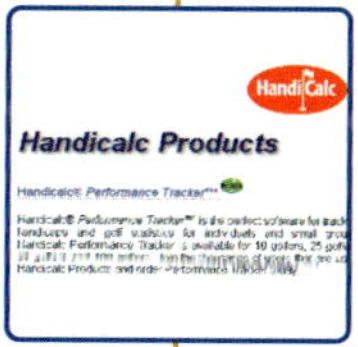

All in all, a well rounded site for what it's there for, and worth a visit.

RATING Refer to pg8 for rating explanations.

Overall Rating	✪✪✪
Ease of Use	✪✪✪
Content	✪✪
Look & Feel	✪
Customer Service	✪✪✪
Site Speed	✪✪✪
Technical	✪✪✪

MAIN POINTS:

>> Free trial versions of the software available for downloading.

Intelligolf

http://www.intelligolf.com

The Intelligolf website showcases the company's scorecard software for palm hand helds, pocket PCs and other platforms. This well laid out and easy to navigate site allows you to purchase this software and also sells a selection of palms and other portable computers which you can carry with you on the course. You can download a three day trial of the software, before you part with your cash. Intelligolf ships internationally and has a site with a very global outlook.

One of the biggest problems with many pieces of golf tracking software is that you have to wait until you get home to enter all your data. This software, which will work just as well on a handheld as a home computer, handles scoring, statistics and shot tracking. There are a few little extras too, such as a feature that will calculate any wagers you set during the game - which will either prove to be a blessing or a curse, depending on which end of the wager you end up.

Apart from the details on the software itself, you can download course information (hole par, handicap, length) from their course database. This has been compiled by visitors to the site and although entries are sporadic, they are scattered from all over the world. If your golf course isn't there you are encouraged to upload the relevant information.

RATING Refer to pg8 for rating explanations.

Overall Rating	✪✪✪✪✪
Ease of Use	✪✪✪✪
Content	✪✪✪✪
Look & Feel	✪✪✪✪✪
Customer Service	✪✪✪✪
Site Speed	✪✪✪✪
Technical	✪✪✪✪✪✪

MAIN POINTS:

>> Well designed site, offering useful golfing software.

Stroke Manager

http://strokemanager.com

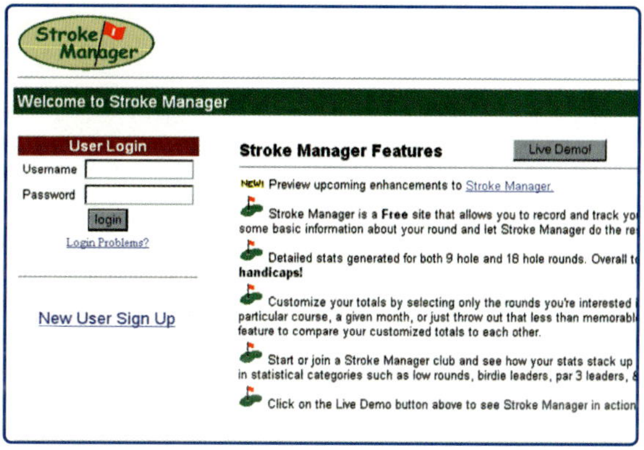

Despite a fairly basic design, this site has lots of interesting features.

Firstly, there's a great little free utility, that allows you to record and track the progress of your golf game online. It's easy to use too, requiring you to simply enter some basic information, while it'll take care of all the fancy calculations, statistics and performance charts. Whether you play 9 holes or the full 18, you can customise Stroke Manager to suit your game, while it'll also take into consideration the handicaps of any players involved.

You're also able to customise things a little further, by viewing your results from either a particular course, month or year. If you're feeling sneaky, you can even delete the odd round that might bring your average down – although that does seem to defeat the object of tracking your game.

Finally, if you need convincing that this piece of software is going to be useful to you, then just click on the live demo button and you'll get a quick preview of what to expect.

RATING Refer to pg8 for rating explanations.

Overall Rating	★★★
Ease of Use	★★★
Content	★★
Look & Feel	★
Customer Service	★★★
Site Speed	★★★
Technical	★★★

MAIN POINTS:

>> Excellent customisable game tracker.

Tourtrak

http://www.tourtrak.com

This site takes a while to load but once in there it's a slick, technically impressive site showcasing the golf software developed by TourTrack.

It's hard to know where to start when it comes to summarising the features found in this great course management software. Indeed, with 9 different editions and counting, each one specifically tailored to suit every golf course manager or tournament organisers needs, there's probably not enough room in this entire chapter, let alone on this page, to cover everything you'll find within.

To scratch the surface, you'll find support for custom score cards, as well as the facility to create your own, an improved interface and a great scoring and reporting facility.

The people who are going to get the most out of this software are likely to be organising several tournaments a year, or maintaining a golf course year-round.

There is an opportunity to order the software online or by phone or mail. Although not without a couple of technical problems on some pages the site covers the software it's promoting from every angle.

RATING Refer to pg8 for rating explanations.

Overall Rating	✪✪✪✪
Ease of Use	✪✪✪✪
Content	✪✪✪✪
Look & Feel	✪✪✪✪
Customer Service	✪✪✪✪
Site Speed	✪✪✪
Technical	✪✪✪✪

MAIN POINTS:

>> Feature packed software, perfect for those within the golf industry.

Other Software Link Listings

Other Software related sites reviewed

		Page
The Golf Channel	http://www.thegolfchannel.com	159
The Golf Warehouse	http://www.tgw.com	198

Other Software related sites

http://golfcap.com
http://northernsystems.com
http://www.goibs.com
http://www.golfbase.com
http://www.golfpac.mcmail.com
http://www.golfsoft.com
http://www.handi.com
http://www.hwcn.org/ac524/golfhelp.html
http://www.linksgolf.co.uk
http://www.meab-mx.se/software/golfstat
http://www.scorekeeper.com
http://areagolf.com
http://members.xoom.com/golfgenie
http://www.aekcomputers.com
http://www.avenet.fi/golfdog
http://www.best.com/shiro/savers
http://www.birdiesoftware.com
http://www.cet.com/cgms
http://www.compusmart.ab.ca/smithr
http://www.creativeicr.com
http://www.easyscoregolf.com
http://www.golfclubmaking.com
http://www.golf-stat.com
http://www.handicapmaster.org
http://www.homealonesoftware.com
http://www.iserv.net/shofman/golf
http://www.leaguescoring.com
http://www.lsigolf.com
http://www.magadraw.com
http://www.mulligansw.com
http://www.netgolfleague.com
http://www.networks911.com
http://www.prizegolf.com
http://www.quadsport.com
http://www.qwikregistor.com
http://www.sports-coach.com
http://www.stratec.ca/golfhand
http://www.tqs.net
http://www.winscore.com
http://www3.sympatico.ca/wbabin/hccalc
http://www.golferrx.com

Reviews

3D Golf

http://www.3dgolf.co.uk

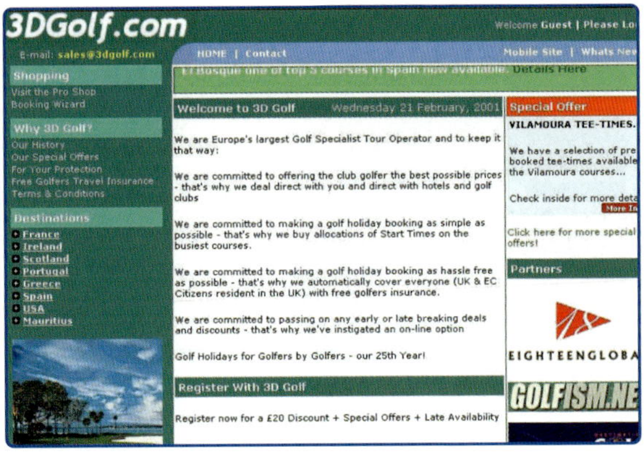

While 3DGolf may sound like a typical title for a golfing computer game, don't be put off. What you're actually getting here is an excellent site for European golfing travel. And when we say excellent, we mean it.

3DGolf boasts a stunning pricing wizard for determining accommodation prices for all the main golfing centres across Europe.

Once you've entered your details in a simple registration form, you can find out the cost of staying at any number of hotels, ranging from the most basic to five star, in any central city in Europe. Impressive stuff. This wizard is very effective indeed, and with a few clicks you can establish exactly how much it will cost you and your family to stay at the hotel of your choice.

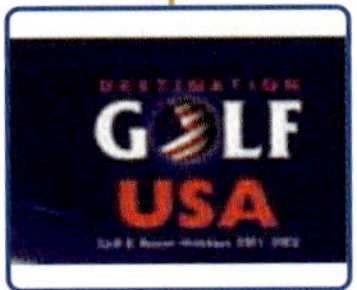

There are also graphic displays and information on golfing travel spots throughout Europe. You name it, you'll be able to find it here.

Another nice touch is that the site also offers free golfer's travel insurance for UK residents, which could be incredibly valuable if the unexpected happens while you're travelling.

All in all, this is a good place to visit if you planning a golfing holiday in Europe.

RATING Refer to pg8 for rating explanations.

Overall Rating	✪✪✪✪
Ease of Use	✪✪✪✪
Content	✪✪✪
Look & Feel	✪✪✪
Customer Service	✪✪
Site Speed	✪✪✪
Technical	✪✪✪

MAIN POINTS:

>> An excellent accomodation pricing wizard.

Destination Golf

http://www.destinationgolf.co.uk

This visually impressive Flash site is a golfing holiday guide to the US and Morocco.

The interface is clear and fast, while most pleasingly it doesn't have the usual problem that most Flash sites suffer from: overly long download waiting times.

The coverage of the resorts is very slick and comprehensive, with almost all areas of the US and Morocco here on the site. Quite a feat when you consider how much ground there is to cover.

There is also as a handy map which can be used to locate the golfing resorts. From deciding which venue you might like to visit, you move onto the planning part of the site. Again, this is comprehensive and easy to use, with all aspects of travel dealt with, including insurance issues.

One of the pages we tried to access wasn't functioning when we visited, but besides this one flaw, which may have been a temporary hitch, the site offers one of the most visually appealing and comprehensive vacation planning sites that you'll ever see. Certainly worth a visit, even if only to see this site's slick and polished finish.

RATING Refer to pg8 for rating explanations.

Overall Rating	✪✪✪
Ease of Use	✪✪✪✪
Content	✪✪✪✪
Look & Feel	✪✪✪✪
Customer Service	✪✪✪
Site Speed	✪✪✪
Technical	✪✪

MAIN POINTS:
>> Comprehensive and visually impressive.

Golf Breaks

http://www.golfbreaks.com

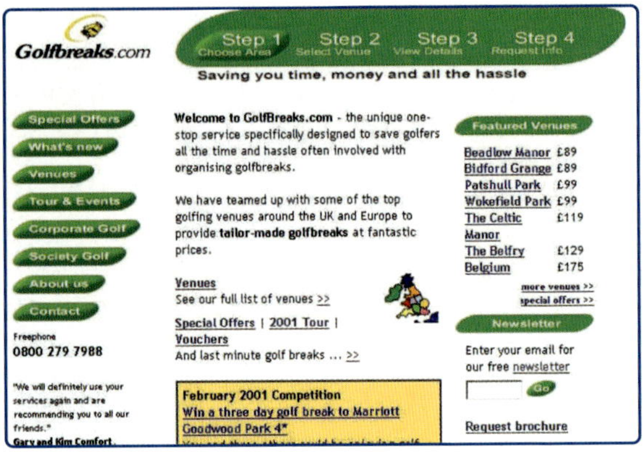

"Welcome to GolfBreaks .com," announces the home page of this online golfing breaks site, which offers a "unique one-stop service specifically designed to save golfers all the time and hassle often involved with organising golfbreaks." Well sounds OK so far, but we're always a bit cautious when dealing with on-site claims.

In this case though, their claims are justified. They've made the process of selecting a break, choosing accommodation and sorting out your travel so easy, even a novice could do it.

The site offers golfing venues in the UK and Europe, although at the time of our visit our visit they did not feature any in mainland Europe.

You can click on a (very busy) map of the British Isles to determine where you would like to take your break.

Contacting them can be done by email, phone or fax, and their response to our attempt to make contact was good.

The site also offers a "last minute" section which is well worth visiting. If you're free to travel at little notice, you could make some real savings on your golfing break.

RATING Refer to pg8 for rating explanations.

Overall Rating	✪✪✪✪
Ease of Use	✪✪✪✪
Content	✪✪✪
Look & Feel	✪✪✪
Customer Service	✪✪✪✪
Site Speed	✪✪
Technical	✪✪✪✪

MAIN POINTS:

>> Great site for sorting out that golfing holiday. Good prices too.

GolfAndTravel.com

http://www.golfandtravel.com

There are some partnerships in life that will always work well together, and golf and travel seem to be one of them. By its very nature, golf can take you to some of the most scenic spots on the face of the Earth, so a working partnership between seeing the world and playing a round or two of golf on the way seems like an excellent idea to us.

We're not the only ones who think this way: Golf and Travel.com thinks so too, because their site explores some of the best golfing resorts and clubs in the world. Yet there's plenty more to make this one stand out from the endless crowd of online golfing holiday sites.

Besides offering tournament results, the site also hosts very attractive graphical and text based information about selected courses.

Another interesting aspect of the site is their online art galley, devoted to golf related work including paintings of world renowned golf courses.

There is also an equipment showroom with access to product descriptions and prices.

The images in this site alone are a worthwhile reason for visiting - some breathtaking images of incredible golf holes.

RATING Refer to pg8 for rating explanations.

Overall Rating	✪✪✪
Ease of Use	✪✪✪
Content	✪✪
Look & Feel	✪✪✪✪
Customer Service	✪✪
Site Speed	✪✪✪
Technical	✪✪✪✪

MAIN POINTS:

>> Great graphics and overall design.

Golfing Ireland

http://www.golfingireland.com

If you've even got the slightest passing interest in playing a round of golf in Ireland, then this site will surely help to make your mind up. After one visit, you'll be eager to pack your bags and start your journey to essential courses like Ballybunion, Portmarnock or Royal County Down.

Golfing Ireland features just about everything you'd possibly need to make the journey – no matter where you're starting from.

There's a guide to the stunning castles that you can call home while on your golfing break, as well as information on the resorts, hotels and country houses where you'll be able to rest your head after a hard day on the course. To ensure you'll fit in with the locals, you can even brush up on your history of the country with an impressively detailed guide to Ireland.

Here you'll also find an indispensable travellers guide, with some great advice on how to make your journey as stress free as possible. Simply by reading the guide to Irish weather you can tell the site isn't sugar coating anything to make the trip seem more attractive than it already is. "It has been known to rain in Ireland, sometimes quite a lot, so a rain suit and an extra pair of golf shoes are recommended," they say. Well, you can't argue with that.

RATING Refer to pg8 for rating explanations.

Overall Rating	★★★★
Ease of Use	★★★★
Content	★★★★
Look & Feel	★★★★
Customer Service	★★★
Site Speed	★★★★
Technical	★★★

MAIN POINTS:

>> Lavish and well designed. Guaranteed to make you long for a golfing break in Ireland.

Golf Miles

http://www.golfmiles.com

You'll no doubt be familiar with the concept of Air Miles. The more you travel, whether it be for business or pleasure, the more "bonus" miles you get, and you can use these for discounted travel later.

Golf Miles works on a pretty similar basis, only instead of clocking up the points by flying from place to place, you earn your Golfing Miles by doing what all golfers love most...playing the game. Basically, for all the "miles" you clock up on selected courses in the US, you can play at others for discounted rates. We thought it was a great idea, but imagined that it would be a mamoth task to administer.

The scheme allows you to take advantage of golf packages at top resorts, offers members preferred tee times and savings on green fees and even use your golf miles to buy selected pro shop merchandise from over 650 US golf courses.

Some parts of the site were under construction when we visited, but the site is worth a look if you're going to be playing at any of the courses they have in the scheme and are interested in clocking up some "golf miles".

RATING Refer to pg8 for rating explanations.

Overall Rating	✪✪✪
Ease of Use	✪✪
Content	✪✪
Look & Feel	✪✪✪
Customer Service	✪✪✪
Site Speed	✪✪✪
Technical	✪✪✪

MAIN POINTS:

>> Runs a golf miles scheme along similar lines to air miles.

Places To Golf

http://www.placestogolf.com

"We strive to be your resource for everything golf related!" raves the very enthusiastic Places to Golf website.

The site offers a national (US) and international golf course guide, golf web site directory, daily news, an extensive pro shop, golf business centre, tour schedules, tips, jokes, bookstore and many other features.

There are interactive message boards and classified ads and the option to subscribe to a free email newsletter that'll keep you up to date with all the latest golfing news and offers from the site.

Yet it's the times when Places to Golf doesn't take itself too seriously that really shine through. The jokes you'll find here, while admittedly can be cringe-makingly bad, will raise a groan or two amongst fellow golfers, while the Fantasy Golf Game will provide a nice distraction from the real thing.

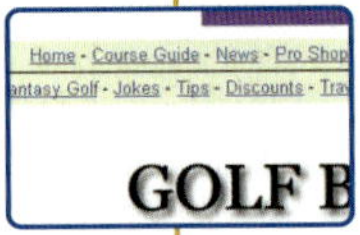

RATING Refer to pg8 for rating explanations.

Overall Rating	✪✪✪
Ease of Use	✪✪✪✪
Content	✪✪✪✪
Look & Feel	✪✪✪
Customer Service	✪✪✪
Site Speed	✪✪✪✪
Technical	✪✪

MAIN POINTS:

>> Plenty to see, including bad golfing jokes.

T-Tours

http://www.t-tours.com

A fast Flash introduction starts things off on the right foot for T-Tours, a travel and holiday guide which specialises in offering golfing holidays in Portugal's Algarve.

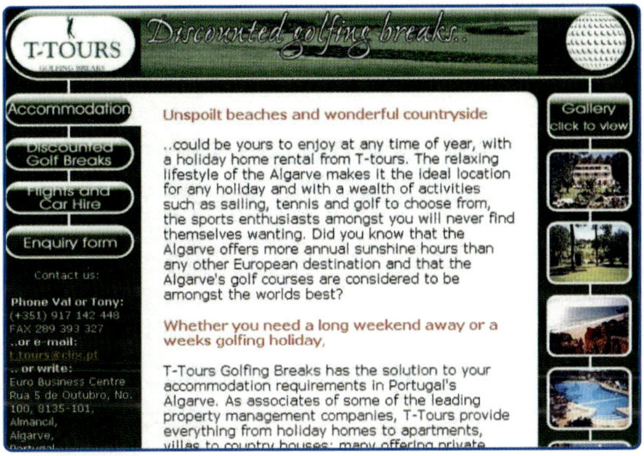

If you're feeling like you want someone else to take all the hard work out of holiday planning, then they can help there too – offering to make any flight or car arrangements for you. Sometimes it's good to let someone else take care of the technicalities, while you get on with the important business of enjoying your break.

The sites main feature is a graphic display of an accommodation area, with rather slow and chunky images. If you imagine what an online version of a accommodation brochure could look like, then you won't be far from the mark here.

Some video clips or a virtual tour of the facilities they offer would have been nicer, but as it stands it is still a useful holiday brochure.

RATING Refer to pg8 for rating explanations.

Overall Rating	✪✪
Ease of Use	✪✪✪
Content	✪✪
Look & Feel	✪✪✪
Customer Service	✪✪✪✪
Site Speed	✪✪
Technical	✪✪

MAIN POINTS:

>> Impressive animated opening sequence.

>> An online holiday brochure.

World Golf

http://www.worldgolf.com

This US based site claims to be international and has lists of golf courses in 46 countries. However, these lists are by no means comprehensive, and the information on each course is often inconsistent. It's not uncommon to find that some of the most well known golfing venues in both Europe and even in the United States, are simply missing from this site.

The courses that are there are reviewed using the comments of visitors to the website (presumably patrons of the said courses), which goes some way to explaining why the layout of each entry, and the overall editorial style itself, is quite inconsistent.

The fact that the course reviews are first hand accounts makes them more useful than just a list of courses.

There are a number of other features on the site, including a page where golfers can celebrate their hole in one glory and the golfing news of the day. It also offers links to other golfing sites in different countries, as well as an online shop.

At present this only ships to within the US. However there is still plenty of information that will be of interest to golfers – no matter where you call home.

RATING Refer to pg8 for rating explanations.

Overall Rating	✪✪✪
Ease of Use	✪✪
Content	✪✪
Look & Feel	✪✪
Customer Service	✪
Site Speed	✪✪✪
Technical	✪✪✪

MAIN POINTS:

>> Tidy layout. Reviews are first hand and from real golfers.

Other Travel & Holiday Link Listings

Other Travel & Holiday related sites

http://agithai.com
http://algarvegolf.net
http://classic-golf.com
http://golfandsun.com
http://golforient.com
http://mckinlay.com/golf
http://phelan.com
http://resort-golf.com
http://scotsgolf4all.com
http://supergolf.com
http://thegolfnurse.com
http://trilogygolf.com
http://www.4seasonsresort.com
http://www.aesir.com

Other Travel & Holiday Link Listings

http://www.africa2000tours.co.za
http://www.agolfing-experience.co.uk
http://www.aircents.com
http://www.albagolftours.net
http://www.allpro-motions.com
http://www.allvalencia.com
http://www.angelsascent.com
http://www.antognolla.com
http://www.ash-golf.com
http://www.ashgolf.demon.co.uk
http://www.atlanticgolf.com
http://www.atlgolf.demon.co.uk
http://www.autoeurope.com
http://www.azgolftours.com
http://www.aztravel.com
http://www.basinharbor.com
http://www.bigeasygolf.com
http://www.billgoff.com
http://www.blacklake.com
http://www.bluffpoint.com
http://www.bonjourtravel.com
http://www.caddygolfsafaris.com
http://www.camdenvalley.com.au
http://www.carolinagolfvacation.com
http://www.carrollvalley.com
http://www.celebritytours.net
http://www.charterhub.com
http://www.chasgolfvac.com
http://www.classic-golf.com
http://www.classicgolftours.com
http://www.coastalgolfaway.com
http://www.conceptgolf.com
http://www.conquerafrica.co.za
http://www.costablanca-golf.com
http://www.destination-golf.com
http://www.destinations.com
http://www.directtravel.co.uk
http://www.eagle-crest.com
http://www.eaglepointe.com
http://www.easy-breaksbrittany.com
http://www.e-golftravel.com
http://www.emeraldhillsresort.com
http://www.escapadegolf-travel.com
http://www.executivesportstravel.com
http://www.experience-irelandgolf.com
http://www.fairwaysgolftravel.com
http://www.frade.com
http://www.global-golf-links.com
http://www.globalgolftours.com
http://www.goireland.com
http://www.goldenhill.co.za
http://www.golfandfishsco.co.uk
http://www.golfdepartment.com
http://www.golfdestinationsonline.com
http://www.golfdownunder.co.nz
http://www.golfescapes.com
http://www.golfexclusives.com
http://www.golf-getaways.com
http://www.golfholidays.co.za
http://www.golfingresorts.com
http://www.golfing-tours.co.uk
http://www.golfinternational.com
http://www.golf-irl.com
http://www.golfisleofman.com
http://www.golfplus.ie
http://www.golfscot.com
http://www.golfscotland.co.uk
http://www.golf-shuttle.com
http://www.golftales.junglelink.co.uk
http://www.golftheworldvacations.com
http://www.golf-time.net
http://www.golftoursandtravel.com
http://www.golf-tours-ireland.com
http://www.golftoursnz.com
http://www.golf-travel.com
http://www.golftravel4u.com
http://www.golftravelinformation.com
http://www.golf-trotters.com

Other Travel & Holiday Link Listings

http://www.golfvacations.co.uk
http://www.golf-vacations.com
http://www.golfvacationsuk.com
http://www.golfworld.co.za
http://www.graciousgolf.com
http://www.greatgorgegolf.com
http://www.greyowlgolf.com
http://www.gti-home-exchange.com
http://www.gvac.com
http://www.hansmerensky.com
http://www.harbourtowne.com
http://www.highcountrygolf.com
http://www.homestead-ut.com
http://www.hope-island.com.au
http://www.hopman.com
http://www.islandgetaway.com
http://www.jackolanternresort.com
http://www.kenya-golf-safaris.com
http://www.kexplorers.com
http://www.kiawahresort.com
http://www.kingsmill.com
http://www.lakemoreyinn.com
http://www.linksland.com
http://www.luxurygolftour.com
http://www.mexicogolftrips.com
http://www.missioninnresort.com
http://www.niblick-golf-tours.com
http://www.nutterscrossing.com
http://www.ocgolfgroups.com
http://www.okanagangolf.com
http://www.outerbanksgolf.com
http://www.par5.com
http://www.pganational.com
http://www.pga-resorts.com
http://www.pgatravel.com
http://www.pgawest.com
http://www.phuketgolf.com
http://www.pinehurstresort.com
http://www.pineviewresort.com
http://www.ramadagolf.com
http://www.rentalresources-ms.com
http://www.resort-golf.com
http://www.resortsuites.com
http://www.rumpointe.com
http://www.runningy.com
http://www.rydercupholidays.com
http://www.sagolf.co.za
http://www.sanmarcosresort.com
http://www.scotislandgolf.co.uk
http://www.scotsgolf4all.com
http://www.scottsdalegolf.com
http://www.seabrookresort.com
http://www.seasidegolf.com
http://www.sghgolf.com
http://www.shakagolf.co.za
http://www.shenvalee.com
http://www.socalgolfsafari.com
http://www.sonoransuites.com
http://www.sportvac.com
http://www.stagshead.co.uk
http://www.stmarlo.com
http://www.swtours.com
http://www.teetimesusa.com
http://www.terracebay.com
http://www.tgtmag.com
http://www.thecarolinagolf.com
http://www.thegolfdesk.com
http://www.thegolfvillas.com
http://www.the-vic.com
http://www.tinakilly.ie
http://www.train-chartering.co.uk
http://www.ttfgolftours.com
http://www.turkishgolf.com
http://www.turnberry.co.uk
http://www.westinriomar.com
http://www.wigwamresort.com
http://www.wilddunes.com
http://www.winebond.com

EZ Webguides

18th hole - womens golf

Reviews

Golf Ladies

http://www.golfladies.com

"In 1995, Golf Ladies began because I did not see the types of products on the market that catered to women and were related to the game of golf," explains Sue Wright, creator of the Golf Ladies site. Run by a woman, for women – but has both the idea and the site paid off?

Well, we're happy to report that they have. Golf Ladies looks really nicely done and the information on it is presented clearly. Even though each item up for sale has its own picture, the site still loads really quickly and since ordering is done on a secure server, you can shop with confidence knowing that ordering won't be a problem. Once you've done so, you'll most likely want to do so again and again, because shopping on this site is hassle free, simple and quick.

This site is located in the US and all the prices are in US dollars. International shipping is offered.

The site has a large number of women's golf products on sale, making it likely that you'll find something that catches your eye, be it a sweater, golf bag or any number of other items.

We highly recommend you give this site a look.

RATING Refer to pg8 for rating explanations.

Overall Rating	✪✪✪✪
Ease of Use	✪✪✪
Content	✪✪✪
Look & Feel	✪✪✪✪
Customer Service	✪✪✪✪
Site Speed	✪✪✪✪
Technical	✪✪✪

MAIN POINTS:

>> Run by women, for women. Long running and reputable.

Ladies Golf Clubs

http://www.ladiesgolfclubs.com

Although the name may not hint at it, iGolfstore & Ladies Golf Clubs sells much more than just woman's golf equipment. In fact, the site offers a large variety of clubs and accessories for golfers of any age or sex including umbrellas, travel cases, bags and the infamous Birdie, which is described as "just a really big umbrella".

The prices are in line with those on most other sites. The merchandise however, does appear to be high quality based on the provided photos.

Shopping online is made easy, their pages load quickly and items are arranged neatly and logically. Adding items to your cart is done in the standard way and credit card information is taken on a secure server.

The overall site itself has a very plain look to it which, aside from the product pictures, features nothing but plain text on white backgrounds. That's not all in all bad, because it adds to the ease of use and speed.

Well worth a visit in our opinion.

RATING Refer to pg8 for rating explanations.

Overall Rating	✪✪
Ease of Use	✪✪✪
Content	✪✪✪
Look & Feel	✪✪
Customer Service	✪✪✪
Site Speed	✪✪✪
Technical	✪✪

MAIN POINTS:

>> Shopping online is made simple and speedy.

Lady Classic

http://www.ladyclassic.com

Lady Classic Internet Pro Shop concentrates on the sale of gloves and accessories, but it's their classic golf gloves which seem to be the main draw on their site.

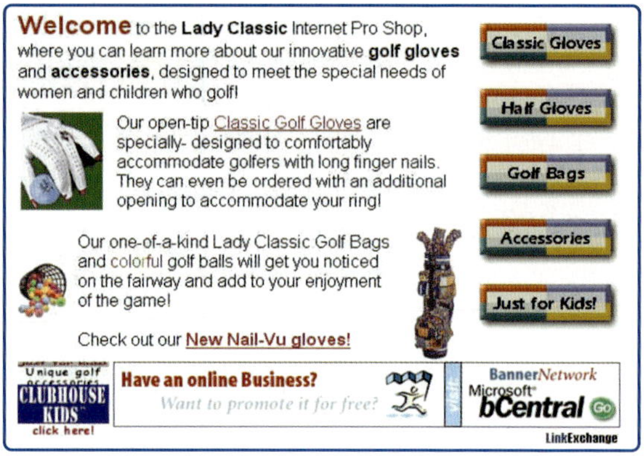

The specially designed gloves have special slits at the tip of each finger, which allow ladies with long fingernails to not have to worry about fitting them into a pair of traditional gloves or breaking them off during their next round on the links.

The other unique feature is a special diamond hole in the fourth finger left hand to allow rings to show through. They also offer a number of other items, but nothing as unique as the gloves.

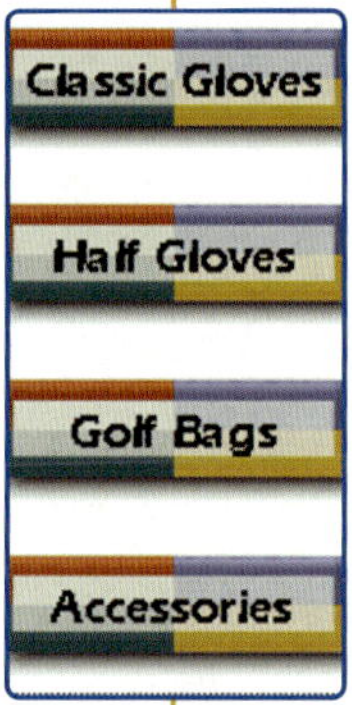

Although plain and lacking an identifying logo anywhere on the site, the overall site is very well organized and has the look of a printed catalogue.

There's also a small kid's section with golf bags in different sizes to suit growing children, children's gloves and colourful golf balls and tees.

RATING Refer to pg8 for rating explanations.

Overall Rating	✪✪✪
Ease of Use	✪✪✪✪
Content	✪✪✪
Look & Feel	✪✪✪
Customer Service	✪✪
Site Speed	✪✪✪✪
Technical	✪✪

MAIN POINTS:

>> The site showcases special gloves for ladies with long nails and those who prefer to keep their hand jewellry on while golfing.

LPGA

http://www.lpga.com

This is the official site of the Ladies Professional Golf Association and as such, should really act as a champion for the people it represents. The flagship for the association, if you like.

Although the design is fairly uninspiring, it does, have plenty of relevant information to hand on the ladies tour, the players within the Association, and golfing news in general.

It's straightforward to use with a list of subjects continually displayed up the left side of the screen, which are then divided into sub-categories when clicked on.

Explore further and you'll find the site features technique tips, an area for juniors (where they are planning a games and activities section, which will undoubtedly liven up that particular part of the LPGA webpages) a history section and a Pro Shop which links to their afilliation shop on another site, www.womensgolf.com, which is also reviewed in this chapter.

RATING Refer to pg8 for rating explanations.

Overall Rating	✪✪✪
Ease of Use	✪✪✪
Content	✪✪✪
Look & Feel	✪✪
Customer Service	✪✪✪✪
Site Speed	✪✪✪
Technical	✪✪✪

MAIN POINTS:

>> Extremely simple to use.

>> Some pages crowded.

She Golfs

http://www.shegolfs.com

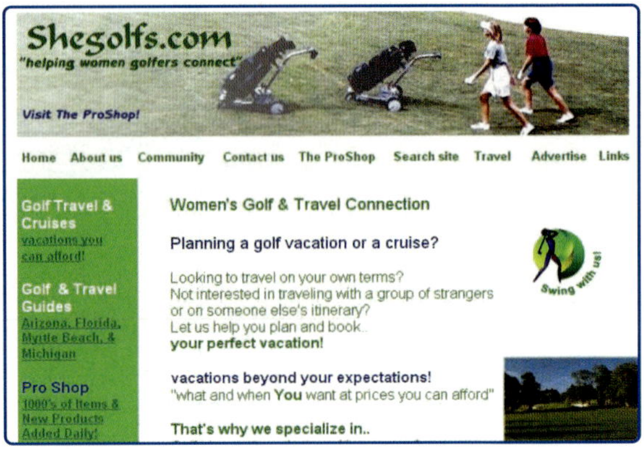

If you're a woman thinking of getting into the game of golf for the first time, then you may want to make Shegolfs.com one of the first places you visit.

Their motto is "helping woman golfers connect" and they definitely seem to live up to that.

For starters, if you're worried about looking like a less than stellar player on your local course, then, through this site, you can arrange a number of golf vacations at courses all over the world, including the US, Scotland and South Africa.

Of course, before you leave for your vacation you'll need to pick up at least some new golf equipment. That's why they give you tips and links to woman's online pro shops (if you order from their sponsor you can get up to twenty percent off).

They also offer a number of other links, such as one that will take you to online guides written by women, that are designed to help you improve your game.

The site itself is somewhat on the plain side, although the nice banner logo and the green-backed control panels add a bit of colour.

Otherwise, the site offers a few pictures and a lot of plain text and we felt was deserving of a visit.

RATING Refer to pg8 for rating explanations.

Overall Rating	✪✪✪
Ease of Use	✪✪✪
Content	✪
Look & Feel	✪✪✪
Customer Service	✪✪✪
Site Speed	✪✪
Technical	✪✪✪

MAIN POINTS:
>> Good meeting place for female golfers the world over.

Women On The Green

http://www.womenonthegreen.com

Women on the Green claims to be your "Hole-in-One for Women's Golf Products & Information," and we found it to be a very good site overall.

One of the features that we like the best is their "Ask Molly" section. Molly James is an LPGA/PGA Teaching Pro that will, after you fill out a short form, personally answer your golf-related questions. You have the option of having your questions answered privately or in a public forum. This is a really useful service, which costs nothing, and is something more sites should think about providing.

Apart from that nifty feature, they also have libraries of golf tips and answers to past questions.

The site also contains a well-stocked women's pro shop, which will take your credit card details on a secure sever.

The homepage has an attractive, if slightly cluttered look to it. They advertise the site's newest features and feature a number of pictures - many of which are links- and a nicely designed control panel which holds the entire site together.

So, while we wouldn't call it a hole in one, it's definitely a solid birdie bordering on an eagle. Certainly give Women on the Green a look.

RATING Refer to pg8 for rating explanations.

Overall Rating	✪✪✪✪
Ease of Use	✪✪✪
Content	✪✪✪
Look & Feel	✪✪
Customer Service	✪✪✪✪
Site Speed	✪✪✪
Technical	✪✪✪✪

MAIN POINTS:

>> Packed with information for women golfers.

Womens Golf

http://www.womensgolf.com

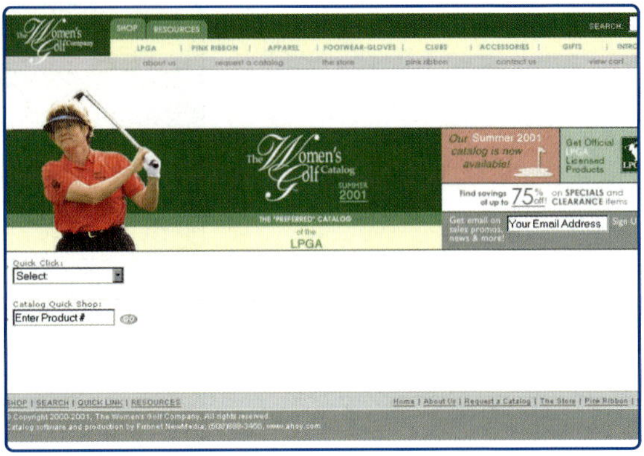

More than just a female specific golf store, the Woman's Golf Company also has a page of "women friendly" resources, such as guides to golf courses, schools and custom clubs.

All their information is focused upon US based business, but you might still want to have a look if you are a golfer from elsewhere.

The shop itself is endorsed as the "preferred" catalogue of the LPGA and offers a wide array of women's golf equipment for older players, young girls and even toddlers.

Everything is nicely sub-divided and moving around is quick and easy. The site foregoes the usual left-hand side control panel and instead has the controls on the top and bottom of your window which is a nice change.

Any shopping you do also takes place on a secure server, or alternatively you can order a catalogue so that you can do your shopping by mail.

Overall, the Woman's Golf Company is an excellent site, that can truly be your one stop for anything the female golfer is likely to need.

RATING Refer to pg8 for rating explanations.

Overall Rating	✪✪✪✪
Ease of Use	✪✪✪
Content	✪✪✪
Look & Feel	✪✪✪
Customer Service	✪✪✪✪
Site Speed	✪✪✪✪
Technical	✪✪✪

MAIN POINTS:

>> Great site, that offers everything women need to enjoy the game of golf.